An incredible look at the astounding journey of a KG[
of the Cold War. Heartbreaking, exciting, intriguing. [
of one of the most difficult careers known to man. E[
spycraft guide, and historical document, *Deep Undercover* perfectly
describes the crippling insularity of the spy's life.

JOE WEISBERG

Creator, showrunner, and executive producer, *The Americans*

Jack Barksy's ultimate act of courage is sharing this intimate story that sheds
light on the true personal consequences of a life in espionage. Gripping and
emotional, *Deep Undercover* peers beyond the Iron Curtain for a look into
the world of a KGB officer illegally living abroad. Instead of romanticizing
the life of a spy, Barsky tells his story with honesty and heart.

JOEL FIELDS

Writer and executive producer, *The Americans*

Our fascination with spies runs deep, particularly those who are under deep
cover, the so-called sleeper agents. Living and operating under aliases, with
elaborate background stories (called legends), they intrigue us for the double
lives they live, sometimes with families—and even children. (The current
popularity of FX Network's award-winning *The Americans* attests to this.)
But what is the truth beneath the often glamorized surface? How are they
selected, trained, and dispatched to foreign countries? What are their secret
assignments? *Deep Undercover* lifts the veil on one such case, giving us a
glimpse of a secret life, showing us the price one man paid for undertaking
such an assignment. Reading his intriguing story, you realize how few of us
would willingly undertake such a mission—or succeed!

PETER EARNEST

Executive director, International Spy Museum

As a double agent who worked against Russia, I thought I had heard it all.
Then I heard Jack's story.

NAVEED JAMALI

Former double agent and author of *How to Catch a Russian Spy*

Jack's honesty and sincerity were clear from the first time I met him. He was
on a journey, and I was privileged to watch something very special unfold.
Jack's story is fascinating, and *Deep Undercover* tells it well. A true story of
redemption and what can happen when God's healing love breaks through
our mind, heart, and relationships.

ROB CRUVER

Senior pastor, Zarephath Christian Church; executive director, Urban Impact;
and author of *The Blue Jeans Gospel*

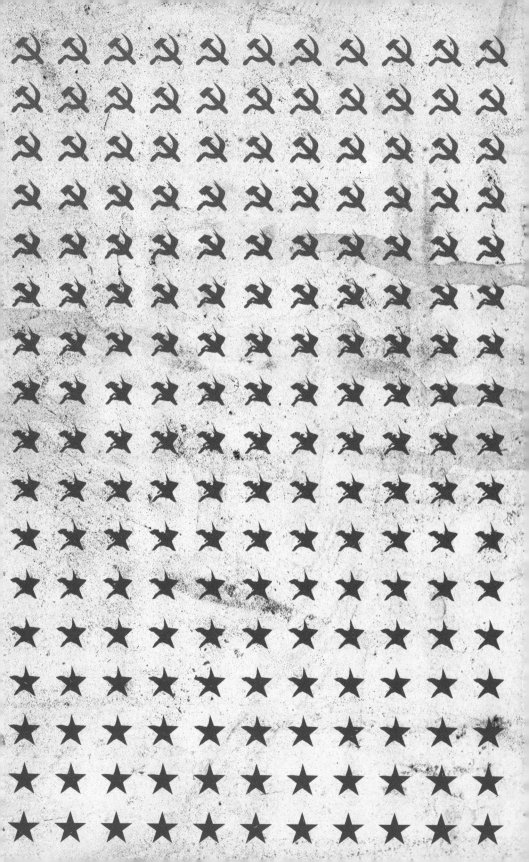

DEEP UNDER COVER

JACK BARSKY

with CINDY COLOMA

MY SECRET LIFE & TANGLED ALLEGIANCES
AS A KGB SPY IN AMERICA

TYNDALE
MOMENTUM

The nonfiction imprint of
Tyndale House Publishers, Inc.

Visit Tyndale online at www.tyndale.com.

Visit Tyndale Momentum online at www.tyndalemomentum.com.

TYNDALE, Tyndale Momentum, and Tyndale's quill logo are registered trademarks of Tyndale House Publishers, Inc. The Tyndale Momentum logo is a trademark of Tyndale House Publishers, Inc. Tyndale Momentum is the nonfiction imprint of Tyndale House Publishers, Inc., Carol Stream, Illinois.

Deep Undercover: My Secret Life and Tangled Allegiances as a KGB Spy in America

Designed by Dean H. Renninger

Published in association with the literary agency of Dystel, Goderich, and Bourret Literary Management, One Union Square West, New York, New York 10003.

Scripture quotations are taken from the *Holy Bible,* New Living Translation, copyright © 1996, 2004, 2015 by Tyndale House Foundation. Used by permission of Tyndale House Publishers, Inc., Carol Stream, Illinois 60188. All rights reserved.

For information about special discounts for bulk purchases, please contact Tyndale House Publishers at csresponse@tyndale.com, or call 1-800-323-9400.

Library of Congress Cataloging-in-Publication Data

Names: Barsky, Jack, date, author.
Title: Deep undercover : my secret life and tangled allegiances as a KGB spy in America / Jack Barsky with Cindy Coloma.
Description: Carol Stream, IL : Tyndale House Publishers, Inc., 2017. |
    Includes bibliographical references.
Identifiers: LCCN 2016048505 | ISBN 9781496416827 (hc)
Subjects: LCSH: Barsky, Jack, 1949- | Spies—Soviet Union—Biography. | Spies—Germany (East)—
    Biography. | Soviet Union. Komitet gosudarstvenno?i bezopasnosti. | Espionage, Soviet—United
    States—History—20th century.
Classification: LCC UB271.R92 B37753 2017 | DDC 327.1247073092 [B] —dc23 LC record
    available at https://lccn.loc.gov/2016048505

ISBN 978-1-4964-1683-4 (Softcover)

Printed in the United States of America

24   23   22
8   7   6   5   4

TO SHAWNA, CHELSEA, AND JESSIE, WITH ALL MY LOVE

CONTENTS

PROLOGUE

DECEMBER 1988

As I walked briskly toward my subway stop at 80th and Hudson in Queens, I glanced casually, out of well-worn habit, at a steel beam near the entrance to the station. What I saw there—an innocent-looking red dot—caused a momentary break in my stride. That dot was a secret message from the KGB: *Severe danger. Activate emergency procedure.*

For almost two years, I had managed to keep my worlds from colliding, but now a decision had to be made.

Two weeks later, I was still stubbornly resisting the extraction order. Instead of retrieving my emergency documents and making my way to Canada, I passed the red dot every morning, boarded the A train, and continued my commute to work. I was stalling, but I knew I couldn't make time stand still. That dot was a stark, daily reminder that I was disobeying orders, and the gravity of my situation pulled at me day and night, like an ever-tightening loop I couldn't escape. How much longer could I dodge the final decision?

Now, on a dreary December morning, as I prepared to leave my second-story apartment, I silently opened the door to Chelsea's room to steal a peek at my little princess. At the window, it was still pitch dark, but the nightlight cast enough of a beam for me to see those beautiful eyes, closed in peaceful sleep, and the riot of dark, curly hair that I never grew tired of caressing. I resisted the urge to bend down and kiss her, not wanting to risk waking her when I really needed to catch my train. Still, how could something so perfect be mine?

Without question, this child had stolen my heart. She wasn't my first, or my only, but she was the first I'd been granted time with, all eighteen months of her life thus far. Whenever she reached for me, fell asleep on my shoulder, or touched my face with her downy soft hands, my heart was overcome with a love I had never thought possible: unconditional and all-consuming.

Checking my watch, I backed out of the room without a single creak in the wood floor. After gathering my briefcase, I left Chelsea and my wife asleep inside the apartment and ventured into the dank December darkness. The city that never sleeps would wait another half hour for the sun to tease the edges of the morning sky.

As I walked toward the subway station, I thought about the web I had created and had now trapped myself within. In America, under the guise of computer analyst Jack Barsky, I had successfully established myself as an undercover agent spying on behalf of the Soviet Union. Back in East Germany, I was a different person with a different name and a different life. And that life was now calling me back. As an embedded agent of the KGB, I was expected to obey authority and follow orders.

The red dot told me to run—my cover must have been compromised—but that little girl asleep at home was holding me here, along with something else that I couldn't quite put my finger on.

After my usual ten-minute walk, I passed the steel beam with the dot and entered the westbound platform at 80th and Hudson. The station was populated with only a smattering of other commuters who, like me, had come early to avoid the morning rush.

As I looked in the direction from which the train would soon appear, I noticed an unusual movement off to the right in the periphery of my vision—the dark figure of a man who did not fit the appearance of a typical commuter. He seemed to be moving toward me, though tentatively, as if stalking an unsuspecting prey. Before I could fully digest the situation, he was at my side.

"You must come home," he whispered with a thick Russian accent as he leaned in toward me, "or else you are dead."

PART I

THE MAKING
OF A SPY

1

MY PARENTS HUDDLED at the kitchen table, pressing their ears toward a small cathode-ray tube radio, a relic that had survived the war but brought in only three stations. As my father fiddled with the knobs, trying to minimize the static, I scooted close to the small wooden table to find out what was going on. My mother rocked my baby brother, shushing him gently so they could make out what was being said on the radio. The dramatic sound of a voice speaking in a language I did not understand rose against the background of Chopin's somber "Funeral March." The equally gloomy German translator was heard on top of that.

On that early March day in 1953, all three radio stations were broadcasting only one event: the funeral of the great Soviet leader Joseph Stalin. Everywhere across the Eastern Bloc, people were spellbound, glued to their radios, just as we were.

"Vati," I asked, "who was this man Stalin? Why is he dead? What is the Soviet Union?"

My father tried his best to explain the situation in terms that my four-year-old mind could grasp.

"Comrade Stalin was a great man. He was the leader of the Soviet Union, a huge country that defeated Hitler. Under Stalin's leadership we were going to build a country where everyone could be happy. Today we are saying good-bye to one of the greatest men in history."

"So is everything going to be okay? Will you still get me a bicycle when I'm ready to start school, as you promised? Will I still get pudding on Sunday?"

"Yes, Albrecht, I think we will be okay. It might get a bit harder without Stalin, but there are some things you will not understand until you are a bit older."

This was his way of telling me that further questions would not be welcomed.

✦ ✦ ✦

Discovering my roots and heritage came to me in increments over the years: some remembered, some overheard, and some retold when I was old enough to ask. Most of the early pieces came in conversations with my mother.

What I know for certain is that I was born in a dreadful place at an unfortunate time—four years after Adolf Hitler's suicide effectively ended World War II in Europe. While the Americans, British, and French were busy rebuilding the western occupied zones in Germany, life in Soviet-controlled East Germany became a daily struggle for survival. The devastation from the war was only made worse by the Soviets' removal of valuable assets that had survived the Allies' aerial bombardment, including entire factories and a large part of the country's infrastructure. As a result, East Germany regressed economically and technologically by at least thirty years. And more than at any other time in the twentieth century, acquiring nutritious food became the number one priority in the land.

My parents first met in January 1948 at a teachers' orientation in the village of Rietschen, which was in a particularly poor area of East Germany not far from the Polish border. Though six years apart in age, Judith Faust and Karl-Heinz Dittrich were both recent graduates of the *Neulehrer* new teacher's program, an initiative introduced by the Allies in postwar Germany to develop teachers not tainted by connection to the Nazi regime, and both had grown up during the Great Depression, Hitler's ascendance to power, and the hardships of the most destructive war in the history of humanity.

For both my parents, their first teaching assignments signaled a new beginning, allowing tentative dreams about the future to begin to germinate in their hearts. Both had traveled to Rietschen from their parents' homes in Kaltwasser and Reichenbach, and it had taken them both the better part of the day to cover the thirty-kilometer distance. In those days, public buses were almost nonexistent and the trains were unreliable—at best, travel was an unpleasant adventure with uncertain outcomes. Schedules weren't worth the paper they were printed on, and the only thing predictable about the railroads was their unpredictability.

As Principal Panzram laid out the curriculum and the assignments for the coming school year, Judith's eyes frequently wandered to the cleanly dressed, bright-eyed Karl-Heinz, who listened to the principal with intensity. His fine features, high cheekbones, piercing gray eyes, and straight black hair gave his face the look of a movie star.

Not yet twenty years old, Karl-Heinz was the youngest member of the group, and his gangly frame made him look even younger, like someone who needed to be taken care of. Unlike Karl-Heinz, who was just starting out, Judith had six more years of life experience and six more years of hardship under her belt.

My mother was born in 1922 in Kaltwasser, where her parents, Bernhard and Zilla, worked as head forest ranger and cook at the estate of a German count. She had two sisters, Ruth and Eva. Those biblical names, and the fact that my mother sang in a church choir prior to marrying my father, lead me to believe that she was raised in a Lutheran family, though I have no other evidence of spirituality among my extended family or ancestors, and God was never mentioned in our home.

Because my mother grew up on a country estate, she never lacked for basic nutrition, a fact that may have accounted for her healthy appearance when so many others during those years looked emaciated. Her sparkling blue eyes projected intelligence and independence, but her plain, loose-fitting, full-length dresses marked her as a country girl. She wore no lipstick, and her shoulder-length hair was tied in a conservative knot at the back of her head.

In spite of their numerous differences, Karl-Heinz and Judith had two things in common: They were both new teachers, and they were strangers in the village of Rietschen. Consequently, they often turned to each other for companionship between classes and sometimes at the end of the school day.

In the spring of 1948, Karl-Heinz caught a virulent strand of tuberculosis. There were no antibiotics available for treatment. The village doctor could only prescribe bed rest and good nutrition. Getting rest was not a problem, but finding healthy food was an almost impossible proposition.

At this point, Judith's maternal instincts took over, and she began to care for her ailing friend and colleague. Every day after school, she stopped by Karl-Heinz's small apartment to keep him company and feed him whatever food she had scrounged up. Somehow she managed to acquire several pounds of rye meal from a local farmer, which she turned into a water-based porridge that became a staple in my father's diet as he convalesced.

After two months of Judith's loving care, Karl-Heinz overcame the disease and promptly fell in love with the woman who, most likely, had saved his life. In October 1948, these two ill-matched friends tied the knot at my grandparents' home in Kaltwasser.

Their marriage was unlikely to succeed in the long run. It rested on the fragile foundation of my father's need for a mother figure and my mother's strong desire to fill that role, as well as her pride at having captured such a handsome young fellow at a time when there was a severe shortage of eligible men in postwar Germany.

It appears that my father, virility restored, expressed his gratitude to my mother in more ways than one before they were married. She most likely knew she was pregnant at the time of the wedding.

✦   ✦   ✦

At the end of April 1949, my mother was granted a one-month pregnancy leave in anticipation of my birth. My father accompanied her to his parents' home in Reichenbach. The plan was that she would give birth there.

My father had recently joined the Socialist Unity Party (*Sozialistische Einheitspartei Deutschlands*—SED) and felt compelled to join the parade on May 1, 1949, in honor of International Workers' Day. He convinced his father to participate by suggesting they have a Sunday morning drink after the parade.

The weather in Reichenbach on that morning was typical for

springtime in Germany—gray skies, temperatures hovering around 60 degrees Fahrenheit, and a steady drizzle. The May Day parade was supposed to be a celebration, but the mood among the motley crowd of marchers making their way slowly through the deserted center of town did not reflect that sentiment. What was there to celebrate? Hitler and the Nazis had turned German pride into utter shame and dejection. Soviet rule was hard and unpredictable, and there was still not enough food for everyone. The average ration across occupied East Germany amounted to just under 1,500 calories.

The effects of this starvation-level diet were particularly apparent among the male marchers, including my father and grandfather, who had dressed in their best suits for the occasion. Their jackets hung loosely from bony shoulders, and their pants were held in place by suspenders. Indeed, these were lean times for bringing a child into the world.

But that all became a moot point late in the evening of May 17, when Judith's contractions began to intensify and my grandmother summoned the local midwife. The three women spent the entire night awake in the small bedroom usually occupied by my grandparents.

My father and grandfather also had a rough and sleepless night. Camped out in the home's tiny kitchen, they bravely consumed several bottles of homemade apple wine—enough to induce a headache so terrible that they both later insisted they had suffered as much pain as my mother had in labor.

Sleep would have been hard to come by that night anyway. Starting at 4:00 am, a seemingly endless parade of Soviet troops passed near the house. The rattling, screeching, and clanking of the Russian tanks on the granite cobblestones of Löbauer Straße was nearly unbearable, and nobody in the immediate vicinity had a good rest that night.

✦ ✦ ✦

I was born into a postwar world in which tensions between East and West were rapidly escalating. Just four weeks after the lifting of the Soviet blockade of West Berlin, which was five days after my birth, the western occupied zones of Germany were combined into the newly formed Federal Republic of Germany, also called West Germany. The subsequent establishment of the German Democratic Republic (GDR) in East Germany formalized the division that would last for the next forty-one years and quickly became a focal point in the Cold War. I was born in the GDR, on the Soviet-controlled side of the line.

The entire trajectory of my life is rooted in the geographic location of my birth. By the time Stalin died, it had become clear that East Germany would continue to evolve into a Communist dictatorship that might one day call upon one of its children to serve the Communist cause—perhaps in a major way. It is indeed an interesting coincidence that my first childhood memory is that of Comrade Stalin's funeral, the man most responsible for the establishment of Communist East Germany.

2

THE SHOVEL MADE A DULL RINGING SOUND as I thrust it desperately into the pile of frozen straw, dirt, and snow. The harsh January wind stung my face and numbed my fingers. My flimsy knit gloves did little to protect my tender young hands as I chipped away at the icy mound in search of the precious potatoes we'd stored there last autumn. Soon my runny nose had frozen—it seemed my nose was always running and my throat was often sore from infected tonsils. But none of that mattered. I had my assigned chore: to dig up the potatoes for our weekend meals.

One by one, I counted ten potatoes, stashing them in a burlap bag, and then dragged myself back through the cold to the school building where my parents both taught and where we had a three-room apartment on the third floor above the classrooms. During the winter, our rooms were heated by two coal-burning stoves, and the kitchen stove burned scrap wood that we collected from a nearby forest. With no indoor plumbing, I spent my early childhood trudging down the stairs and across the yard to the school latrines. But at least we had running cold water in our home and a solid roof over our heads. We may have been poor, but my brother and I didn't know it. Everyone we knew lived in similar or worse conditions.

Reaching the third-floor landing with my precious cargo of potatoes, I pushed open the apartment door and kicked off my muddy shoes.

"Shut the door!" my mother said before I was even inside. I was used to her sharp commands and knew she expected immediate compliance.

That apartment was the first home I remember. I took my first steps there, but because of poor nutrition, constant illness, and the pathetic state of medical care in the GDR, those steps didn't come until I was eighteen months old.

I dropped the dirt-clad potatoes into a bin in the kitchen and carefully removed the gloves from my frozen fingers.

"Did you count the potatoes?" my father asked.

"Yes—exactly ten."

"Good. Now wash up and get to the table."

"Can I warm up my hands first?" I asked, glancing toward the kitchen stove.

"They'll thaw while you eat," my father replied.

Over at the dingy sink, the ice-cold water felt surprisingly warm on my frozen hands. With that task completed, I headed to the kitchen table, where my mother waited with the dreaded spoonful of cod-liver oil, a torturous nightly ritual introduced by my grandfather, Opa Alwin, who had been served a daily dose of that wretched, dark brown—"but it is good for you"—goop while languishing with his fellow Wehrmacht soldiers in the bitter Norwegian cold during World War II.

Mother poured tea into my father's tin mug and served us all thick slabs of rye bread slathered with rendered pork fat. I watched as Hans-Günther, three years my junior, listlessly played with his food. Apparently he did not like the taste.

As was typical in Germany, supper was a light meal, usually consisting of sandwiches. The main meal was served around noon, and our food was supplied by the school. Often it was barely edible, but it was food.

Up until fourth grade, the students all went to school with small beat-up aluminum pots attached to their backpacks. The meals were cooked somewhere off-site and transported in aluminum milk cans on a wooden handcart drawn by a dwarf woman named Ulla. When Ulla arrived at the schoolyard, we were already lined up single file and greeted her with a clanking cacophony produced by beating our small pots with our metal spoons.

"Ulla, what you got today?" we yelled at her.

"Nothing special," she would answer honestly.

There was one meal that was worse than "nothing special." It consisted of a spoonful of watery scrambled eggs, a little bit of mashed potatoes, and a generous helping of an overcooked greenish pap that had once been spinach. On the days when that meal was served, most of my classmates and I emptied our small pots surreptitiously behind the bushes and chose to go hungry in anticipation of a slice of bread and a piece of sausage at the evening meal.

Saturday was soup day, and Sunday was the only day of the week when either meat or fish was served. The scarcity of food meant there was an ironclad rule in our home: "You will not leave the table until you have finished all the food on your plate." "I don't like it" or "This makes me sick" were not acceptable excuses.

Besides raw tomatoes, there were two vegetables I absolutely hated: red beets and celery root. Though I was able to choke down the beets, celery root was a different matter.

One day as I forced the dreaded root down my throat, it came back up with everything else. My mother jumped up from the table, threw a wet cloth at me, and made me clean up the mess.

"Now get back to the table and finish your meal," she said.

I wanted to protest, but her pressed lips and narrowed eyes sent me silently back to my plate. I took a deep breath and swallowed another bite—and it came right back up as the previous portion had.

Faced with a choice between enforcing the rules and having a mess on the table, my mother finally relented and changed the rule. I still had to eat my beets, and everything else on my plate, but thankfully no more celery root. Just the thought of it today makes me feel a bit queasy.

✦ ✦ ✦

Life continued to be hard in the mid-1950s. Building a new life in the GDR required both intelligence and survival skills. My parents had both.

My mother was well-prepared for the task of supporting a family during times of limited resources. She had acquired all the necessary skills during an apprenticeship as a domestic aide. Her darning ability came in handy in the management of our limited supply of socks and stockings. We Dittrichs were never caught with holes in our socks.

Somehow, she got her hands on a prewar mechanical sewing machine, and with the help of that contraption she repaired and altered our clothes. For years, we wore silk undergarments fashioned from the remnants of a parachute my father had found in the woods.

All food was rationed, including staples such as milk, bread, flour, sugar, and meat. Coupons were printed by the central government and distributed by local leaders.

One day, at the start of the month, my mother sent me to buy milk and handed me a wallet with some money and all the food coupons for the entire month. When I returned to the apartment, I realized with great horror that I no longer had the wallet in my possession. There was no hiding the fact that our entire monthly ration was gone.

"Mutti, I have to tell you something, but please do not get angry."

My mother gave me that stern look I was so afraid of and said, "What did you mess up this time?"

"Mama," I said, using my most endearing voice, "the wallet is gone."

The horror on my mother's face was frightening. "*Ach du meine Güte!*" she exclaimed. "Do you know what you have done? That was the food for the entire month, and anybody who finds the wallet can use those coupons. Go to your room. There will be no supper tonight!"

With head hung low, I went to my room and cried myself to sleep. The next morning, my mother stated matter-of-factly, "Albrecht, you are in luck. One of the neighbors found the wallet and returned it to us. But you have to learn a lesson: No sweets for you for the entire month!"

So for the next thirty days, I went to bed without being able to satisfy my sweet tooth.

+   +   +

Our evening routine was always the same, regardless of the time of the year or day of the week. At 6:00 p.m., all play had to stop. Even if it was still light enough to play outside, my mother would stick her head out the third-floor window and yell, "Albrecht, bedtime!"

My friend and playmate Reiner was allowed to stay out longer, and he was always baffled by this clocklike rigidity. But I would trudge up the stairs, get cleaned up for supper, swallow the hated cod-liver oil, eat my sandwich, and get ready for bed.

Most nights, "getting ready" meant washing my hands and face with a washcloth and cold water. Saturday was the day we got a thorough cleaning, either in a wooden bathtub filled with water that was heated on the kitchen stove or at a communal bath at the local factory.

Every night, after I said "good night" to my father, my mother followed me to my room, tucked me into bed, and gave me a good-night kiss. Then she turned out the lights and closed the door behind her. There was never a bedtime story or a lullaby, just the most efficient routine to get the boys into bed.

One night, when I was about five years old, I playfully averted my face to avoid my mother's kiss and said, "Mutti, I am bigger now. I do not need a good-night kiss anymore."

She raised her eyebrows for a brief moment but quickly regained her composure.

"All right then," she said curtly, and turned away.

Left alone in the dark, I was distraught. Did my mother not understand that I was trying to be funny? I was craving *more* hugging and kissing, not less. I wanted to take back my foolish joke, but the dark room and the fear that my mother would not understand my innermost thoughts and feelings held me back. Instead, I cried quietly until I fell asleep.

For years, my mother proudly shared this moment with others as proof of my early maturity. Her friends would chuckle as if I'd done something both comical and praiseworthy, while I would grin and duck my head. But my yearning for affection did not subside, no matter how many times my mother told that story.

From that night on, there were no more kisses for me.

3

EVERY GERMAN CHILD ANTICIPATES the day when he or she will receive *die Schultüte*, a large, brightly decorated cardboard cone filled with school supplies and sweets, which marks the first day of elementary school. Even with the scarcity of so many goods in the GDR, this was one tradition that could not be pushed aside.

On the table beside the large cone my parents had prepared for me, I noticed a smaller cone of goodies for my brother to keep him happy and an eight-by-ten-inch erasable slate set in a wooden frame, which was essential for our lessons with paper still in short supply.

Despite my mother's admonishments to slow down, I gobbled up the clumpy rye-meal porridge she served for breakfast, and I was ready to go. Since we lived in the school building, I only had to go downstairs to get to my new classroom, and when I arrived, I took a seat in the front row, as I would in every classroom from then on.

Now that we were school age, my classmates and I immediately joined the Communist youth organization, the Young Pioneers. Wearing the triangular blue necktie over a white shirt made me feel very special. My mother taught me how to iron the necktie and tie the knot so that I would always be ready for the Monday-morning salute to the flag.

I worked hard to memorize the Ten Commandments of the Young Pioneers, which we recited periodically during our meetings:

1. We Young Pioneers love the German Democratic Republic.
2. We Young Pioneers love and respect our parents.

3. We Young Pioneers love peace.
4. We Young Pioneers are friends with the children of the Soviet Union and all other countries.
5. We Young Pioneers study diligently and keep order and discipline.
6. We Young Pioneers honor all working people and help out where we can.
7. We Young Pioneers are good friends and help one another.
8. We Young Pioneers like to sing, dance, and do projects.
9. We Young Pioneers like sports and keep our bodies clean and healthy.
10. We Young Pioneers proudly wear our blue kerchief.

Young Pioneers was the first link in the chain of Communist organizations we would join as we grew up. In fifth grade, the Young Pioneers advanced to what was called the Thälmann Pioneers (named after Ernst Thälmann, the head of the Communist Party of Germany, who was killed by the Nazis at Buchenwald in 1944). In high school, we advanced automatically to the Free German Youth, and almost every working person later moved on to the Free German Trade Union. A select few might become members of the Communist Party itself.

Beginning with second grade, my class was moved from the building where we lived to a place at the very edge of town. Every morning at 7:30, the entire class gathered in the center of Rietschen to make the kilometer-and-a-half trip to school together on foot. Rain, shine, cold, or snow, we dutifully walked to class, without supervision, on a road without a sidewalk.

By the start of third grade, we were taught by a team of specialized educators. My absolute favorite was Herr Lehman, our new math teacher. Math did not feel like school at all. To me, it was fun and games, and the "accidental" outcome was that I hard-coded the fundamentals of arithmetic into my brain.

One morning in October 1957, Herr Lehman came to class even more excited than usual. He was holding a metal box with a bunch of dials and gauges. When he turned one of the knobs, the box made a *beep, beep, beep* sound. He let that go on for some time while we patiently waited for an explanation.

After about thirty seconds, Herr Lehman turned off the sound and said excitedly, "That, boys and girls, is your future!"

Our future was a bunch of beeps?

Herr Lehman explained that the beep originated from something called *Sputnik*, a satellite that could circle the entire earth in about ninety minutes.

I couldn't quite grasp the enormity of the event, but I understood that something really big was going on. The fact that this Sputnik thing had been launched by the Soviet Union, our closest friend and ally, cemented our budding belief that the future was on our side.

✛   ✛   ✛

Also in third grade, an optional class—Religious Instruction—was added to the curriculum. The class met at noon every Saturday at the end of the regular school day.

When I asked my father if I could attend this new class, his immediate reaction made it clear what the answer would be. As an active member of the SED, which viewed religion and spirituality as something only to appease the uneducated masses, he could not allow his son to participate in such a class.

"But, why not?" I asked.

"Albrecht," my father said with a glance at my mother. "The stuff they teach in that class is mostly fairy tales. It's not good for you."

I looked at him quizzically. "Fairy tales are not good for me? I just finished reading the entire Brothers Grimm, and I like fairy tales."

My father seemed annoyed by my precocious argument and tried to explain further.

"The Christian fairy tales make people believe in things that are not good for them. In the past, this has helped the rich to suppress the poor. I don't want to explain anymore—just believe me, this stuff is bad for you."

With that, the conversation was over, without a convincing argument—which was something that happened often when I asked questions that made my father uncomfortable. But the lack of any real information in his reply only intensified my curiosity.

The next Saturday, when the regular class was over, my friend Reiner and I left the school building while the rest of our classmates stayed for Religious Instruction. Reiner's father was head of the local police and a member of the SED, and he, too, had forbidden his son from attending the class.

"What do you think it's all about?" Reiner asked as we lingered outside of the building.

"My father said it's harmful to people," I said.

"Why would they have it then?"

The way his eyes widened, I knew that he, too, wanted to know about this dangerous class.

"What did your dad say?" I asked.

"Nothing. Just that I cannot attend."

Once the class started, we tiptoed along the outside wall of the building and planted ourselves below a half-open window. From there, we were able to follow along with the class.

Indeed, the teacher seemed to be sharing a fairy tale with the students, but instead of using the Brothers Grimm, he used a book called *The Bible*. We listened with rapt attention as the teacher told a story about three kings who went on an arduous journey, riding camels through the desert, guided by a bright star, to visit a newborn baby by the name of Jesus.

The story was just getting good when Reiner failed to suppress a sneeze. We heard giggling from inside the classroom, and a moment later our teacher peered out the window.

"Albrecht, Reiner, go home right now!"

We jumped to our feet and scurried off.

When I got home, I saw my father feeding the chickens and tried to engage him in a conversation.

"Dad, do you know anything about the Jesus fairy tale?"

His face showed instant disapproval. "Where did you hear about Jesus?" he demanded.

"Well . . . Reiner and I overheard the teacher through an open window," I said.

My father had a way of swirling his tongue inside his lips whenever something I did met with his disapproval or anger. When he spoke, his words were terse and unequivocal. "From now on, you come straight home after your last class. Do you understand?"

I nodded and backed away before he could decide on a harsher punishment. Reiner got a similar tongue-lashing from his father, and we were sufficiently scared not to pursue the subject any further. Every Saturday after that, Reiner and I hurried straight home at noon.

✢   ✢   ✢

A few months later, I had an opportunity to find out more about the Bible for myself.

We had gathered for Christmas at Opa Alwin's and Oma Hedwig's house, which was always my favorite destination for any holiday.

Opa Alwin was the only adult in our family who seemed to like me. He was a kind man, and it sometimes seemed strange to me that my father was his son. Opa's muscular six-foot frame made him look like a giant to me, but he always had a twinkle in his sparkling blue eyes.

I remember once watching him shovel coal through an open window into the school basement, part of his job as the janitor. He showed me where it landed and where it would be used to heat the school throughout the next winter. As I stared at that enormous pile, I couldn't fathom how only one person could have done all that work.

"Opa, I can't believe you finished that big pile all by yourself. How did you do it?" I asked.

"One shovelful at a time," he said with a proud smile.

My grandparents had an apartment at the far end of a huge regional high school that also included a dormitory. The expansive school facilities included a tennis court, a soccer field, a gym, and a park. Of course, at Christmastime, the entire building was empty because all the students had gone home for the holidays. I had the long tiled hallways all to myself, and I would either bounce a ball off the walls or race up and down on my rubber-wheeled scooter.

Christmas was the biggest holiday of the year for us, yet there wasn't even a hint of Christ in our celebration. Our traditions were purely pagan, including a meticulously decorated fir tree and an occasional appearance by Santa Claus, whom I easily identified as a neighbor in disguise.

When I was old enough to be trusted with such an important task, I was put in charge of dressing up the tree. First, wax candles had to be placed carefully so as not to be directly beneath an overhanging branch. Heavy tinsel (which contained a percentage of lead to make it hang down straight) was added strand by strand (and also removed strand by strand to be reused the following year), and all other decorations were added last. Presents were opened on Christmas Eve.

Among the several packages with my name on them, there was really only one that was of interest. Socks, shoes, and other articles of clothing were quickly set aside in search of the one box that contained the *real* present. And whether it was a Tinkertoy construction set, a soccer ball, a toy fire engine, or a model train, there was always only just one.

It was still a few days before Christmas, and I had come inside the house to warm up after playing in the cold, empty halls of the school. My brother rarely joined me in my adventures, and my parents spent much of their time in the kitchen talking with Oma Hedwig.

After a cup of peppermint tea to warm me up, I went to search Opa's bookcase for something interesting to read. As I scanned the shelves, a title caught my eye: *Die Bibel*. It was the very book that the Religious Instruction class revolved around. The Jesus fairy tale was within those pages.

Looking around to be certain that no one was nearby, I eased open the cover and flipped through the delicate pages. The words were printed in the outdated and difficult-to-read Fraktur font, just like the Brothers Grimm book I enjoyed so much.

My heart picked up a beat as I turned the pages of this forbidden book and began reading from the beginning. I didn't see any mention of Jesus. By the time I reached Genesis 10 and 11 and the lineages of Noah and Abraham, I had yawned enough times that I decided to close the giant book.

What could make this book interesting enough for an entire class? And why was I forbidden to read it? I couldn't ask my parents, or even Opa Alwin, about the Bible, and so I left it behind to pursue more interesting subjects.

I didn't open another Bible for the next forty-five years.

4

A FEW INCIDENTS FROM MY CHILDHOOD will serve to illustrate how my parents unwittingly taught me to ignore my pain and suppress my emotions—characteristics that gave me the independence needed for a successful career as an undercover spy but did not necessarily serve me well in my relationships.

When I was about nine, I went to summer camp and had a terrific time—playing soccer and other games with my friends, swimming in an ice-cold river, visiting a local zoo, singing songs, and telling stories—until three days before it was time to go home.

That day, a few of us were out playing soccer in a grassy field. As usual, we all played barefoot. At one point, I went into the bushes to retrieve an errant ball and suddenly felt a stinging pain in the sole of my left foot. I don't know what I stepped on, but my foot was bleeding like crazy as I hobbled back to the main building and alerted a teacher. She appeared more frightened than I was when she saw the blood streaming from my foot.

With no medical staff at the camp, the teacher retrieved a bandage from the emergency kit and dressed the wound as best she could. For the next three days, I was doomed to stay indoors because my bandaged foot wouldn't fit into a shoe.

Despite my injury, I remember that the bus ride home was still a lot of fun. We sang all the songs we had learned at camp, and the four hours passed quickly. But when the bus dropped us off at the school building, which was about a mile from our apartment, the teacher was worried about how I would get home.

To my surprise, my father showed up on a brand-new, shiny black Jawa motorcycle he had purchased while I was gone. Noticing my bandaged foot, he said, "What kind of trouble did you get into this time?" When I explained what had happened, he said, "Well, I hope you learned a lesson about not going into the bushes without shoes on. Come on, let's go home."

I climbed onto the back of the motorcycle, wrapped my arms tightly around my father's midsection, and off we went.

When we arrived at home, my mother and brother were outside the building. Hans-Günther showed immediate concern as I hobbled toward the door, but my mother got right down to business.

"Let's go upstairs so I can take a look at this mess," she said.

Once inside our apartment, I dropped my backpack of smelly camp clothes under the kitchen table and sat on a stool while my mother removed the dirty, bloodstained bandage. The last bit stuck to the scabbed-over wound, and I winced as she tugged it from my foot.

"This is probably infected," she said as she glanced up at the clock on the wall. "You need to get to Dr. Harbers before he closes for the day."

"Now?" I said. Surely she didn't mean for me to walk the twenty minutes to the doctor's office.

"Yes, now. I will put a smaller bandage on your foot so you can fit into your sandals."

"But—"

I thought about my father's shiny new motorcycle and how it would take him only a few short minutes to drop me off at Dr. Harbers's doorstep, but a mixture of guilt for having gotten hurt and a desire to appear tough kept me from asking him—and he didn't offer.

"Put on a new sock before you go," my mother said as she returned to her household chores.

I hopped on one foot to my room, carefully pulled a new sock onto my injured foot, and slipped into a pair of sandals. Then I limped out the door without another word to my parents. I felt like a wounded snail making that journey, and every step was more painful than the last.

When I finally reached Dr. Harbers's office, the waiting room was cluttered with other patients. I sat waiting on a hard wooden bench as my foot throbbed a drumbeat of pain. When my name was finally called and Dr. Harbers examined the wound, the flicker of concern on his face spoke volumes.

"We need to clean this out. Where is your mother?"

"She's at home," I said.

"You walked here?"

I nodded.

Dr. Harbers frowned but said nothing. Instead, he rose from his stool and called the nurse, a strapping, middle-aged woman who barely acknowledged me as she came into the room. No friendly greeting or words of comfort. After a short instruction from the doctor, her vice-like hands pinned me to the examination table.

"Wait, wait—"

Dr. Harbers dug in, and the pain shot through every inch of my body like hot fire. I twisted and fought against the nurse's hands as the doctor burrowed mercilessly into my foot for what seemed an eternity. There was a brief moment of relief when I thought it was over, but then I saw a solid object in Dr. Harbers's hand that looked like an oversized tube of lipstick. A moment later, I cried out in pain at the searing heat and the smell of burning flesh as he cauterized the wound.

As the doctor dressed the wound and pushed away from the table, the nurse gave me a curt nod and left to go torture some other hapless patient.

"After you get home," the doctor said, "try not to walk on it very much while it heals. Come back immediately if it isn't better in a day or two."

As the sunlight faded behind me, I hobbled home, alternating between hopping on one foot and trying to walk on the side of my left foot—then the heel, and then just my toes. Every step sent a fresh shot of pain up my leg until I began to feel nauseated. That was one of the longest, and certainly most painful, walks of my life.

As it turned out, that would not be the only time my parents would send me to the doctor on my own for an injury. At the age of fifteen, I suffered a contusion on my left knee, which made the joint completely inflexible and landed me in the hospital. After four weeks there, I was entirely on my own to get home—with a severely atrophied leg.

At seventeen, I developed a severe case of appendicitis. The pain was so intense that I was not able to stand or walk straight. My mother simply advised me to take the bus to the hospital, where a surgeon performed an emergency appendectomy.

Throughout my upbringing, my parents provided me with food and shelter—and they made sure I toed the line—but when pain was involved, I was on my own. I learned early in life not to rely on others for assistance or comfort.

+ + +

My father's hard work and his commitment to Marxist Leninist principles finally paid off when he was summoned to an after-school meeting by Principal Panzram. Those meetings were almost never a good thing.

When my father returned from the meeting, my mother and I were doing the dishes—she washed them and I hand-dried them with a towel. My mother turned around and asked, "What did he want?"

"He said there is a position for a principal at the upper Bad Muskau middle school. The district school administration and the party leadership decided I was the best man for the job.

"Will you take it?" my mother asked.

"Of course. It means a promotion and more money—but also, you say no to the Party only once."

In May 1959, we loaded our belongings on a rented farm truck and made the twenty-four kilometer move to our new home. Twenty-four kilometers (about fifteen miles) was a huge distance in those days of limited transportation options, and I knew that I would never see my old friends again. But the excitement of moving to a much better place overcame the sadness of those final good-byes.

Our new home was an old two-story country school, divided into three sections: the classrooms, where grades 1–4 were taught, and two apartments—one for teachers and one for us. The building was in good shape, even though its dirty gray facade was pockmarked with bullet holes, a grim reminder of the combat action that had damaged much of the town during World War II. On the northern face of the school building, the Russian phrase Вперед на Берлин (Forward to Berlin) was painted in large red letters.

Compared to the tight space in Rietschen, our new apartment was huge: It had a kitchen, bedroom, living room, and study downstairs, and the bedroom for us boys was upstairs. The bedroom was not heated, and when the indoor temperature dipped below freezing, as it often did during the winter, my brother and I depended on the heavy, ten-inch-thick German feather beds to keep us snug and warm. Only our noses got cold.

Though the building had cold running water, we still had no in-house toilet facilities, and the trip across the backyard to the outhouse was often a scary adventure, particularly during the dark and bitterly cold winter nights. Toilet paper was not widely available, so we used square sheets cut from old newspapers. Still, by East German standards at the time, this was a luxurious place.

That fall, I entered the Bad Muskau middle school where my father was the principal and also taught biology and English. It required only a minimal effort for me to excel at my studies, though I was up against more than just the curriculum. I once overheard my father tell a neighbor, "The only student who deserves an A in biology is Albrecht, but as his father, I can't give him that." That bothered me quite a bit.

✦ ✦ ✦

As the school year wound down, I started counting the days until summer recess, which began the first week of July and ended promptly the last week of August. I couldn't wait for summer camp and a long visit to Opa Alwin's. He always smiled whenever he saw me, and we shared an emotional connection that I had with nobody else in my family.

When I visited, Opa Alwin would show me what he was growing in his garden that year, and I would stuff myself with luscious ripe strawberries. Or he would take me to a quarter-acre wheat field and let me watch him mow the golden stems with a sharp scythe, just as the peasants had done for hundreds of years.

But the most excitement came when he would stampede his four pigs from their muddy daytime pigpen into the sty where they spent the night. I'll never forget the first time he asked me to help by planting myself in the middle of the path to prevent the pigs from bolting into the street and forcing them to turn toward the sty instead.

"Opa," I said. "What if they run me over? They are much bigger than I am."

"Just be brave," he said with a gleam in his eye. "Pigs respect people, but only if they stand their ground."

Taking a deep breath, I prepared myself for the onslaught. However, just as my grandpa had predicted, when the lead pig saw me, she made a sharp left turn and ran into the sty. Opa came over and softly tousled my hair with his calloused hand.

"Well done," he said. "Well done."

I beamed with pride at my glorious achievement and the rare words of encouragement.

✦   ✦   ✦

One brisk autumn day in 1960, I was playing outside when my father called me in. I followed him into the kitchen and sat down at the table. He did not say anything for quite a while, but from the swirling motion of his tongue inside his lips, I knew he was uncomfortable.

Finally he said, "Opa Alwin is in the hospital. He had an operation, but don't worry. He is a strong man and will be well soon."

I knew this was true. My entire life, I'd seen just how strong Opa was.

But two weeks later, the news was disastrous. Again, I was summoned into the kitchen. But this time we did not sit down. My father had a somber look on his face, and he gently touched my head—something he very rarely did.

"Albrecht, I am sorry to tell you that your grandfather passed away yesterday."

I stood confused as my father broke down and cried. It was the only time I ever saw him cry.

"What do you mean, 'passed away'?" I asked after a respectful pause.

"He died, Son."

"But, but . . . you told me he was strong and would be well soon," I said with tears welling up in my eyes.

"I was wrong."

As my father turned and walked out into the garden, I ran to my room and cried for a long time. Nobody followed. Nobody came to console me.

When the small funeral party gathered around the freshly dug grave, I stood between my father and mother, desperately wanting to hold one of their hands. But I was conditioned not to ask. As we waited for the hearse to arrive, I felt chilled to the bone, partly from the cold wind and partly from the loss to my soul of the one person who had affirmed me and encouraged me.

When the casket had been lowered into its final resting place, an official said a few words and ended his eulogy with the customary "ashes to ashes and dust to dust." Then each person walked forward and tossed a ceremonial shovelful of dirt into the grave.

When my turn came, my father nudged me and I went forward, staring down at the cold ground. As I dropped a little more dirt into the hole, I saw my hero laid to rest "one shovelful at a time."

Back at my grandparents' home, Oma Hedwig and her sister-in-law served a meal, and the beer and wine soon lightened the mood and loosened the tongues of the mourners. This was unbearable to me, so I left the living room and mourned in solitary silence. I wanted to understand life and death, but there was no one to talk to. Once again, I was on my own, and once again I buried the pain as deep as I could—a habit that, sadly, I would perfect into adulthood.

5

BY THE TIME I WAS TWELVE, our standard of living had improved significantly. Food was no longer rationed, and meat was much more common, even in school lunches. Teachers were treated well in East Germany, and my parents' combined incomes produced a stash of savings available to acquire items that not long before had been unattainable luxuries.

I was playing outside one day in the spring of 1961 when a shiny dark-green car slowly entered our yard. It was a Wartburg 311, the best passenger vehicle produced in East Germany and a prestigious automobile indeed. I had never gotten close enough to a car to even touch one, much less ride in one, so you can imagine my shock and surprise when my father emerged from behind the wheel.

"Vati, wow, what is this all about? Did you borrow this thing?"

"No," he answered with a smile that barely concealed his pride. "I just bought it."

Getting a car at that time in the GDR was next to impossible. It was not uncommon for people to wait ten or fifteen years for the opportunity to purchase one. But apparently the ten thousand marks in cash that my father had shown to the seller had done the trick. And thus we became the first family in the entire village to own a car.

That summer, we took our first vacation that wasn't to one of our grandparents' homes. Our new Wartburg was perfect for the 395-kilometer trip to the seaside resort town of Heringsdorf on the Baltic Sea.

When I caught my first glimpse of that vast expanse of water and saw ships in the distance, I wondered what was on the other side and if it were possible to get there. My parents explained that we would not be allowed to travel on one of those ships because they were going to foreign countries, but to me that only made the prospect more enticing.

Our two weeks at the seashore came and went in no time, and on August 13, we loaded the Wartburg, said good-bye to paradise, and started our homeward journey. Because Berlin was directly on our way, my parents decided we'd make a stop in the capital and perhaps take a quick trip to the western side of the city to buy some things we couldn't get in the East.

After about two and a half hours of driving, we found ourselves on a busy section of the Autobahn, one of the main arteries connecting the northern coast with the rest of Germany. My father looked over his shoulder at my brother and me and said, "We're almost to Berlin. Get ready for the big city."

I sat up quickly and looked out the window at the road ahead. I had never seen so many cars before, but traffic was moving swiftly.

Suddenly, my brother and I were thrown forward into the back of the front seat as my father unexpectedly slammed on the brakes. And from that moment on, traffic slowed to a crawl, and the minutes turned to an hour as the sun heated up the inside of our dark-green car. There was no air-conditioning, and we had to keep the windows closed to avoid the thick, stinking exhaust from the inefficient two-stroke engines of the East German cars.

Though other cars began turning around ahead of us, my father stubbornly held his course, all while mumbling words I had never heard him say.

Finally, we saw two soldiers in camouflage up ahead with machine guns at the ready. They were flagging people down and pointing in the opposite direction.

My father cranked down the window and said, "What's going on here? How much more of a delay should we expect?"

The taller of the two soldiers responded with a smirk, "Delay? *Hier geht's nicht weiter.* You can't continue." From the tone of his voice, it was clear who was in charge.

My father tried again, "Can you tell us what's going on?"

"You'll find out soon enough," the soldier replied. "Now turn around and go home. That's an order."

We were all disappointed to miss out on the Berlin visit, but there was also a measure of fear that accompanied the unknown. What could have happened? A military confrontation with the occupying forces on the western side of the city? Or worse, the outbreak of another war? We were mostly silent for the next few hours as my father drove us around the outskirts of Berlin and south to Bad Muskau.

We found the answers to our questions when we arrived home and turned on the radio. The regular programming had been replaced by classical music, which was interrupted periodically by strident news bulletins.

> Today is an important day in the history of our young antifascist republic. Under the wise leadership of Walter Ulbricht and the Politburo of the SED, we have begun securing our border with an antifascist protective wall. This measure will protect the first German state of workers and peasants from the assaults by the West German neo-Nazis and their Anglo-American patrons. Long live the GDR, long live the SED, and long live Walter Ulbricht!

When the music started again, my father said with a nod, "It's about time. We need to protect what we've worked so hard for."

The Berlin Wall never had much significance to me during those years. Far more exciting things were going on, such as the first manned space flight, which had happened four months before the wall was erected. Yuri Gagarin's orbit of the earth was one more conspicuous sign that the Soviet Union had moved ahead of the United States in the area of technology. It was additional evidence of the inevitable triumph of communism over capitalism. For a young man growing up in the GDR, there seemed to be nothing but promise ahead.

✦ ✦ ✦

At the end of eighth grade, the educational path split into two tracks. Most students continued for another two years of formal schooling and then went on to learn a trade. But the top ten percent continued their education at a regional *Erweiterte Oberschule* (EOS—an advanced secondary school), which was the East German equivalent of the traditional four-year gymnasium or prep school. The primary purpose of the EOS was to prepare students for entry into university.

My mother had attended a boarding school, and she was determined that I would do the same. My application to EOS Karl Marx in the nearby town of Spremberg was granted, pending successful completion of a written entrance exam demonstrating my proficiency in math and German.

My father drove me the twenty-seven kilometers to Spremberg, and I was one of the last students to arrive in the classroom where the exam would be administered. The moment I stepped into the room, I felt uncomfortable, as if I had arrived at the wrong place. The boys all seemed bigger and stronger, and the well-dressed, well-developed girls were even more intimidating. As they mingled in little groups and interacted among themselves, they seemed like citizens of another world.

By contrast, with my shorts held up by suspenders, I looked like a scrawny beanpole of a country boy. Which I was. Luckily, no one paid any attention to me as I silently made my way to the last row, sat down at a bench near the window, and waited for the test to begin.

As soon as the teacher gave the word, all heads bent forward and the room fell silent except for the scratching of pencils on the test forms. Completely in my element, I moved quickly and easily through the questions and finished long before the allotted time. I always had a good sense of how I did on exams, and as I left the room that day, I knew I had passed. Sure enough, when the results were published, I was one of forty applicants admitted to the school.

On September 1, 1963, my father and I loaded my bedding, school supplies, and other necessities into the Wartburg and made the thirty-minute drive to the dorm at EOS Karl Marx.

As my father parked the car on the street, I stared out at the enormous building that would be my home for the next four years. Compared to everything I was used to, the place looked like a castle. Set back a hundred feet from the road and surrounded by lush greenery, the three-story villa rose up majestically to rule the surrounding neighborhood. The stucco front, unusually large windows, and complex steep roofline made the building a true standout in the entire city of Spremberg.

I later learned that the mansion, built in the 1920s, had been owned by a wealthy textile businessman and his wife. At the end of the war, both the textile mill and the villa had been declared *Staatseigentum*—property of the state. I don't know what happened to the businessman, but the authorities allowed his wife to stay in a two-room apartment on the second floor of the villa and share the grandiose mansion with twenty-five lively and disrespectful teenagers. The dowager kept to herself, and the students treated her like a ghost from the past, passing in silence on those rare occasions when our paths crossed.

Though I was impressed by the grounds and the beautiful building, what mattered most to me was that the dorm was coed. Though this arrangement caused many headaches for the live-in headmaster, for me it opened up glorious possibilities. Finally, I would be closer to those elusive and magnificent creatures known as *girls*.

Once school began, classes filled the day until 2:00 p.m. There were no electives in the EOS system, only a heavy emphasis on the following subjects in order of importance: math, German, chemistry, physics, Russian, English, history, biology, geography, physical education, civics, philosophy, art, and music. We also had school-sponsored extracurricular events in the Communist Youth Movement and Communist Military Sports Movement to strengthen our belief in the Communist cause.

Religion was absent from the curriculum, and even the study of philosophy was limited to the fundamentals of Marxist dialectical materialism—the idea that the material world has objective reality independent of mind or spirit.[1] Giants of German philosophy such as Kant and Hegel did not even get honorable mention. The concepts of open debate, point and counterpoint, and Socratic dialogue were unknown to us. Thus, the intellectual blackout extended far beyond spiritual matters.

There was one truth and one truth only: the teachings of Marx, Engels, and Lenin, as interpreted by the Communist leaders of our time. Dialectical materialism was elevated to the status of an exact science, on par with mathematics and physics. Therefore, its findings and conclusions, as applied to the history of mankind, were unassailable.

Moreover, because capitalism was certain to fall and yield to communism—the pinnacle of societal evolution—we were clearly on the right side of history, and there was no further need for critical thought. Existential issues were, by and large, off-limits.

This single-track approach to life could not help but stunt both our spiritual and intellectual growth. We were hungry for answers but often did not even know the questions.

After dinner each night in the dorm, there was a mandatory viewing of the evening news program, *Die Aktuelle Kamera*, which was primarily government propaganda with two minutes at the end for weather and sports. The top story was invariably something about the heroic efforts of a group of workers or farmers to help fulfill the goals of the central plan laid out by the Communist Party. Not even the most ardent supporters of the Communist regime (which included me) took this stuff seriously.

On the evening of November 22, 1963, I stepped away to the bathroom just prior to the start of the newscast. As I reentered the room through the sliding double doors, my friend Helmut jumped up from his chair and yelled, "Kennedy got killed!" The entire room, usually filled with banter and laughter, fell silent as we looked at one another in disbelief.

Though Kennedy, as president of the United States, personified our ultimate enemy—as we had seen clearly during the Cuban Missile Crisis in 1962 and his visit to West Berlin in June 1963 when he gave his famous "Ich bin ein Berliner" speech—he still had a certain mystique that reached even behind the Iron Curtain. JFK and his wife were attractive and elegant—an irresistible contrast to the stodgy East German leaders and their dour wives. And there was some hope that he might start the process of easing tensions between East and West.

Even though the media coverage of the assassination and funeral was cold and factual, and even though most East Germans lacked a deep understanding of what was going on in the world at the time, we sensed that Kennedy's untimely death was a big loss to humanity. Students and faculty alike were sobered by this tragic event.

The next day, a small group of students shuffled along a sandy back road to the railway station to catch the weekend train to our respective hometowns. The cold November drizzle and leafless trees reflected our somber mood. Even the transistor radio that usually blared rock-and-roll music during our walks was silent.

6

I WAS SITTING AT THE TABLE in my dorm room on a hot June afternoon, wrestling with a pesky math problem, when Rosi stepped into the room. Rosi was one of the girls in the dorm who often mingled with the guys. She was bright, funny, attractive, and friendly.

"Hey, Albrecht, a bunch of us are going to see *The Three Musketeers* at the open-air theater tonight. We got permission to stay out late. Do you want to come?"

I stared at her in surprise and said shyly, "I don't know. I have a lot of homework left to do."

Rosi let out a hearty laugh. "Since when do you have a problem with homework? I wish I had your smarts. Come on, it will be fun!"

Rosi was almost a year older than me, and she was already a fully developed young woman. For a scrawny, awkward country boy, she was clearly out of my league. And yet . . . was this for real? It wasn't exactly a date, but had this pretty girl just asked me out?

Up until that moment, girls had been creatures to secretly admire from afar. From kindergarten on, there had always been a pretty girl or two that I wished I could have as a special friend, but I was always too shy to ask. To me, girls were to be adored, admired, and treated with kindness and love—especially the dainty ones.

And now, here was my chance. A beautiful young lady had shown enough interest in me to ask me to join her. I hoped that Rosi couldn't detect my accelerated heartbeat as I leaned back, scratched my head, and said with phony equanimity, "All right, you talked me into it. When are we leaving?"

"Now!" she said.

I felt suddenly light-headed, and all thoughts of staying back to work on math problems fled from my mind.

For this special outing, the dorm administrator had moved the curfew from 10:00 p.m. to midnight. As nine o'clock approached, we began the twenty-minute walk to the outdoor theater. There were a dozen boys and girls in our group, but as if by secret agreement, Rosi and I stayed a few yards behind the others, walking silently side by side along the meandering back path through a garden ablaze with late spring flowers. The temperature outside was still near eighty degrees, and Rosi was wearing a sleeveless summer dress with a flowery print design.

Emboldened by her proximity, I "accidentally" brushed her hand, and to my surprise and delight, she took hold of mine. For the remainder of the walk, we held hands but didn't say a word.

After viewing the movie—of which I remember nothing—we began the homeward stroll, again lagging behind the group. Under the cover of darkness, I awkwardly tried to find her lips. When I did, she responded passionately and (in hindsight) with experience. Before we withdrew to our respective dorm rooms at midnight, there was one more sweet good-night kiss and our first embrace.

The next morning, my lips were sore and my jaw hurt, but I was walking on air, and the blissful grin that seemed permanently engraved on my face was a dead giveaway to anybody who cared to look. After sixteen years without meaningful love, and many years of yearning for female companionship, I was certain I had found the love of my life and the girl I would one day marry. What was probably only a casual flirt for Rosi was head-over-heels passion for me.

To my dismay, only two weeks remained before summer vacation, so I focused the grand sum of my pent-up emotions on my new girlfriend and spent every possible minute in Rosi's presence. When we were apart, I daydreamed about her and wrote her name on books, bags, desks, my hands—whatever suitable object could be victimized by my smudgy ballpoint pen. I sent her little slips of paper with love notes, including one that said, "I am you and you are I."

It was going to be a long summer without her, but I would write to her and think about her the entire time. And I was certain she would do the same.

✦ ✦ ✦

Although the school year was winding down, I still had time to get in trouble before the summer break began.

My mother always declared proudly to anyone who would listen, "Albrecht is very, very smart and easy to handle." But given the occasional lashings I received from my father, the "easy to handle" part may have been more fiction than fact. In any case, parental discipline at home did nothing to change my behavior when I was away at school. And as my ability to think, reason, and respond had improved, I had begun to challenge authority.

Oma Hedwig always advised me to count to ten and take a deep breath before I opened my mouth, but that wisdom was not on my mind one warm afternoon in June when I threw out a challenge to my math teacher in front of the entire class.

We were slogging through a stretch of the most boring mechanical algebra: square roots and logarithms. As Herr Traubach was filling the blackboard with formulas copied from a large notebook, I raised my hand.

"Yes, Herr Dittrich?" Our teachers always used the polite form of speech to address us, and in keeping with customary practice, I rose from my seat to reply.

"Can you tell us why we have to learn all this *quatsch*?" I said.

Herr Traubach's face turned beet red, and there was dead silence in the classroom.

"Sit down!" was all he could muster, and we finished the final ten minutes of class under a cloud of severe discomfort.

The following day, I was moved from the front row to the back and was also summoned to the principal's office. The principal was a short, wiry man with penetrating eyes, an aquiline nose, and a full head of wavy, dark-blond hair. He exuded authority and was one of the few people at the school whom I truly respected. When I closed the door behind me and stood in front of his desk, there was no mistaking that I was in trouble.

"Herr Dittrich, your behavior in class is unacceptable. You are such a smart young man, but your performance does not live up to your potential. High school is a privilege. Do not squander it by clowning around. You must shape up or we may have to resort to punishment."

Blah, blah, blah, I thought on my way back to the classroom. *My father's hand is a lot more dangerous than your mouth.* But I would soon get a painful reminder that a principal's words must be taken very seriously.

On Monday of the last week of school, the students gathered for the customary general assembly. As usual, I paid no attention to the announcements until I was rudely awakened from my daydreaming by the sound of my own name.

"Herr Wlochal and Herr Dittrich, step out in front of the assembly!"

I had barely enough time to come forward before the principal began reading a statement to the students and teachers. "Herr Dittrich, you are herewith receiving a strong reprimand for lack of discipline, disrupting class, and inciting your classmates to behavior unbecoming of a young Communist. We are placing you on probation. Failure to turn things around will result in expulsion."

The "blah, blah, blah" had become a real threat. Expulsion from high school would have a severely negative impact on my future. I had a sinking feeling in my stomach, and throughout the day I was unable to produce a single coherent thought. On the walk from the classrooms to the dorm—normally a joyful, chatty occasion—I trailed behind the group, hanging my head and brooding.

This was the first serious crisis of my life. When I met up with Rosi, she said, "Albrecht, if you care about me and about yourself, please, please improve your behavior!"

Well, I would show her I was worthy of her love, a motivator stronger than all the others taken together.

✦ ✦ ✦

I filled the two months of summer vacation with activity—going on camping trips and working in a local factory—but life seemed entirely meaningless without Rosi. We had promised to think about each other every night by looking at the brightest star in the sky at exactly

10:00 p.m. This I did faithfully, every night, often overcome with emotion. The few letters we exchanged made the wait more bearable, but I was incredibly anxious to return to school in September.

+ + +

One Sunday morning, I woke up early and proceeded gingerly down the creaky steps of the wooden staircase connecting the main living quarters to the second floor. My parents often slept in late on Sundays, so I tiptoed into the study in search of a book to read until it was time for breakfast. To my surprise, my parents were already awake and arguing rather intensely, albeit in hushed voices, in the adjoining living room. As I got closer to the door, I could hear what they were saying.

"I've had enough," my father said. "I'm filing for divorce."

I heard my mother laugh and say, "Calm down already, Heinz. It is normal for couples to have arguments. Let's stop this silly discussion before we wake up the boys. Should I make breakfast?"

This response infuriated my father, and he raised his voice.

"You don't seem to understand: I am getting a divorce. I am sick of your mothering and setting all the rules in this house. I want to live! I want to breathe! I am getting a divorce!"

With that, he walked out the door, got into the car, and drove away. I tiptoed back up the stairs, stunned and guilt-ridden for having eavesdropped.

Before reaching the second level, I heard a loud thud in the living room and rushed back down to find my mother passed out on the floor. I sat her up and pulled her onto the sofa, which was not an easy task for a skinny sixteen-year-old. Before I could think of what to do next, my mother came to and sat up in silence. There was a dazed, otherworldly look on her face as she stared into nothingness for what seemed an eternity. Finally, she raised herself with a forceful jolt and hurried up the stairs.

When I heard heavy footsteps in the attic just above me, I couldn't ward off the ghoulish vision of my mother dangling from a rope attached to the rafters. So I went up the attic steps and took a peek through the half-opened door. To my relief, she was engaged in some routine cleaning activities.

My mother and I barely spoke the rest of that Sunday. I didn't ask where my father was, and if my brother asked, I didn't hear him. Over the next week, conversation was kept to the bare minimum required to manage the logistics of the household.

My brother and I were never given any insight into the divorce proceedings. One day, my father called me into the living room. As we stood across the table from each other, he said, "Albrecht, the court will soon make a decision on the divorce. Since you are sixteen years old, they are willing to give you a voice in deciding who you want to live with when you're not at school."

In my mind, the decision had already been made, and I wasted no time in making that clear.

"Vati," I said, "Hans-Günther and I would like to stay here with Mutti."

By the characteristic swirling of his tongue inside his mouth, I knew that my father was displeased with my response, but he didn't say a word. Instead, he nodded curtly and walked out the door.

In late July, he moved into a one-bedroom apartment near the school in Bad Muskau. And though I went to visit him one time at his request, it was clear we had nothing left to say to each other. The relationship that had never really been had now reached its final destination—a dead end. After a few minutes of awkward silence, I made an excuse about having to help a friend with some bike repairs, and I got up to leave. He seemed almost grateful to see me go. I never saw my father again after that day—and never gave him much thought, either.

✦ ✦ ✦

On our first day back at school, I didn't see Rosi until after class was out. We walked back to the dorm together, across the Spree River and along a dirt road. I was ecstatic to be reunited with my one true love, but something didn't seem right.

When Rosi finally opened up, she spoke hesitantly at first, and then quickly got to the point.

"Albrecht, you know I really like you . . ."

I looked over at her, but her eyes were averted and her head was down.

"What is it, Rosi?"

She took a breath and started over. "Albrecht, I had a boyfriend before you and I got together. He's from my village, and he's in his second year studying medicine at the university. He came looking for me this summer, and now we are back together."

I stopped dead in my tracks, and for a moment everything was a jumble. Finally I managed to sputter, "But . . . but . . . what about your promise? What about the star? What about everything we had? Don't you know how much I love you?"

Rosi responded gently, with her eyes still averted, "I thought we were just having fun. You took everything too seriously. But I should have told you. I'm really sorry."

Despondent at the thought of losing her, I could already feel the distance between us growing wider.

"Well, can we still be friends?"

"Yes, of course," she said with relief in her voice, and for the first time since we had left class, she made eye contact with me.

For me, her answer left the back door ajar, and I decided I would win her back. We still had two full years of school together, which gave me the advantage of physical proximity. During my entire junior year, I hung around Rosi and made myself useful whenever and wherever I could. I helped her with her homework, carried her bags on the walk to school, and made myself available to talk whenever she wanted to. I was dogged in my pursuit and even faked a fainting spell one time. Yet nothing worked, and when we parted company at the end of the school year, we were still just friends. But I wasn't giving up.

7

AT THE END OF OUR JUNIOR YEAR, my class took a trip to the city of Weimar and visited nearby Buchenwald, one of the largest concentration camps from the Nazi era. This mandatory class trip was an idea conceived by the East German authorities to raise up future generations of leaders who would be firmly committed to the antifascist, pro-Communist heritage of our nation.

There were forty of us on the tour bus to Weimar, and we were a happy bunch, singing songs and joking during the four-hour drive. But all good humor quickly fell away when we got off the bus and stood before the entrance to the former concentration camp with its infamous inscription on the wrought iron gate: *Jedem das Seine* ("To Each His Own"). A heavy silence hung over us as we followed the guide into the large inner yard, where roll call had once been held. The guard towers, surrounded by razor wire, loomed ominously above us. The guide led us through the museum, which had been created in one of the buildings that used to house the camp's administration. We walked by walls with countless pictures showing emaciated, half-naked inmates, piles of corpses about to be bulldozed into a mass grave, and other gut-wrenching images of unspeakable cruelty.

In the next room were exhibits of lamp shades made of tattooed human skin and even two shrunken heads. This was too much to bear. I heard several of the girls begin to sob as they covered their mouths and tried to stifle their tears. Like most of the other boys, I hung my head in horror at what had been done here but remained outwardly stoic.

But the tour was not yet finished. On we went to the crematorium, where the dead were incinerated until nothing but ashes was left of the prisoners who had been alive only hours before.

Cleverly planned by the museum leadership, the tour ended in a room called the *Genickschußanlage*, which means "facility to shoot somebody in the neck." Unsuspecting victims were led into that room under the pretext of having their measurements taken. As soon as the victim was put up against the wall, a hole opened and an executioner on the other side of the wall killed the person with a bullet to the neck. We were told that Ernst Thälmann, the head of the German Communist Party, had been executed in this manner.

Thälmann was a hero of mythical proportions in East Germany. He had been a fighter against Hitler and the Nazis early on, and he was said to have been an all-around good person who died fighting the scourge of fascism.

For me, the loop was closed: Hitler was Satan incarnate; the Soviet Union had defeated Hitler; Ernst Thälmann had died fighting Hitler; and the East German Communist Party was now continuing Thälmann's fight against the neo-Nazis in West Germany and their American patrons.

At that moment, I swore that if I ever got a chance to make a major contribution to the destruction of the evil forces of fascism and capitalism, I would do my best. This vow became a driving force behind decisions I would make in future years.

After we left Buchenwald, we visited Weimar, where two preeminent German writers and poets, Johann Wolfgang von Goethe and Friedrich Schiller, had resided for many years. From there we went to the nearby city of Jena to see the university and the famous Carl Zeiss Planetarium. I immediately fell in love with Jena and thus made another life-shaping decision: I would attend the university there and study chemistry.

✦   ✦   ✦

Summer vacation came and went, and soon it was time to begin my final year of high school. By now, my grades had improved significantly and I was on course to graduate with highest honors. I had learned how to operate successfully within the system, and all the teachers now treated me with respect.

For me, this was the beginning of a ten-year period during which I pursued academic excellence and seemed destined for stardom and a glorious career within the East German system. Unfortunately, the combination of academic success and the lack of a father figure—or mature mentor—who could offer some guidance and infuse me with a desperately needed dose of humility, allowed me to develop a level of self-confidence bordering on pure arrogance, a fierce independence, and a deep-rooted sense of invulnerability. All of these qualities, it turned out, were critical elements of the psychological makeup that made me an excellent candidate for a career in espionage.

When I returned to Spremberg to start the school year, I was delighted beyond words to discover that Rosi had broken up with her medical school boyfriend. I was now in the clear, without a rival, like a soccer player on a breakaway who has outmaneuvered the entire defense and needs only to nudge the ball gently past the goalie.

By Christmas, my patience and persistence finally paid off and Rosi was once again my girlfriend. As the school year progressed, we talked about taking our relationship to another level, and shortly after my eighteenth birthday, we became lovers. But as final exams approached and the future opened up before us, our lives were moving in different directions. Rosi was headed to Berlin to study psychology, and I would keep my vow to move to Jena and study chemistry.

Although Jena was an eight-hour train ride from Berlin and access to phones was very much restricted, I ignored these inconvenient facts in my unbridled enthusiasm. I was convinced it would not be long before Rosi and I would be reunited and eventually married. I failed to notice that Rosi wasn't equally upbeat about our future together.

June 16, 1967, was an exceptionally dreary day in Spremberg. Heavy clouds hung over the town, and a steady, chilling drizzle punished anyone who ventured outside. The gloomy weather reflected my mood as I faced my last day with Rosi before we would go our separate ways. Most of the other students had already left, and the dorm was deserted. Having packed the last of our belongings, we sat on my bed and just looked at each other.

Then, in a desperate attempt to make time stand still, we engaged in one last intimate embrace before Rosi had to go. I watched her as she walked along the pathway and disappeared from view, but she never once looked back for a final good-bye.

After she was gone, I grabbed my suitcase and staggered out into the dismal afternoon, hot tears merging with the cooling raindrops. By the time I reached the train station, I was soaked through, but the misery of my condition paled in comparison to the incredible void that had opened up in my soul.

Perhaps, deep down, I knew what had to come. Still, when I received Rosi's final good-bye letter, which came in August, it hit me hard. This was her first letter since the last day we'd spent together, and I opened it with a mixture of hope and fear.

Dear Albrecht,

I am very sorry to tell you that our relationship has come to an end. We had a great deal of fun during our time together at high school, but it is now time to go our separate ways. Please understand that this is really the end—there is no other way. I am very sorry if this hurts you, but in the end it will be the best solution for both of us.

Greetings,
Rosi

The void I had felt for the past two months took on another dimension— the future. Though I would later make one last attempt to win Rosi back by visiting her in Berlin, in the end I failed miserably, and I finally had to come to terms with my defeat.

The end of our relationship left deep and indelible marks on my soul. For the first two years in Jena, I buried myself in my studies at the university and avoided female companionship altogether. After opening myself up to love only to be kicked squarely in the teeth, I vowed to myself that I would never let it happen again. From now on, nothing and nobody would penetrate my armor. Later I would discover that the ability to keep marching toward a goal without being held back by feelings or relationships was absolutely essential to building an undercover identity in another country. But at the time, I had no idea how profoundly my relationship with Rosi would influence the course of my life.

8

ON A SULTRY DAY IN EARLY SEPTEMBER, I dragged my heavy bags the final 800 meters from the train station to the student dorm in Jena. My stomach was growling, my mouth was dry, and my muscles were weary, but my mood was upbeat. After all, this was the first day of my life as an adult.

Jena was a dream come true, a real city with public transportation and multiple establishments of every kind—butchers, bakers, clothing stores, and restaurants. And then, of course, there was the magnificent university with its ten thousand students and four-hundred-year history.

When I finally arrived at Nollendorfer Straße 26, I paused for a moment and looked up in wonderment at the oddly configured three-story hotel, built in the early 1900s, that now served as a college dorm. I checked in at the desk, received my room assignment, and made my way upstairs to the two-hundred-square-foot bare-walled rectangle, with three metal bunks, a worn wooden table, and a roughly constructed armoire that I would share with five other bright young men for the next ten months. When I saw that I was the first to arrive, I claimed what dorm experience had taught me to be the best sleeping location—the upper bunk of the bed furthest from the door.

Famished by now, I devoured the two sandwiches my mother had packed me for the trip and climbed onto my bunk to wait for my roommates to arrive. While eating, I was suddenly overcome with thankfulness for my mother. Even though she had not given me the love I was looking for as a child, she had taken very good care of me and my brother. So I pulled out a pen and a piece of paper and wrote a letter expressing my sincere gratitude and also apologized for any trouble I may have caused her in the past.

When my roommates began to trickle in, I watched with some amusement as they tried to cram their belongings into the overflowing armoire. Most of their belongings stayed in their suitcases, which were stowed beneath the beds. As cramped and sparsely furnished as our living quarters seemed, we soon found out that we were the lucky ones. The rest of the first-year male chemistry students—East Germany's best and brightest—were housed together in a single large room in a building at the other end of town.

The last of my roommates to arrive was Klaus, a redhead with intense, deep-set eyes. I would soon find out that Klaus was a rarity on campus: a Catholic who made no attempt to hide his faith in God. But he knew better than to try to proselytize his five atheist roommates. Klaus was the only Christian I met during my six years at the university. Whatever remained of a once-vibrant theological faculty had no voice on campus now, and in our philosophy classes we were taught Marxism-Leninism to the exclusion of any other philosophy or religion.

✦ ✦ ✦

Once classes began, the workload was overwhelming. We had science coming at us from every angle—through lectures, seminars, and labs, along with copious amounts of assigned reading and a seemingly endless series of lab reports to submit. Knowing that the students admitted to the program were drawn from the top 10 percent in the nation, the elite faculty had put together a curriculum that amounted to a full-frontal scientific assault. The demands of this "chemistry boot camp" were so high, in fact, that one quarter of the freshman chemistry majors would resign by the end of the year.

We soon fell into a schedule that had us on the go from 6:00 a.m. till 11:00 p.m. on weekdays, with a mandatory four-hour lab session on Saturday morning. After that, most students who had families close enough to school went home for the rest of the weekend. In my room, only Spencer and I, who both lived long hours away, stayed back on the weekends.

I often hung out with my new friend Günter, who lived in Jena. His family welcomed me with open arms. Günter and I would play chess, shoot the breeze, or listen to records from his eclectic music collection—everything from classical to beat to jazz. On Saturday evenings we would often head to the Rosenkeller student club for beer and dancing—well, mostly for beer. Going in, the hope was always that I might connect with a pretty young lady, but invariably I would walk back to the dorm around midnight, somewhat inebriated, without having met anyone.

One of the first things I did after arriving at the university was seek out the basketball coach. Although my experience consisted of exactly one game in high school, I knew this was a game I should be playing. At six feet three inches, I was one of the tallest people on campus, and I could run and jump with the best of them. Coach Stange put me on the second team for my freshman year, but after holding my own in practice against our six-foot-seven-inch starting center, I earned the respect of my teammates, and by the beginning of the next season, I had worked my way up to the first team.

For the next four years, I enjoyed all the practices, games, and tournaments—and, above all, the camaraderie. This was the very first time I had ever been part of a team that had to work together to be successful. I loved it. We were united in our beefs about the coach, and we won and lost as a cohesive team. Either way, there were always a few beers involved.

The basketball team became a family for me, a family to which I developed more of an attachment than to my real family at home. During my university years, basketball was the most important thing in my life emotionally. I felt cared for and appreciated, even on days when I didn't play very well. The teamwork and camaraderie were connections I had never experienced before, and I came to appreciate the value of being part of something bigger than myself.

✤ ✤ ✤

Even as I worked to fit in and find my place with the basketball team, in the classroom I found ways—intentionally or not—to set myself apart. Though I was not necessarily the brightest among this elite group of achievers, I managed to establish a reputation for brilliance through hard work, cleverness, and a bit of serendipity.

During our freshman year, the most important interactive small group session was in our general chemistry class. The instructor, Dr. Walther, was a short man whose distinctive features reminded me of Pinocchio. Dr. Walther was a classic example of the breed of elite academicians who rose to prominence in the GDR: smart, incisive, and oh-so-full of himself. He treated us students as if we were on borrowed time—which many of us were, I suppose. Most of our peers seemed intimidated by the mighty Dr. Walther, but Günter and I saw him more as a challenge, and we wore our own self-confidence on our sleeves.

When Doc, as we called him, advised the class to memorize a key formula of thermodynamics in preparation for an upcoming test, I opened my big mouth and blurted out, "No problem. If you forget the formula, you can always just derive it from scratch."

Günter, who usually sat next to me, pulled at my arm in horror and whispered, "Are you crazy?" He knew what was coming, but what he didn't know was that I had spent the night before memorizing the fifteen steps needed to derive the formula.

The expression on Dr. Walther's face said it all: *I've got you now, you arrogant twit!* With a smirk, he stepped grandly to the side and invited me up to the blackboard.

"Well then, Herr Dittrich, derive away!"

I walked calmly to the front of the room and picked up the chalk. After glancing back at my classmates, I began to write out the formula, step by logical step. When I was done, I underlined the final result with a bit of a flourish and turned around to bask in the glory of my accomplishment. Dr. Walther appeared dumbfounded, and the class could barely contain their joy over the defeat of their tormentor. Günter gave me a big grin and flashed a victory sign just above his desk.

Doc's respect for my performance was clear when he turned to the class and said, "You have just witnessed the performance of a student who will one day be a real scientist."

From that point on, I became the go-to guy in class discussions when other students responded with silence to a difficult question.

Occasionally, the professor would sigh and ask rhetorically, "Do I have to go to Dittrich again?" Of course, this meant I always had to be prepared. But I learned to focus on the toughest subjects and often didn't know the answers to more basic questions. Still, this "trap" I had set for myself taught me how to discern what was useful and most important.

Continuing to work hard and get good test results bore fruit at the university. Apparently, my reputation as a whiz kid carried over to other sections of the chemistry program as well, and the professors were always looking for ways to trip me up. Once, during organic chemistry, the lab professor gave me a mystery liquid to analyze. Normally, this would have been some kind of organic liquid such as benzene or an ester. But after three days of futile testing, it finally dawned on me: It was tap water. Now, to prove that I had discovered what the substance was, I had to deliver a derivative, another substance made from the original. When I handed the professor a boiled egg, the Dittrich legend continued to grow.

✦   ✦   ✦

When it came to lab work, I was a sloppy—and sometimes dangerous— scientist. As one of my professors once remarked, "It seems that Albrecht's theoretical genius is way ahead of his practical prowess." That pretty much summed up my performance.

One day I was talking with Günter across the aisle. Rather than turn around on my stool, I sat down on my worktable with my back close to a flaming Bunsen burner. When I felt unexpected warmth, I turned slowly to my neighbor and said matter-of-factly, "I think I'm on fire."

"You *are!*" he shouted.

Günter immediately put out the flames with a very liberal dose of water, and other students stepped in and "helped" until I was soaking wet. Then we all had a good laugh.

On one particular day in the lab, the assigned experiment gave me pause. I consulted the scientific literature to make sure I had not mis- understood. No, it was all correct. In order to conduct the experiment, I was required to use mustard gas—a chemical weapon that had been used during World War I. It causes severe burns and blistering to every tissue it touches and often results in a painful death.

As with many difficult lab assignments, I consulted with Günter.

"Listen," I whispered. "I got this task which seems rather simple, but it involves mustard gas."

"Are you joking?" Günter responded.

"No, I'm not joking. Take a look." I showed him the page in the chemical journal where I had found the recipe.

"Don't do it—this is nuts!" Günter said adamantly.

"But—but if I go to a secondary assignment, the best grade I can get is a B."

"So you get a B," Günter responded, "and we all live to play chess on Sunday."

Clearly he did not understand that a B was unacceptable for Albrecht Dittrich. I thought about it for a moment and created a plan. As I walked toward the exit, I called back to Günter, "I'll be careful, and on Sunday I'll beat you at chess."

After securing the proper permissions from my professor, I went to find the janitor, who would retrieve the mustard gas for me from a basement bunker in one of the buildings. My confidence took another hit when he dragged out a heavy, medium-size gas tank that looked just as scary as its contents—with peeling, light-green paint and some sizable rust spots.

Determined not to back out now, I set up my equipment in the outdoor lab. The configuration was rather simple: a flask on a tripod filled with a solvent and covered with a stopper with two holes, one for the intake of the mustard gas, the other for the gaseous new compound to be piped into another flask that was sitting on a bed of dry ice. The stopper did not fit very well, but getting another stopper from the supply room meant a half-hour delay, so I decided to go ahead with what I had.

I donned my gas mask and turned on the Bunsen burner. Moving over to the tank of mustard gas, I slowly turned the valve until I saw bubbles going through the now boiling liquid.

There was only one problem: the janitor's very large dog, who was sitting under a tree outside the building. As soon as he saw me with the gas mask on, he got spooked and charged at me, barking violently. With my heart pounding, I hurried away from the lab setup and removed the gas mask. The dog immediately settled down and trotted away.

As I looked around for the janitor, in hopes that he would take his dog away so I could put the gas mask on again, I suddenly saw flames shooting out of the flask with the bubbling solution.

Cursing the faulty stopper, as if it were the fault of that little piece of rubber I had not placed correctly on the flask, I weighed my options: I could either put on the gas mask and risk being attacked by the dog again, or I could leave the mask off and risk mustard gas poisoning.

Choosing the latter option, which somehow seemed the less risky, I took a deep breath, ran over to the tripod, doused the flames, closed the mustard gas valve, and shut down the experiment.

For the next twenty-four hours, I checked my skin, mouth, and eyes for signs of poisoning, but I also had to admit to the professor that my experiment had failed. He gave me another assignment, and I got the dreaded B, but I lived to tell about it. Then, to add insult to injury, Günter trounced me in chess that weekend after telling me in so many words, "I told you so."

9

ONE DAY, IN THE SPRING OF 1968, Günter told me to meet him outside the lab for a cigarette break. After offering me a cigarette from a pack of filterless Karos, by far the most noxious cigarettes on the market in East Germany, he got straight to the point.

"Albrecht, you need to join the Party."

His directness surprised me. This was the second time since high school that someone had attempted to recruit me into the elite organization that essentially ruled the entire country. By instinct, I was not much of a joiner, but my father's example had shown me that Party membership was a great career booster.

"Why?" I asked Günter.

"Because you're the smartest guy in our group and we need people like you in the Party. We will be the leaders of the future," he said, appealing to both my logical mind and my ego. "So what do you say?"

"I'll think about it. But don't push me."

"Fair enough."

Unbeknownst to me, Günter had engaged an ally in the recruitment process, our professor of Marxist philosophy, Siegmund Borek. Professor Borek was a firm believer in the Communist cause—so much so that he had chosen to teach Marxism rather than chemistry, the subject he had majored in.

One day, he pulled me aside after class.

"You really ought to think about joining the Party, Albrecht. You have great potential. How would you like to work closely with your friends Günter and Matthias?"

"You aren't the first one to bring this up," I said, "but tell me what will be expected of me and how Party membership would benefit me personally."

"It's very simple," Professor Borek said. "You will participate in leading the affairs at the university. You will be privy to information before it is shared with the general public—if it is shared at all. And you will be prepared to become one of the leaders of your generation. Does this not sound good?"

Before I could reply, he took his recruiting efforts to another level by inviting me to his apartment.

"Tell you what," he said, "come for dinner one night and we'll talk things through and answer all your questions."

An invitation to dinner with a professor—now that was something! And though the apartment turned out to be a typical dimly lit, one-room, third floor walk-up, and the lukewarm mutton the professor's wife served for dinner left something to be desired, the fact that I, a mere freshman at the university, was able to spend time with a professor in his private home was far more significant. Our conversation centered on the future of the world. As a philosopher, Professor Borek had the big picture in mind.

"Think about it, Albrecht. We're going to put Marx's theory into practice, and we will finish what Lenin started. We will build a just world that is free of any kind of oppression, and we are inviting you to participate in this great endeavor."

His enthusiasm was contagious, and soon after that evening at his home I applied for Party membership, sponsored by the professor and Günter. After an interview with the leadership of the Party organization within the chemistry section, I was voted in as a candidate of the Party for the standard one-year probationary period.

Once I began to understand what I had joined, I was delighted to be part of a group of intelligent people who believed in the same ideals I did and who were in a position to put those beliefs into practice. Party members believed in the cause, and we all understood that bumps in the road were only minor obstacles to building a fully functional Communist state. The sincere efforts at intellectual honesty along with the openness of this group were the final blocks in my ideological foundation. I believed wholeheartedly in the Party's objectives, and I never would have expected that, in the decades to come, I would come to see the world completely differently. At the time, it was all very clear to me:

1. Marxism-Leninism is a science with a sound economic and philosophical foundation. Mankind moved from slavery to feudalism to capitalism. The logical next and final step is communism.
2. Capitalism is based on the exploitation of workers by the rich owners of the means of production. The Marxist maxim, "From each according to his ability, to each according to his needs," would guarantee happiness for all human beings regardless of their innate capabilities.
3. The Soviet Union and its allies would succeed in freeing the world from the scourge of capitalism. Signs of progress were already visible all over the world as newly freed Third World colonies often wound up with socialist-leaning governments.
4. The working class would take the leading role in overthrowing capitalism, and the working class had taken its rightful leadership role in the Soviet Union and the Eastern Bloc countries. The Communist Party was the key instrument of the working class to fulfill its destiny.
5. West Germany was the successor state to Hitler's Germany. It was fully supported by the ultimate enemy of all mankind, the United States.

Certainly, there were some questions that contained seeds of doubt: How could the working class be in a leadership role when most of the workers I knew were not very bright? Why did our leaders, Walter Ulbricht and, later, Erich Honecker, sound so unintelligent and boring? Why did our teachers have *no convincing answers to the question of the meaning of life?*

But as a newly minted member of the elite, with a vested interest in the success of the established order, and because my fundamental beliefs were rock solid, I easily swept those questions and doubts under the carpet.

After attending my first Party meeting, I joined Günter, who was already a full member, for a cigarette in front of the building.

"Hey, this was great," I said. "Thanks for inviting me in. This is a very good place for me."

Günter smiled proudly. "Yes, my friend, this is a very good time to join the Party. All of the hard work has already been done by the older generation, and it will soon be up to us to finish the job. Look how far we've come since the war. We have better consumer goods now, my parents just bought a color TV set, our athletes are among the best in the world, and the GDR is getting respect from everywhere."

Soon I was recruited to take a prominent role in the Freie Deutsche Jugend (FDJ), the Communist youth movement. Prior to college, I had stayed under the radar by volunteering for the modest role of treasurer, but this was the big leagues now. I could not, and would not, evade the call to duty any longer.

At the beginning of our sophomore year, I was elected secretary of our twelve-student youth group. The following year, I became first secretary of the entire class of approximately sixty-five students, and by my senior year, I had been elevated to first secretary of the Communist youth organization of the entire chemistry section, comprising nearly four hundred students.

In May 1970, because of my volunteer work and my outstanding grades, I was nominated for and received the Karl Marx Scholarship, a prestigious grant that was awarded once a year to approximately seventy students nationwide. The award included a stipend of 450 marks per month, which was a fortune to me.

Through my first three years at the university, I essentially aced the entire program, and I was a well-respected student leader in the chemistry section. As such, several enticing career options quickly presented themselves to me. Though I still held to my dream of becoming a tenured professor in chemistry, a goal that now seemed well within reach, there were competing interests pointing me in the direction of a career within the Party or with the government. I had been approached by university Party officials about possibly taking over leadership of the Party group in the chemistry section. It was highly unusual to offer such an important position to a man of my limited years. At the same time, I was recruited to become the deputy youth leader for the entire university. The typical succession pattern would have led to my becoming the leader of approximately ten thousand students within two years.

But there was another unexpected option that would soon appear on the scene, an opportunity that began with a simple knock on my dorm room door.

PART II
THE TRAINING OF A SPY

10

THAT LIFE-CHANGING KNOCK came in September 1970, just after the start of my fourth year at the university.

I'd done some dorm hopping in the previous years and currently lived very close to the cluster of chemistry buildings in a three-story dorm at August Bebel Straße 26. Spencer, my roommate from the beginning, shared a room with me on the second floor, with windows overlooking the street.

One Saturday afternoon, I was alone in our dorm room because Spencer had decided to make the long trip home to visit his parents that weekend. Günter wasn't around, so I decided to work on some lab reports until it was late enough to head over to the Rosenkeller for my usual Saturday night of partying.

When I heard the knock, I looked up from my papers and waited for the door to open. It was customary among the students to announce ourselves with a knock, but then to immediately enter.

Unusual, I thought when the door didn't open, and after about ten seconds had passed, I called out, "Come on in."

The door opened slowly to reveal a short, almost diminutive man with short-cropped hair and a peaked nose that made him look like a weasel. His left forearm was in a cast. This was definitely not a student and not one of our teachers.

"Are you Albrecht Dittrich?" he asked before I could open my mouth.

"Yes?" I replied in a questioning tone, as if to say, "And what do *you* want?"

The man entered the room, pulled out one of the old wooden chairs, and sat down to my right.

"I'm from Carl Zeiss Jena," he said. "I would like to talk with you about your career. Do you have a few minutes?"

I recognized the name of the large local optical company with an international reputation, but this introduction was odd. Companies did not recruit students, and my visitor had not even mentioned his name.

The word *Stasi* flashed through my mind. There was no other possible explanation: This man had to be from the Ministry for State Security, the East German secret police.

"Ja, I have a few minutes," I said slowly, gathering my lab reports in front of me.

He continued the conversation with banal small talk.

"Working hard, I see—even on a Saturday." He nodded toward the collection of loose-leaf pages I had by now neatly stacked together.

"Sure," I responded. "Chemistry is a tough subject, especially since we are required to spend twenty hours in the lab every week."

"So, what are your plans after graduation?"

"Well, get my doctorate and then become a tenured professor. I love Jena and this university."

He nodded as if encouraging me to continue.

"I think I have a good chance of reaching this goal. I have the best grades in the class, and I was awarded the Karl Marx Scholarship." I couldn't resist a bit of bragging.

"Congratulations," the man said with a hint of a smile. "I was aware of that. In fact, that's the reason I'm here. We know that you are very special, and you have a great future ahead of you, regardless of where you wind up. And now I have a confession to make: I am not from Carl Zeiss. I actually work for the government." He leaned forward, as if trying to create a common secret space for the two of us.

Now the cat was out of the bag. Even though I instinctively did not like this man, I decided to play the game by subtly leaning into our private space.

"Oh, how interesting!" I said with excitement in my voice. "What part of the government?" I was still thinking he had to be Stasi.

"We'll get to that later. Right now I have only one question. Could you imagine working for the government one day?"

I put my left hand on my chin, as if I were thinking it over carefully. After a pregnant pause, I responded, "Yes I could, but not as a chemist."

He had cast the line, and I had willingly, and knowingly, taken the bait. I was curious where this might lead. Perhaps something unusual and exciting. I was always up for a challenge.

The man was visibly delighted with my answer. He leaned back out of our common space and flashed a warm smile. "That's all I wanted to find out today. Why don't we meet again, next Thursday evening at Die Sonne. Do you know that restaurant?"

"Yes, of course. I usually eat there on Sundays. It is rather expensive, but I can afford it once a week. With the cafeteria food here, you've got to have at least one decent meal a week."

With an affirming nod, my visitor rose from the table, shook my hand, and walked out the door. After he was gone, it occurred to me that I still didn't know his name.

So I now had an appointment with an anonymous stranger, whom I really didn't like and whose true intentions were still cloaked in mystery. Intriguing. My mind raced with possibilities, and I could no longer concentrate on my lab notes. Where was this all going?

✦ ✦ ✦

Thursday seemed to drag on forever, and when the clock finally struck five at the end of our lab time, I quickly packed up and set out on foot toward the center of town, where the restaurant Die Sonne was located.

Once inside, I spotted my weekend visitor at the far end of the main dining room. I assumed he had intentionally positioned himself to be out of earshot of neighboring diners, but I was surprised to see another man seated at the table. Not knowing who he might be, I approached the table carefully. My contact rose from his chair and, once again neglecting to introduce himself, stated matter-of-factly, "I would like to introduce Herman. We are working with our Soviet friends."

No more, no less. So now I would be "working" with the Soviets? With the introduction of a representative from one of the world's two superpowers, this opportunity became even more intriguing.

Herman, a blond-haired, blue-eyed man of average height in his midthirties, rose from the table and extended his hand. "Nice to meet you, Albrecht." I detected only a touch of a Russian accent.

I shook his hand and settled into a chair.

"Take a look at the menu," my nameless German contact suggested as he pushed the printed menu under my nose.

"I know what to eat here—it is the best dish on the menu." Then somewhat shyly I added, "It is also the most expensive."

"Not to worry," said Mr. Nameless with a touch of grandeur that seemed out of step with his weasel-like face.

"*Danke.* In that case, I'll have the rump steak with herb butter and French fries. You ought to try it. It's really good."

Meanwhile, Herman had ordered a round of beers for the three of us and we toasted the German-Soviet friendship. Then we got right down to the serious part of the conversation. Herman carried the ball while Mr. Nameless sat back, sipped his beer, and listened.

"We've heard a lot of good things about you," Herman said amiably. "The Karl Marx Scholarship? That tells me you are one of the brightest and most socially active students in the entire country. Perhaps we can work together in the future. How do you like Jena and the university?"

"I absolutely love it here," I said. "This city feels more like home than any place I've ever lived. The people are nice, I have a lot of friends, and I enjoy playing on the local basketball team."

"What about your career plans?" Herman asked.

I repeated my plan to become a tenured professor, knowing that the Stasi guy had surely relayed my interest in other opportunities.

"Well," said Herman with a touch of a smile, "perhaps we can offer you something slightly more interesting. Do you like to travel?"

"Certainly. Last summer my friend and I went camping at the Black Sea."

"Ah, the Black Sea. Beautiful. The Soviet part?"

"No, I was in Bulgaria. Varna."

"Any interest in seeing other places?"

"I'd love to go to France someday. I want to see the places that Honoré de Balzac wrote about in his famous novels."

Herman's smile grew into an agreeable grin. "We should talk about this some more when we meet again."

I understood that this was the end of our official discussion for the day, and I was too cautious to ask any more questions. We ended the meal with a cup of coffee and some awful Russian cigarettes offered by Herman. We agreed to meet again in a week. Same place, same time.

Even though our discussion had been rather noncommittal, I felt certain this was an attempt to recruit me as a *Kundschafter für den Frieden*—a "scout for peace," to use the politically correct East German phrase for *spy*.

On my walk back to the dorm, my mind raced in overdrive, conjuring all kinds of exciting scenarios. Was it possible I would be able to make a significant contribution toward the triumph of communism throughout the world?

I thought about the larger-than-life aura the Soviets and East Germans had built around historical spy figures. They were an important part of the overall mythology of the struggle against the enemy of the people.

In history class, we had learned about *Die Rote Kapelle* (the Red Orchestra), the antifascist group that had operated inside Germany during Hitler's reign. We were told about Richard Sorge, who had spied for Stalin but was caught and executed by the Japanese during World War II. Through literature I had read, I was acquainted with Rudolf Abel, the Soviet spymaster who was exchanged in 1962 for Francis Gary Powers, the U-2 pilot the Russians had shot down while he was flying a high-altitude mission over Soviet territory. There was also superspy Kim Philby, who made a mockery of MI6, the British counterpart of the CIA, and got away with it.

That very month, the East German political journal *Der Horizont* had run a feature on the escape by George Blake, another prominent KGB spy, from an English prison.

There were also a number of movies and books that featured undercover heroes. And now, apparently, the door was slightly open for me to join this pantheon of heroes, an opportunity that commanded serious consideration.

The promise of something new and completely unexpected hung in the air as I walked back to my dorm alone.

✛ ✛ ✛

Herman and I met again the next week at Die Sonne. This time he came alone, and I did not inquire about Mr. Nameless. I liked Herman much better anyway.

After another rump steak and fries, Herman suggested that we get more serious about our future collaboration.

"Listen," he said. "The things I want to talk with you about cannot be discussed in a restaurant. From now on, we will meet every other week in my car."

Though I was sorry to have to give up my favorite meal on the KGB's dime, I was intrigued by the secretive nature of whatever Herman wanted to discuss with me. We decided to meet the following Wednesday at noon, at the corner of Beethovenstraße and Ebertstraße, not far from my dorm in a residential section of town that was unlikely to be frequented by students.

Thus, a week later, I set out for the first clandestine meeting of my life. I made a wide loop around the meeting place, checking frequently to make sure there was nobody in the area who knew me. Though there was absolutely no danger, my heart was beating rapidly as I approached Herman's brand-new beige Wartburg. As he opened the door, I turned my head one more time to check my surroundings and quickly disappeared into the car.

Herman drove about ten minutes out of town and parked the car on a dirt road in the woods, just off a deserted country road.

"Albrecht, first of all, you must know that everything we will discuss is top secret. Nothing can be shared, not even with your mother or your best friend. This is not just *your* secret, but a state secret of the Soviet Union, and you must keep it safe."

"No problem," I responded eagerly. "I know how to keep a secret."

"Today we are starting a very long process to *possibly* prepare you for undercover work in enemy territory."

Finally, what I had suspected all along was now out in the open. The realization that I was under consideration for a secret mission by the mighty KGB made my chest swell with immense pride.

Herman continued, "We have reason to believe that you are well-suited for such work, but there is much to be done before you or I can make a decision. We need to get to know you, and you need to find out if you can handle this type of demanding assignment. Believe me, the decision will ultimately be yours. An agent who is forced into service will invariably be a bad agent. And one more thing: All agents need a code name."

"A code name?"

"All agents have a code name, and I have decided to call you 'Dieter.'"

I thought a moment. "How about something a little more fancy, like Stingray?"

The grin disappeared from Herman's face. Apparently he did not appreciate my lighthearted approach to this very serious enterprise.

"This is not the movies, Albrecht. This is very real."

I nodded and said, "Dieter it is then."

Over the next fifteen years, nine volumes labeled "Dieter" would accumulate in the KGB archives. No doubt the very first pages of those records included a report about this very meeting.

Relieved that a final decision seemed far in the future, I asked, "So how do we start?"

"We'll talk about that next time we meet. In our business it is important to be thorough and deliberate. You will know what you need to know when you need to know it."

After concluding the official part of our meeting, we spent another half hour engaged in small talk before Herman started the car and drove back to the city. Along the way, we passed a few grazing cows and a potato field before reaching the road leading into town, which was lined with attractive single-family homes.

One day, I said to myself, *I will live in one of these homes.*

Thus began my unofficial relationship with Herman and the KGB. For many months, these meetings were a mere diversion and had little effect on my studies at the university. For the most part, life went on as usual—with one exception. Every Monday morning at 8:30, I called Herman and he told me whether, when, and where we would meet. At first, we just met in his car, but after three months, he moved the meetings to a safe house—an apartment occupied by a single, middle-aged woman, a Party member, who served us cookies and tea before leaving the place at our disposal for the next two hours.

Herman always brought some West German magazines, notably *Der Stern* and *Der Spiegel*, which I thumbed through while we were together. This was my first taste of being above the law because West German publications were not allowed in the GDR and if discovered would result in an investigation by the Stasi.

With time, Herman gave me small intelligence-related tasks, mostly for practice, but occasionally with some significance. To assess my observational skills, he asked me to write reports about the political situation at the university and to submit profiles on a number of fellow students with whom I had regular contact. He also introduced me to the basics of the spy trade, such as secrecy protocols, field operations, and clandestine investigative techniques.

After about three months of somewhat informal conversations and some high-level theory, Herman gave me my first real task.

"We are interested in a certain individual who lives in West Germany," he said. "He has relatives in Jena. I want you to make contact with those relatives and find out as much as you can about the West German target."

I was a bit confused. "How do I do this without those folks getting suspicious?"

"You are smart enough to figure this out—think about it for a moment."

I spent a few minutes analyzing the situation and then said, "I guess I'll have to come up with a cover story to make contact and then move the conversation subtly in the direction of the target."

"Excellent," Herman said. "That's how it's done. The subject should never have the slightest idea what you're really after. Go to it—I am expecting a written report the next time we meet."

This type of task made me very nervous and uncomfortable. First of all, I had to lie, which did not yet come easily to me. Second, I had to make contact with strangers, another difficult task. So I practiced extensively in a remote section of a nearby park by talking out loud.

Once I was ready, I walked to the address, took a deep breath, and rang the doorbell. The door was opened by a middle-aged woman dressed in clothes appropriate for household chores. I launched into a friendly opening.

"Good afternoon, I am Volker, and I am studying sociology at the university. My professor assigned a paper on family relationships, so I am conducting a survey to collect data. Would you be so kind as to spend a few minutes and answer some simple questions? The survey will be anonymous; there will be no names in my notes."

"No problem, young man. Come on in. I am Frau Reimann—so what is this survey about?"

I opened a notebook and read to her a number of innocent questions about family relationships. I pretended to write down the answers. Gradually, I managed to zero in on the target of our investigation.

"So your nephew, Klaus, who lives in Hamburg—does he ever come to visit?"

"Yes, as a matter of fact he'll be with us this Christmas."

At that point, I thought I had enough to satisfy Herman. If there was more to be done about this target, my colleagues in the KGB or I would have to make contact with Klaus himself when he came to Jena for a visit.

I used this technique of clandestine investigation several times during my training, but never in the United States.

11

BY 1971, I WAS READY FOR AN ADVENTURE. I'd been in Jena for nearly four years and had dedicated myself to my studies, basketball, the Party, and assignments from Herman. Günter was also game for something new, so we planned a summer hitchhiking trip to Bulgaria—some 1,900 kilometers in all.

When I informed Herman of the plan, he supported it and asked that I take notes on the journey. As summer approached, I bought some hiking shoes and borrowed a pair of Levi's from a friend. Günter and I procured a couple of large backpacks and attached our sleeping bags to the outside. We didn't know it yet, but we would learn to appreciate those sleeping bags on the nights we spent outdoors—wherever our last ride for the day dropped us off. With a stack of maps to plan an approximate route, we hiked to the outskirts of town and stuck out our thumbs.

And thus began "Günter and Albrecht's Excellent Adventure."

The trip gave us a view of what life in the southern part of the Eastern Bloc was like. Czechoslovakia and Hungary were quite civilized, with a standard of living comparable to what we were accustomed to in East Germany, but Romania and Bulgaria were a different matter.

In Prague, I had my first real Coca-Cola—*delicious!*—and I was able to buy my first pack of American cigarettes, a pack of Kents. In Budapest, we entered the lobby of the Hilton and got our first taste of an American-owned hotel. When Günter returned from a trip to the bathroom, he exclaimed, "Those toilets start flushing as soon as you open the door!"

Once we reached Romania and traveled on into Bulgaria, we found that both countries were very rural. Many of the buildings looked as if they were a hundred years old. The people, too, seemed as if they were from another century, dressed in mostly dark, well-worn clothing and wearing shoes that even my fashion agnostic mother would have rejected. In the summer heat, almost all the young children were walking around half naked and barefoot.

"It's like we've traveled back in time to the Middle Ages," I said, leaning toward Günter as we rode in the back of a truck through a village.

On our second day in Romania, one of our rides dropped us off in a small village in front of a ramshackle building made of discolored bricks. The wooden sign over the front door said that it was a restaurant, but judging by the weatherworn facade and a straw roof in desperate need of repair, my expectations for the quality of food we might find there were not very high. Still, we had been on the road since early morning and both Günter and I were hungry and thirsty.

As we stood in the street and considered our options, we saw some shady characters entering and leaving the establishment. I looked at Günter, and he looked at me.

"Should we?" I asked.

"Why not? The sign says *restaurant*, so they should have something to eat and drink."

We cautiously opened the front door and found a roomful of swarthy and unkempt Romanian villagers who appeared to be having a drinking contest—saluting one another with shot glasses containing a clear liquid that they quickly tossed down. The room was buzzing with energy, but as soon as the revelers saw us standing at the doorway, the place fell silent. They looked at us with hooded eyes, as if to say, *You'd better have a reason for coming in here, boys.*

There was no turning back now.

Günter and I dropped our backpacks against the front wall and settled in at a nearby table. There were forks, spoons, and dull knives attached to the table with chains to prevent casual theft.

"We should have brought a Romanian dictionary," I said, staring at the grease-stained single-page menu.

"Just pick something," Günter replied.

I waved over the hostess, a wrinkled, dark-skinned woman of indeterminate age, who was wearing a short apron over an ankle-length black dress. Pointing at one of the items on the menu, I held up two fingers and nodded in Günter's direction to make it clear I was ordering for both of us. Without a word, the woman disappeared through a doorway that I assumed led to the kitchen.

At that point I noticed one of the locals edging closer to where we were seated.

"What does this guy want?" I said.

"Why don't you ask him?" Günter responded facetiously.

"He's staring at the pack of Kents in your shirt pocket," I said. "Why don't you give him one?"

With a sigh, Günter parted with his last American cigarette, which the young man received with an appreciative nod. But instead of lighting up, he began to pass the precious gift carefully around the room. Everyone was allowed to admire, fondle, and sniff the cigarette before it was returned to the original recipient, who tucked it gingerly behind his left ear.

The waitress arrived with the food, a barely edible dark-brown mash. She returned a minute later with a couple of shot glasses filled with the clear liquid and set them in front of us.

"Did you order this stuff?" Günter asked.

"Are you crazy—schnapps in the morning?"

Across the room, I saw the fellow with the cigarette behind his ear raise his glass toward us and say something in Romanian.

"Looks like your new friend bought us the drinks," I said to Günter.

We returned the salute and bravely knocked back the horrible-tasting liquid, which was probably a version of *rakia*, a fruit brandy common in the Balkans. We were gamely forcing down a few more spoonfuls of our meals when a second round of shot glasses appeared.

"We better get out of here while we still can," I said. "I think another round of this stuff will make me dizzy."

I dropped enough money on the table to cover the cost of the food, and we picked up our backpacks and moved toward the exit, smiling and waving at the rowdy crowd. Outside, we hiked down the dusty road at an expedited pace, glancing back from time to time to make sure we were not being followed.

✦ ✦ ✦

Two days later, we once again witnessed the magical power of American cigarettes.

The bridge over the Danube River connecting the border towns of Giurgiu, Romania, and Ruse, Bulgaria, was called the Friendship Bridge. However, friendship was not in the air as we sought to cross.

As we traversed the 2.2-kilometer bridge on foot, we faced one last Romanian border guard, who had planted himself in the middle of the road, waving a bayoneted rifle in the air.

Somewhat intimidated, I said to Günter, "What in the world does this guy want?"

"Beats me," he replied. "He keeps pointing at your back pocket. Do you have your wallet back there?"

"Yes, but I don't have any more Romanian money. Do you think he's trying to collect a personal border-crossing fee?"

"I don't know," said Günter. "But I have an idea."

He reached into his shirt pocket and handed the guard the Kent box, which he had filled with a few awful Romanian cigarettes.

Thinking he was getting a gift of prized American smokes, the guard's face lit up with an ear-to-ear grin, exposing several gaps in his tobacco-stained teeth. We smiled back at him and walked briskly toward the Bulgarian side of the bridge.

As soon as we passed the sign welcoming us to Bulgaria, we looked back across the bridge in time to see the Romanian border guard discover our deception. With a look of pure disgust, he threw the pack of "Kents" onto the roadway and began stomping on it and cursing us. We quickly turned and continued on our way into Ruse, narrowly escaping what could have become a three-nation border incident.

After visiting the capital city of Sofia, we turned toward our final destination, the Black Sea city of Burgas. Along the way, we visited the Rila Monastery and took a three-day hike through the Rila Mountains. When we finally arrived in Burgas, Günter and I congratulated each other for succeeding on this adventure. We knew of no one else who had even attempted such a journey. We would have much to brag about once we were back in Jena.

From Burgas, we made our return trip by train, taking two days to reach the university. We returned totally exhausted but fully tanned and bearded. With only two days left to recover before the fall semester began, I took the time to send a lengthy, detailed report of the trip to my mother, who was delighted to read about my travels. She even shared the report with Frau Greiner, my first-grade teacher.

+ + +

On September 6, I reported back to the university, where I now had a permanent lab space at the Institute for Photochromism, headed by Professor Pätzold, my all-time favorite instructor. There I would conduct original research that would eventually lead to a thesis on the way to the coveted diploma.

Like me, my fellow students had chosen various specialties within the chemistry department, and we were now dispersed across multiple buildings on campus. As a result, we rarely saw one another anymore. One day, as I walked toward the cafeteria at lunchtime, I spotted Edeltraud, who had been part of my lab group for the past three years. I waved at her from across the road and was ready to continue on my way. However, she crossed the street and planted herself right in front of me.

"Albrecht," she said in an unusually sharp tone of voice, "we need to talk."

"Do you need help with something?" I asked innocently.

"I sure do," she responded. "Let's go have a seat on the bench over there."

As soon as we were seated, she blurted out, "I'm pregnant, and I'm 100 percent sure that you're the father!"

I immediately felt the blood drain from my face, and I was glad I was sitting down. Earlier that year, following a lively party with our fellow students, Edeltraud and I had spent the night together. She was now informing me of the consequences.

"Are you sure?" I managed to ask after a long pause.

"Absolutely. I've already been to the doctor."

The next pause was even longer. A child and possibly a marriage to a woman I liked but wasn't in love with was not part of my plan for the future. I simply wasn't ready for that kind of commitment.

When I finally raised my eyes, I noticed a look of strong determination on Edeltraud's face. She was going to be a mother, marriage or not! We both knew that the East German state was very supportive of single mothers, and there was even a dorm at the university for women with small children. Edeltraud would be able to finish her studies, albeit with an additional burden.

"Of course I will pay child support," I said haltingly. I felt awkward and defeated—and I realized I had nothing more to say. We parted ways with everything unresolved.

I didn't see Edeltraud again until after our son, Günther, was born. I went to visit her and the baby in her dorm room after being notified of the birth by a mutual friend. I held little Günther, but I felt distant from him and no more ready to be a father than I had before. Rather than face up to the situation and work things out with the mother of my child—who also hadn't planned for this—I took the approach of a callous coward and simply walked away. It was possibly the most shameful moment of my life.

It was interesting to note that the Communist Party, which usually paid close attention to the moral behavior of its members, never said a word to me about this situation. Apparently I was too much of an up-and-coming star to be pushed off the pedestal they were erecting for me.

During her pregnancy, Edeltraud wrote a letter to my mother, who subsequently went to visit her in Jena. This led to the establishment of a relationship between the two and allowed my mother to be a grandmother to Günther when he was a young boy. But the relationship between my mother and Edeltraud eventually soured because my mother proved to be—surprise!—too bossy.

After college, Edeltraud got married and was fortunate to find a husband who raised Günther as if he were his own. I'm confident that this man was a much better father than I would have been.

+ + +

For my thesis, I had chosen to study a number of indigo-type dyes that change their configuration, and consequently their color (mostly from blue to red and red to blue), when irradiated with light of a certain wavelength. At the time, photochromic chemicals were thought to be the future of computer storage, but that hope was never realized.

After six months of experimentation, I recorded my findings and had my paper typed professionally. I then submitted the document to a committee, and at 2:00 p.m. on February 1, 1972, I appeared before a panel of sixteen faculty members to defend my thesis.

After forty minutes, the results were unanimous. I received an A for my final grade and graduated summa cum laude four months ahead of my class. It had already been made clear that I would be hired by the university as an assistant professor immediately after graduation. The timing of my graduation was accelerated to allow me to take over as first secretary of the Communist youth organization of the chemistry section, an assignment that required about half of my time.

Even though I was done with the program, I occasionally attended lectures by Professor Hartman, who taught organic chemistry and gave additional lectures on special subjects from time to time. On one of those occasions, he embarrassed me greatly.

"Herr Dittrich, would you please come to the front?" he asked. I felt awkward, but at least I was wearing my favorite rust-colored jacket with the Party pin on the lapel.

I was wondering if Herr Hartman was going to test me, but instead he launched into what amounted to a grand tribute.

"Class, on behalf of the entire teaching staff of the chemistry section, I want to express my appreciation for this fine young man. He is smart, a hard worker, and he is a great leader, someone I expect will make great contributions to our country and world communism."

I wanted to run out of the classroom and hide somewhere, but the hearty applause of my fellow students helped me get over what I thought was going to be a very awkward moment.

I was now on a path to receive my doctorate around the time of my twenty-sixth birthday. And if I wanted it, I was also on a path to fulfill my dream of becoming a tenured professor at one of the best universities in Europe. But, of course, there was another opportunity drawing my attention. Herman and I continued to meet, and I would soon be faced with the most important decision of my young life.

12

"BERLIN WANTS TO SEE YOU," Herman said when he arrived at the safe house. This piqued my interest, but I waited for him to continue.

"We are getting close to decision time. Can you get a leave of absence from the university for three weeks?"

I sat down on the back of the couch and thought a moment.

"Sure, but only if I get some kind of official document," I said.

"No problem."

Herman showed up for our next meeting with an official requisition ordering me to report to a military installation near Berlin for three weeks of extraordinary defense training.

As we discussed the details, I felt my blood flowing with excitement.

"What can you tell me?" I asked Herman as we sat at a small table in the kitchen.

"You'll meet with agents in Berlin and possibly be introduced to one or two senior officers," he said. "And for this assignment, you will have a clandestine meeting with an unknown counterpart in a big city. I'll give you a place, a time, and a passcode that you'll need to memorize."

I knew this was my first opportunity to enter into the murky, but ever so enticing, world of undercover operations. There would be no fallback plan. If I missed the meeting or messed up the details, the entire trip would have to be scuttled, with uncertain consequences for my career as a secret agent. Punctuality was never a problem for me so I had no doubt that I would make the meeting. I've often jokingly said that I have a clock where others have a heart.

I took the train to East Berlin and traveled to the meeting site in the Karlshorst district of the city. It turned out to be a residential area, and there was little traffic. My contact and I would both carry a copy of the East German sports weekly in our left hand as a sign of recognition.

At the appointed time, I approached the street corner, identified my contact, and greeted him with the passcode sequence: "Excuse me, I am looking for Lindenstraße."

"Is that where Helmut lives?" he responded with the corresponding code.

Having established our credentials, we introduced ourselves as "Dieter" and "Boris."

Boris was a stocky man of average height, in his late forties, with a typically round Russian face. He proved to be much like Herman, even-tempered and very kind and friendly.

He walked me to his car, and we discussed our meeting schedule for the next three weeks. We would meet every three days at a specified time and location in the Lichtenberg section of Berlin. He then told me to take two days to familiarize myself with the city and find accommodations—and that the KGB would pay the rent.

I quickly found a private house where I could rent a room and spent the remainder of my free time exploring my new surroundings.

Ah, Berlin, our great capital and a metropolis of international prominence. This was where the action was—and I was *here*!

By 1972, parts of East Berlin had been freed from some of the architectural constraints of the Stalin era, which dominated the main boulevard, the Karl Marx Allee. In particular, the Alexanderplatz, a large public square at the center of the city, had undergone a massive overhaul and now boasted the second-tallest TV tower in the world (which is still the tallest freestanding building in Germany today), a world clock, an ornate fountain, and other architectural details that gave this part of the city a certain modern feel not found anywhere else in the GDR.

A visitor from the West would quickly notice the lack of a human touch—there was no commerce, no entertainment, nothing to do but wander about and perhaps sit at the edge of the fountain for a chat—but for those of us in the East, Alexanderplatz was a sign of real progress and a source of great pride. As soon as twilight approached, however, the people quickly scattered, leaving the square a spooky, bleak expanse of lifeless monuments in a scarcely lit city that seemed to draw inward as darkness descended.

During my three weeks in Berlin, Boris and I spent many hours discussing the details of an undercover existence. He emphasized that the mechanics of spying could all be learned, but the psychology was a different matter.

"You will have to disappear from your current life, and nobody— not even your mother—will know where you've gone. As far as most people are concerned, you will have vanished into thin air. Wherever you go, you will be in hostile territory. You will have to befriend your enemies and pretend to be one of them. Communication with Moscow will always be indirect and will always take time, and you will have to make many decisions on the spot without the benefit of advice."

I listened intently, nodding my head occasionally as Boris studied how I took in the information. Looking at a passing streetcar filled with East Berliners, I realized that normal life was not the path for me.

"Lastly—and I want to be quite honest about this—a large percentage of undercover spies get caught and go to jail. Could you handle this? Are you hesitant or afraid? Think about all of that, and try to put yourself into that scenario. This should be the very foundation of your decision."

As I absorbed these words, I was surprised at the lack of fear I felt.

Before we parted company, Boris reached into his briefcase and pulled out a stack of West German magazines. My eyes widened at the sight. I had thumbed through plenty of Western periodicals with Herman, but he had always taken them with him when he left.

"Read them," Boris said. "There will be more."

I loved reading those publications. Unlike our magazines and newspapers in the East, they were colorful and entertaining. I chalked up their anti-Communist rhetoric to capitalist propaganda and viewed my reading as gathering useful information about real life on the other side of the wall.

✦ ✦ ✦

One morning, when I met Boris in his car, he handed me a manila envelope.

"You are going to the West," he said.

I remained unfazed on the outside, but excitement was coursing through my veins. I was being allowed to go where most East Germans could not. The wall ensured that. The West was a world that was taboo for us—and the explorer in me could not have been more thrilled.

From inside the manila envelope, I slid out an East German passport and thirty Deutschmarks, the equivalent of about $50 today. This was the first time I'd had Western currency in my hands. The colorful pieces of paper were the equivalent of a magic wand; they could buy all kinds of wonderful goods that were otherwise not available to us.

The next day, I entered West Berlin by way of the Friedrichstraße subway station. The crossing was guarded only by Soviet military, making it an ideal spot for the KGB to slip people in and out of West Berlin.

Even though the uniformed guard who studied my passport was from a friendly force, my heart still pounded as I waited. Finally, he handed my documents back to me and waved me through.

As I emerged from the subway, I felt as if I had entered a different world. In the first hour of exploration, I noticed a certain cheerfulness in the way West Berlin presented itself, and it made me realize how poorly maintained the historic buildings were in the eastern part of the city and how drab the multistory East German tenements were. West Berlin's architecture and streets were clean and modern. Even the people looked nicer, and they were much better dressed. Moreover, the streets were packed with automobiles of every variety, with makes and models I'd never heard of. Much later, when trying to explain the difference between the eastern and the western sides of Berlin, I would say, "The East was a movie shot in black and white. In the West, they had color."

The purpose of this trip was strictly to get my feet wet. Boris had told me to walk around, visit some stores, smell the air, and get used to the place. It was all innocent enough, but as I walked and observed, my nerves were a jumbled mess. The mere knowledge that I was on a training mission for the KGB made all the difference. My heart skipped a beat every time I noticed a policeman in his inconspicuous light blue uniform. In the East, we could recognize the Polizei from a distance by their bright green uniforms, but not here. Could they sense that I was not one of them? Did it show on my face or in the way I walked? Would they recognize me as an unwelcome intruder and haul me in for interrogation?

My last stop before returning to the East was an outdoor snack stand, where I consumed a delicious bratwurst chased down with an equally delicious glass of beer. Then I walked to the train station, went through the checkpoint, and crossed back into East Berlin. As I came out on the other side of the wall, I had a sense of pride. I'd done it!

Months later, I ran into an old high school classmate who had been recruited by the Stasi to go undercover in West Germany. As we talked, I sensed that he knew I was involved in something—either the Stasi or something else—but he seemed to have that knowledge without our directly talking about it. I told him nothing about my trip to West Berlin, but he told me a story about being let go by the Stasi after falling apart on a practice trip like the one I had taken. There was no direct punishment for him, he said, but he lost his chance to be part of the German secret service and was unable to resume his career in engineering, which he had started before signing up with the Stasi.

✣ ✣ ✣

My foray into West Berlin had served its purpose. I had proven to myself and to my handlers that I could withstand the psychological pressure of being on the other side.

On my next to last day in East Berlin, Boris told me I would be introduced to a very important KGB official. When he picked me up at the usual meeting spot, we drove to the Soviet military complex in the Karlshorst district.

Boris drove up to a fenced-off complex with a guarded entrance. He parked the car and motioned for me to follow him. As I took in the scenery, a complex of large buildings with weathered gray-green facades, every trace of cheerfulness drained from my demeanor. This was serious.

Once past the guards and inside the main building, we walked along a dark hallway and entered what seemed to be an anteroom to a larger office. Boris and I sat down on a wooden bench and waited in respectful silence. Ten minutes later, an attractive young Russian woman opened the door to the office and waved us in.

"Войдите пожалуйста," she said. "Please come in."

I followed Boris inside the spacious office, which had a large dark wooden desk in the center. On the wall were two portraits: Vladimir Lenin and Felix Dzerzhinsky—founder of the Cheka, the early predecessor of the KGB. Dzerzhinsky also had a presence on the desk in the form of a bronze bust.

Behind the desk sat a surprisingly diminutive man in his late fifties. He was dressed in a rumpled suit over a white shirt with an unattractive tie. The little hair he had left was cropped short and combed straight back.

This fellow is a big shot? I thought.

Then he spoke.

"*Guten Tag,*" he said in a loud, steely voice in highly accented German. Those were apparently the only two words in German that he knew because the remainder of his communication to us was in Russian. But there was no question as to who was in charge here. He waved Boris and me toward two upholstered chairs off to the side.

This little man, in all probability the director of the espionage section of the Soviet contingent in Berlin, started the "interview" with a five-minute lecture on the class struggle and the importance of the KGB in the fight against the enemy of the proletariat. My school-level Russian allowed me to follow at least part of what he said, and I managed to respond with a few befuddled nods. But most of the time I had to rely on Boris to provide the translation.

After some compliments concerning my academic achievements and recognition of the praise I had received from Herman and Boris, he wasted no time in going for the kill.

"So, are you ready to sign up? It is time to make a decision. Are you *in* or *out?*" This part of his communication needed no translation; it was accompanied by the universal thumbs-up and thumbs-down gestures.

I was not prepared for this direct frontal assault, and now this impos-ing little man was staring at me, waiting for an answer.

"I—I really like the idea, but I don't think I am trained well enough."

The director let out a hearty laugh that quickly degraded into a lengthy coughing fit. He had probably smoked too many of those poi-sonous Belomorkanal Papirosi cigarettes, which were the cheapest and most popular Russian cigarettes during the war and for many years thereafter.

Taking a gulp of water from a glass on the desk, he said, "Don't worry about that. We will give you all the training you will need. For now, we need a decision. True revolutionaries are decisive. You have until tomorrow to let us know."

With that, he waved dismissively toward the door, indicating that the meeting was over.

I kept silent for most of the car ride to the Hirschgarten rapid tran-sit train station, where Boris dropped me off. I had witnessed my first display of ruthless authority.

Before I left the car, Boris reminded me, "We need your decision by tomorrow. Consider this an ultimatum."

"What do you mean by that?" I asked somewhat innocently. "You're not giving me any more time to think this through?"

"No. The boss has spoken, and when he speaks we had better listen. We shall meet here tomorrow at three, and I expect a firm answer."

Usually, the walk from the drop-off point to my temporary residence was a ten-minute jaunt along a winding dirt path through a nearby park. This time, however, I took my time, walking as slowly as possible.

It was a typical fall day in Berlin. The trees had lost all their leaves, and the empty branches stretched toward the overcast sky as if reaching for an answer to the question "What's next?"

To my overactive imagination, this was an almost surreal scene. I desperately wanted those trees to be alive, to be someone I could talk to and get advice from. But advice was not forthcoming. I had arrived all alone at this ultimate fork in the road, with no possibility of turning back.

On the one hand, I had been looking forward for years to a career as a college professor, and I had worked hard to achieve my goal. Moreover,

I *liked* teaching. I liked being a somebody and being in the limelight. I liked chemistry, I liked living in Jena, and most of all, I liked being part of my basketball team.

To become an undercover spy, I would have to give all of this up. I would also have to completely disappear, leaving behind family and friends to possibly never see them again.

As I kept walking, a decision began to form in my mind. This opportunity was one of the greatest honors imaginable. There were no human ties strong enough—not even the ties to my beloved game of basketball or my teammates; not to my friend Günter, or even my mother—to counter the lure of a once-in-a-lifetime opportunity to do something special and be somebody special.

Kim Philby expressed my innermost thoughts precisely when he was asked why he joined the KGB. He said, "One does not look twice at an offer of enrollment in an elite force."[2]

The next morning I met Boris for the last time before my departure from Berlin.

"Have you come to a decision?" he asked.

"Yes, I'm committed. Let's do this."

13

CHRISTMAS OF 1972 was the last holiday I would spend with my family. My brother had recently volunteered for the army, and my mother was getting remarried after the holidays, so we decided to meet at her new apartment in the town of Weißwasser to celebrate the holiday and attend the small civil wedding she would have a few days later. My mother and I had kept in touch through letters while I was at the university, but this would be my first visit in some time.

Her apartment was typical for the GDR at that time—a cookie-cutter, four-story walk-up with a kitchen and adjoining living room at one end, a bathroom in the hallway, and two small bedrooms at the other end. The government had built thousands of these units all over the country to deal with a severe housing crisis. For my brother and me, this was not home; we came primarily to be together and to get another taste of our mother's cooking. On Christmas Day, she served her special brand of seasoned pork chops with potatoes and sauerkraut. I stuffed myself to the gills.

As we were sitting around the table sipping after-dinner drinks, I broke the news.

"Mutti, I'm changing careers."

She looked at me as if I had slapped her. What was this nonsense from her golden boy, her straight-A student who had won the Karl Marx Scholarship? If there was one thing my mother had known for sure, it was that her elder son would one day be an honored professor at a prestigious university.

"Change careers?"

The question sounded more like a challenge.

"Why would you throw away the great career you have ahead of you?"

"In February I am joining the Ministry of Foreign Affairs to become a diplomat. Think about it, Mutti. I will move to Berlin, and eventually I will be able to travel to many foreign countries."

She stared at me, uncomprehending, from across the table. Finally, she blurted out, "Are you a spy?"

Now it was my turn to be stunned, but Hans-Günther came to the rescue without realizing what he was doing.

"Not our Albrecht! He would never do something as sinister as that."

My mother frowned, then rose to clear a few dishes from the table. I couldn't tell if she believed me, but that was the end of our discussion about my career, and the subject was never taken up again.

At the end of January, I quit my job at the university and handed my SED Party membership booklet to a representative of the secretariat. I wasn't certain why it was necessary to turn in the booklet, but it seemed they would keep it on my behalf to be reclaimed when or if I needed it again. As I spoke for a moment with the secretary, he made a knowing comment about unsung heroes. Apparently, it was not the first time this comrade had collected a Party booklet.

The next day, I stashed my belongings in a suitcase and a large briefcase and boarded the train for Berlin. As we made our way toward the capital city, I realized I was on a trip to nowhere, without a return ticket. There would be many more trips like this one, but this train ride was the starting point of a most unusual journey. The destination on the map of my life was clearly marked with a hammer, a sickle, and a big question mark.

✦ ✦ ✦

On Monday, February 5, 1973, early in the afternoon, I arrived at Berlin Ostbahnof, one of the city's major train stations. After stashing my bags in a locker, I proceeded to the prearranged meeting place at a Karlshorst intersection, where I would connect with my new handler. The meeting protocol was identical to the one that Boris and I had used for my practice trip three months earlier, and everything proceeded as planned.

At three o'clock sharp, I spotted a stocky middle-aged man wrapped in a thick coat, smoking a cigarette near the side of a building just down the street from where I stood. After the usual exchange of passcodes and a few introductory niceties, we went straight to his car to discuss our next steps.

Unlike Herman, who had become a friend, and Boris, whose demeanor was always kindly, this new fellow, Nikolai—a Ukrainian national with a square face and a thick neck—talked and acted like a tough boss.

"Welcome to Berlin, comrade. I can tell you, your training won't be easy." Nikolai shifted in his seat so he could look me in the eye. "Let's start as close to reality as possible. Imagine you just arrived in a new country and have to find a place to live."

"Okay . . ."

"That is your first task—find a place to live and call me at this number next Monday at 9:00 a.m."

I was dumbstruck. After living in dorm rooms with roommates for the past five years, I had been looking forward to settling in to my new accommodations. Surely the almighty KGB would provide their new spy-in-training with a nice place to live. But now Nikolai had just made it clear that I was on my own—and I knew that the housing shortage plaguing the entire country was most severe in Berlin. Communal living was not uncommon, particularly for young people—who often had to stay with their parents while languishing for years on a waiting list before they could find a place of their own.

What have I gotten myself into?

I kept a straight face, but my mind was spinning.

Is this how my great career as an undercover agent begins—looking for a place to live where there is nothing to be had?

I memorized the phone number and got out of the car, joining the stream of pedestrians making their way home from work on the cold streets of Berlin. It was too late to begin my apartment hunt that day, so I retrieved my luggage and rented a hotel room for the night. Tomorrow would be the official start of my new life, and a very unpleasant one at that.

The next day, I began my search by asking myself a question: How does a newcomer go about finding a place to live in a huge city where hundreds of thousands of people are waiting for a place of their own?

The answer was simple: Go door-to-door.

I knew the closer I searched to downtown Berlin, the more impossible the search would be. So I took a commuter train to the town of Erkner, forty-eight kilometers southeast of the city center and the last stop on the line out of Berlin. When I stepped off the train onto the cobblestone-paved platform, the drab terminal was deserted. This was encouraging. The fewer the people, the better the chance of finding a place—or so I hoped.

Exiting the terminal, I made a sharp left turn and walked toward a cluster of detached single-family houses. For the next three hours, I knocked on doors, rang doorbells, and talked with residents. Eventually, my efforts yielded a lead. One homeowner directed me to a small house on a street lined with beautiful birch trees. The street was appropriately named: Unter den Birken (Under the Birch Trees).

The woman who answered the bell appeared sickly, with loose strands of uncombed dirt-blonde hair and a two-tooth gap in her upper front teeth.

"I have a space I can rent out," she said, "but . . . it is not very comfortable."

I would soon discover that "not very comfortable" was the understatement of the year.

The woman led me across the yard to a ramshackle outbuilding divided into two rooms—one with a bed and a chair and the other with a coal-burning stove and a sink with running cold water. There was no other furniture. The toilet was an outhouse in the backyard.

So this was it, my very first apartment: a bed, a stove, a chair, and running water. Not exactly what I had dreamed about, but at least I could say I had a roof over my head and a bed to sleep on.

The spartan conditions didn't bother me. During childhood, I had gotten used to asking for little and getting even less. And sacrifices had to be made for the cause. After all, my ultimate hero, Vladimir Lenin, had suffered through three years in a Siberian prison camp before triumphantly returning to Russia to take the reins of the first Communist state. I could not have known that my KGB bosses were living in luxury while lazily handing out orders to new recruits to find their own housing in a crowded and unfamiliar city.

I moved into my humble abode in Erkner with the kind of faith instilled in me by my parents: Good things will happen if you perform well. So I embraced these new circumstances with youthful optimism. This place was not a home; it was just a place to sleep.

Each morning, I took the train to the city and spent my time at the library or museums, or exploring the various neighborhoods on foot to establish a foundation for future operational exercises. I also joined the basketball team at the College of Economic Studies in Karlshorst, which provided me with some stable social interactions and guaranteed me at least one shower a week. I never told Nikolai anything about my living conditions, and that was instinctively wise. Bosses do not like to hear complaints or problems; they prefer solutions.

✦ ✦ ✦

For one who was eager to get the ball rolling, my training unfolded at a painfully slow pace. There was never a written or structured plan with timelines, deliverables, and performance criteria. Nikolai gave me an outline of the subjects we would cover, but the implementation seemed to be a week-by-week, ad hoc exercise. The only constant in my training was my weekly time with Nikolai. Every Monday at nine o'clock sharp, I called him from a phone booth near my home, and he told me where and when we would meet. The only permanent feature of our meetings was the reports I had to turn in every month: an activity report and an expense report.

During our second meeting in Nikolai's car, he handed me my first month's pay—a stuffed envelope with 800 marks inside. This amounted to a 200-mark pay raise from my net income at the university.

"We pay in advance, and we do not take out taxes," Nikolai said with the smallest hint of a grin.

At first, our meetings took place in Nikolai's car, which he parked on Fürstenwalder Damm near the Friedrichshagen train station. He always brought me a stack of West German newspapers and magazines, and I looked forward to reading these interesting publications cover to cover, a true highlight of my otherwise mundane existence.

Our meetings generally lasted only twenty minutes, during which we engaged in small talk before Nikolai gave me my next set of instructions. It took me a couple of decades to realize that there is really no such thing as small talk between a spy and his handler. Nikolai was analyzing every word I said.

I quickly learned not to ask any questions about my training. I simply listened and learned. But it didn't take long to see that the training was roughly divided into two categories: technical skills, or spycraft; and soft skills, which were about developing me as an individual.

All the technical skills were taught by highly proficient experts. I always worked one-on-one with my instructors, and Nikolai was the only other person allowed to attend. Because most of the technical specialists spoke neither German nor English, Nikolai often served as our translator. The seemingly vast resources required for my training led me to believe that the number of thoroughly prepared undercover agents had to be rather limited. I couldn't imagine that there were thousands of us—and possibly not even hundreds—worldwide. Also, I never once met an active colleague—though, of course, such a meeting would have violated the fundamental rules of conspiracy.

The training covered the following subjects:

a) *Shortwave Radio and Morse Code.* The Morse code training was strictly focused on receiving. After I mastered the ten single digits and the alphabet at a slow speed, we concentrated on building up my receiving speed. I eventually topped out at a respectable 100 digits per minute. I was also instructed on the types of commercially available radios and how to use them to receive shortwave transmissions from my handlers in the KGB during my time in the West.

b) *Cryptography.* All transmissions I received via shortwave radio were encrypted, and I was taught to encrypt every specific piece of information (names, addresses, phone numbers, etc.) contained in my secret messages to KGB headquarters. The algorithm they taught me involved a double encryption. First, all letters were translated into digits, which were then randomized by adding or subtracting another set of digits derived by a separate algorithm. The fact that the only KGB document I ever signed with my full real name was a promise never to disclose any information about these algorithms speaks to the value the KGB attached to their code. According to my instructor, the code was unbreakable and good for about two hundred uses.

c) *Secret Writing.* The practice of secret writing, or the use of invisible ink, is as old as the written word. What changed over the years was the technology. The chemicals I used were almost impossible to detect. The process of creating a secret message started with writing a letter to a fictitious friend. This was called the *open text*. That sheet of paper was then placed on a plate of clean glass, or a mirror, and covered with a sheet of special contact paper and another sheet of regular paper. The secret message was written on the top sheet, using a #2 pencil and a light hand to avoid leaving any visible impressions on the bottom sheet. The letter containing the open text, which now also included the secret message, was sent via regular mail to a foreign address (the addresses I used were in West Berlin, Colombia, and Austria), where a trusted middleman would hand the letter over to a resident KGB agent, who in turn would forward it via diplomatic pouch to headquarters, where the writing would be developed in the lab. The entire process of getting a message to Moscow took two to three weeks.

d) *Photography.* As an avid amateur photographer, I didn't need to be told how to use a camera or develop black-and-white film. I did, however, receive training in the use of a microscope to create a microdot—a negative no larger than a square millimeter that can easily be hidden under a postage stamp or glued into the inside of an envelope.

A great deal of attention was given to the area of field operations, which included surveillance detection, clandestine meetings, and dead-drop operations.

a) *Face-to-Face Meetings.* These meetings were used to give oral instructions, exchange passports, and hand over money. They were subject to a stringent protocol, including recognition signals and mutually known passcodes. My usual signal was that I would carry a copy of *US News & World Report* rolled up over a brown briefcase. To indicate danger, I would carry the magazine and the briefcase in separate hands. My meeting partner would always initiate the passcode sequence by saying, "Excuse me, are you looking for Susan Greene?" I would respond, "Yes, you must be David."

b) *Dead-Drop Operations.* A dead-drop operation is a scheduled, indirect (no face-to-face contact), one-way transfer of material, such as money, a passport, microfilm, or a valuable document. The item to be transferred would be placed in an inconspicuous container, such as an old oil can or a stone made of plaster of Paris, and left in a prearranged drop location (a remote spot with little traffic). The person making the drop would set a signal for the recipient, such as a chalk mark on a utility pole, in a known location that the recipient would be certain to see. Once the pickup had been made, the recipient would set a responding signal for the person who made the drop, indicating the successful completion of the operation.

c) *Surveillance Detection.* Meetings, dead-drop operations, and other operational activities, such as mailing a letter with secret writing, would be preceded by a thorough surveillance-detection procedure. This involved traveling on a two- or three-hour route across the city to determine whether anyone was following. The most effective method of surveillance detection involved a series of small trips via public transportation. If the route was properly selected, it was virtually impossible for even the most sophisticated surveillance team to remain undetected.

Soft subject training involved five elements: ideological foundations, study of West Germany, human contact, learning a language, and cultural enrichment.

To build my understanding of Communist ideology, I was given a three-volume *History of the Communist Party* and a biography of Lenin to study.

I dissected the West German constitution, read West German publications, and watched their television programs. TV was especially rewarding because not only did it provide entertainment, but it was an activity I might otherwise be punished for, a clear indication of my above-the-law status.

Our mantra became "contacts, contacts, contacts," which I heard often during my tenure with the KGB. This was indicative of the high value they placed on human intelligence. I had an ongoing task to meet, get to know, and report on as many new people as possible.

I was told that every KGB operative had to become proficient in a second language. Given the opportunity to choose, I picked English. The KGB paid for private tutors, and I dove into my language studies with the same zeal with which I had studied chemistry at the university.

I happily took advantage of the requirement for cultural enrichment. The KGB wanted their star agents to be broadly educated in order to fit in with the upper strata of any society. I attended the theater, ballet, opera, and museums, and the KGB reimbursed all tickets and entrance fees as part of my expenses.

In particular, I spent a lot of time on Berlin's Museum Island, home to five world-renowned museums. My favorite was the Pergamon, particularly its collection of classical antiquities, which reminded me how, as a twelve-year-old, I had devoured a German transcription of both *The Odyssey* and *The Iliad*.

Occasionally I was given additional tasks, some strictly for practice and others meant to yield real results. Among those were several investigations of individuals with relatives in the West, including a couple who lived in Bernau, some twenty kilometers northeast of Berlin.

In order to accomplish that task, I took up temporary residence in the town, under the guise of a doctoral student of history doing research concerning certain events in Bernau's past. The full beard I sported in those days made the cover quite believable. I interviewed a number of residents until one of them recommended that I also interview the target couple.

I now had a point of reference, which made my approach very natural and allowed me to strike up a conversation with the couple that turned into a brief friendship, during which I was able to extract the desired information concerning their relatives in the West.

Two other investigations took me into West Berlin, and the successful outcomes gave me confidence that I was not distinguishable as someone from the East. I was also asked to infiltrate the National Democratic Party of Germany (NPD), an East German political party, by profiling some of their leaders and writing a general report about the party. I gained access to several midlevel functionaries in the NPD by befriending an active member, the curator of the Gerhart Hauptmann Museum, which was located in my new hometown of Erkner. Given that the NPD was closely allied with, and probably even supervised by, the Communist Party, this was very likely a practice task.

During the early months of training, Nikolai acted like a hard boss, someone to be feared rather than liked. The underlying tension in our relationship came to a head in the summer of 1973.

Somehow, my last girlfriend from Jena had gotten ahold of my mailing address. At first, she sent me a very sweet love letter, which she concluded by saying, "And now everything is in your soft, warm hands."

When I did not respond, she decided to surprise me in person. I could not have been more shocked when I answered a knock at the door of my humble abode and found Gabriele standing there. Though I was rather ashamed of my living quarters, I felt I had no choice but to invite her in. We sat next to each other on the bed, and she initiated the conversation.

"Albrecht, I cannot forget you. I should never have left Jena when I did. You know I never wanted to leave you. I just had to get away from that hateful chemistry lab. Please, let us give it another try—we can make this work." By now, tears were running down her cheeks.

Despite my laser-like focus on the future, it was hard to watch a beautiful woman cry—and cry over me. But this was an impossible situation. I could not have a girlfriend from the past while I was preparing to leave my entire past behind. Such a relationship would jeopardize everything.

With a coldness that belied my true feelings, I said what had to be said, even though I knew it would hurt her. "Gabriele, I liked you a lot, but I never loved you. There is no foundation for a lasting relationship."

"But—" she answered meekly, and then her tears began to flow freely as she realized that it really was over.

For the remainder of her visit, I managed to keep the conversation casual, and at the end of the day, I put her on a train back to her hometown of Leipzig.

When I confided to Nikolai what had happened, he straightened up immediately, and his face turned red with anger.

"Well, you can get back together with that girl if you want, but if that's the case, you may want to consider a career in farming."

"The relationship is *over*, completely over," I said emphatically until finally he seemed to believe me. I had no intention of endangering the path I had chosen, but the message from Nikolai was clear: *We own your private life.*

Although the matter was never mentioned again, I was certain that in his next report, Nikolai would note that I was honest to the bone and that I had a weakness for the fairer sex. Such a notation may have later played a role in the KGB's allowing me to get married, possibly to prevent me from falling victim to the wiles of a female counterintelligence agent. As hardened and focused as I would become, there was a chink in my armor—not the temptation of a woman, but the innocence of a child—that one day would lead to my downfall . . . and also to my salvation.

14

ONE OCTOBER MORNING IN 1973, I hurried through the driving rain with an umbrella that offered little protection. It was a ten-minute walk from the commuter train station to Fürstenwalder Damm, where Nikolai regularly picked me up in his car. Finally, sopping wet, I pulled open the passenger side door and jumped inside. I expected Nikolai to complain about my messing up the interior of his car, as he had done on previous occasions, but this time he pulled out an envelope from his briefcase and handed it to me with a big grin.

"Open it," he said.

I tried to dry off my hands before taking the envelope. Inside, I saw a big aluminum key.

"What is this for?" I asked.

"That, young man, is the key to your new apartment. You have worked hard these past nine months, and you deserve it. I will drive you there right now."

The drive to Eitelstraße 31, in the Lichtenberg district, took half an hour. Nikolai parked on the street outside the building, which was a typical four-story prewar tenement with a brownish-gray facade that had multiple entrances. As if to welcome me to my new home, the rain stopped right on cue.

Entering a courtyard through the front entrance, we found a staircase off to the left that took us past the bombed-out first floor and up to the second landing. Nikolai used the key to open a wooden door and then stood aside as I stepped into my first real apartment.

"What do you think?" he asked with a proud look on his face.

"Very nice," I said. I walked straight ahead into the kitchen, which had a gas stove, a sink with running cold water, and two ancient and well-worn pieces of furniture: a table and a cupboard. To the left was the living room, with a tiled coal-burning stove, a huge oak chest of drawers, and an armoire. Though not quite in live-in condition, this place was a big improvement over the dump in Erkner.

"The WC is outside, down one flight of stairs, but not bad," Nikolai said. "And . . . ," he paused and handed me another envelope with yet another wide grin, "here is something to help you with the furniture."

The envelope contained a thousand marks, two hundred more than my monthly salary. Nikolai was full of surprises today.

We left the apartment separately, so as not to be seen together again, but that day marked a significant change in our relationship. Though I didn't know the reasons, from that point on Nikolai acted more like a friendly mentor than a demanding boss. Apparently, I had survived the probationary period.

I put the money to good use, buying a blue sleeper sofa, a coffee table, two chairs, a small refrigerator, and a used color television set, which was useful to further my understanding of West German culture. Compared to what was available on East German television, the programs in the West were much more lively and entertaining. One of my favorite shows was the German version of *Sesame Street*, which never failed to make me laugh.

My new apartment now served as a primary meeting place for my times with Nikolai—a major improvement over meeting in his car. Every other month, he brought visitors from Moscow who had taken an interest in my development. One such visitor immediately asked me, "How's your English training coming along?"

"I've always been good in English," I replied with a touch of arrogance, "but I'm learning a hundred new words every day, and I can already read English novels without using a dictionary."

"Really? That sounds promising."

At our next meeting, Nikolai gave me a tape recorder and asked me to create a recording.

"Read some English text from one of your novels, and talk freely about a topic of your choice."

A month later, I was invited to KGB headquarters in Moscow—which we always referred to as the Center—specifically to assess my progress in English. This was the first inkling I received that I might not be deployed in West Germany after all.

✦ ✦ ✦

Because of the nature of my "job," and because my future was so uncertain, I pretty much kept to myself between training sessions. Even at the peak of my training, I had plenty of free time. As the weeks stretched into months, I began to realize that I was lonely in the big city. Soon after moving into my new apartment, I decided to seek some companionship—at least someone to spend some time with—but I realized I needed to have a plan.

One Saturday afternoon, I got to thinking, *What better place to meet someone than at Die Melodie?* The famous dance hall was at the center of the city, about a ten-minute walk from the Brandenburg Gate. *And what better time than now?* Putting on my best suit, I gathered up my courage and took the downtown train to Friedrichstraße.

It was still early, so very few people were at Die Melodie when I arrived. As I pushed through the huge double doors, a large hall opened up before me with a parquet dance floor in the middle, a dais for the band straight ahead, and enough tables around the perimeter to hold about two hundred people.

I planted myself at a table for eight off to the side and away from the music. The other chairs were empty, but it wasn't long before two attractive and well-dressed ladies sat down at the other end of the table. They certainly caught my eye. Based on the elegance of their attire and the fact that they were sharing the most expensive bottle of wine on the menu, I concluded that they were visitors from the West and should therefore be kept at arm's length.

But before I could move to a different table, one of the women initiated a conversation with me. Unable to hear what she was saying over the rock music pounding from the speakers, I moved closer and leaned forward.

"Are you from around here?" she asked.

"Sort of. I moved to Berlin from Jena about a year ago," I said.

"So what do you do, if I may ask?"

A nosy one, I thought, but I provided her my stock answer: "I work for the Department of the Exterior. And where are you two from?"

"Oh, we're neighbors from the Prenzlauer Berg area, and we like to hang out with each other."

"Oh, I see." Internally, I breathed a sigh of relief. Prenzlauer Berg was firmly in the heart of East Berlin. I didn't have to worry about getting mixed up with someone from the West.

I glanced at the woman's friend and was instantly intrigued. She was exquisitely beautiful, with a face like a movie star. Her sparkling light-blue eyes highlighted delicate features framed by locks of golden-blonde hair.

"Would you like to dance?" I asked when she caught me looking at her.

"Sure, why not?"

As we walked toward the dance floor, I noticed that she was slightly taller than average—not a bad thing for someone of my height. She told me her name was Gerlinde and that she worked as an administrative assistant at Humboldt University. To be heard over the music, she leaned in close to my ear, and the breath of her words sent a powerful surge of electricity running down my neck. The band played song after song, and we kept dancing as if we were the only two people in the room.

When the band played a version of "The Tennessee Waltz," I put my hands on her waist, and she reached up around my neck. As we danced close together, her head found my shoulder. Her sweet perfume was intoxicating, and I held her a bit tighter.

When the evening was over, I walked her home, completely forgetting that she'd come with a friend. At her doorstep, I gave her a shy good-night kiss, and she smiled warmly at me. As she turned to go inside, I said, "Are you available tomorrow night?"

Her smile widened as she nodded, and my heart took off like a racehorse.

The next evening, we enjoyed a light meal at a nice restaurant, and after further conversation at her apartment, we fell passionately into each other's arms.

When I returned to my place the next morning, I felt as if I had arrived in a different universe. The air seemed fresh and full of promise, and even the birds seemed to have scored a clear victory over the noisy, smoke-belching vehicles that crowded the streets. Overnight, the world had become a better place, and I was lucky to be in it. In the span of twenty-four hours, Gerlinde had managed to penetrate the armor I had maintained for eight years since the loss of Rosi.

For the next several months, there was hardly a night when I was at home. After my "workday," I joined Gerlinde at her apartment, and in the morning I accompanied her to Humboldt University before continuing on to my fictitious job at a nearby government building. Gerlinde didn't know what I really did during the day, or why I took a trip to Moscow.

+ + +

Before my first trip to the Soviet Union, I had never been on an airplane. So I faced this great adventure with a mixture of excitement and fear. In 1975, for a twenty-six-year-old spy-in-training, a plane trip was a special occasion. I dressed accordingly in a suit, white shirt, and tie.

When Nikolai came to pick me up at my apartment, he sat down at the kitchen table, and I joined him there. For the next several minutes, I waited for him to say something or do something, but he just sat with his head bent forward, not saying a word. After a while, he stood up, walked to the door, and off we went.

This "moment of silence" soon became a routine that Nikolai followed for the rest of the time I knew him. None of the other Soviets ever did anything like it, and I always wondered what was going on in his head during those moments.

We arrived at Schönefeld Airport, on the outskirts of Berlin, ninety minutes prior to departure. After checking my suitcase at the counter, I headed in the direction of a sign reading Passport Control. But Nikolai tapped me on the shoulder, smiled, and said, "This way. Follow me."

He led me to a door with a sign that said *Eingang Verboten* (Entry Prohibited) in big red letters. Apparently, the warning did not apply to Nikolai and me. Behind the door was a uniformed East German border guard, who saluted Nikolai as soon as he saw his credentials and let us pass without further ado. In years to come, my East German passport would never have even a trace of evidence that I had ever been to the Soviet Union.

After we walked into a waiting room, Nikolai gave me a quick good-bye nod and disappeared through the same door we had entered. I joined the dozen or so other passengers who were waiting for a bus to take us out to the plane, which was parked on the tarmac.

With so few passengers on the flight, it took no more than five minutes to board the plane and find an empty seat. After the cabin doors were closed, the pilot made a request over the intercom.

"We have a very light load today, and for safety reasons I'm asking everyone to take a seat at the front of the plane during takeoff."

The passengers all looked at one another, but we all moved forward. The pilot's announcement did nothing to dispel my anxiety. I found a new seat in one of the first few rows and tightened my seat belt against my lap.

To fill the time until takeoff, I pulled out the safety instructions and emergency procedures from the seat pocket in front of me, but reading all that information only served to make me even more nervous. When the plane began to taxi out to the runway, every bump and unexplained noise raised my level of anxiety until a cold sweat ran down my forehead. To make matters worse, a rowdy group of young men in the row behind me began to banter back and forth about the flight.

"Did you hear that?"

"Yeah, I think a wheel just fell off."

"Have you ever heard of gathering everyone to the front to distribute the weight properly?"

"I'm telling you, something is wrong with this plane. Hey, stewardess, can I have another drink?"

I wanted to reach back and shut those guys up, but instead I sat as calmly as I could with my hands gripping the armrests. To settle my nerves, I consumed a few drinks of my own and smoked almost an entire pack of cigarettes during the two-and-a-half-hour flight. I arrived in Moscow safe and sound, but with a throbbing headache.

As I entered the airport terminal, I was immediately intercepted by a handsome young man about my age, with very dark eyes and a full head of jet-black hair. He introduced himself as Sergej.

"It's very nice to meet you, Albrecht," he said in excellent German with only a hint of an accent. He had grown up in Moldova. "I will be the host for your stay here. We have heard a lot of good things about you."

"Thank you, and it's nice to meet you, too. But can I trouble you for an aspirin? The flight gave me quite a headache."

"Certainly, but first we'll get your luggage."

Sergej smuggled me past customs and passport control via a side door into the main hall of the airport and motioned me over to a corner to await my bags. In the meantime, I took a look around. By comparison with Berlin's Schönefeld Airport, Sheremetyevo was huge. There were hundreds, if not thousands, of passengers milling around in the main hall. Not only was I in the most powerful country in the world, but I was there by invitation of the government. My chest swelled with pride and I almost forgot my headache.

When a uniformed soldier delivered my suitcase, Sergej immediately took it and led me outside to the curb, where a black Volga limousine was waiting for us. As the limo raced down the left lane of Leningrad Avenue toward the city center, I was thoroughly impressed by the expansive layout of the boulevard and the row of gargantuan buildings that lined both sides. Berlin's Karl Marx Allee was a junior-varsity version of this magnificent avenue.

"So, Sergej, we are allowed to go one hundred kilometers an hour in the leftmost lane while all that traffic to the right seems to be crawling?"

"Special people deserve special treatment," he said.

He further explained that our car had special license plates that allowed the driver to use the restricted lane. Anyone else who ventured over would be hunted down and fined. With that affirmation of my special status, my headache disappeared completely.

I leaned toward the window as we moved past the fascinating inner city. I recognized the famous structures I had seen in books and magazines. We passed the fortified complex of the Kremlin, with its huge spired tops, the vast Red Square, and the impressive gingerbread-and-frosting St. Basil's Cathedral, built by Ivan the Terrible in the sixteenth century.

Ten minutes later, the limo pulled up in front of a typical Khrushchyovka apartment building. I followed Sergej inside to the elevator, which took us up to the fourth floor.

"You'll stay here for the next two nights," Sergej explained as we entered the tidy and well-appointed apartment. He motioned for me to sit down, and a short, elderly woman brought in a light meal of dark bread, smoked fish, and tea. Sergej said she'd take care of all the meals during my stay. After she left, Sergej and I discussed the upcoming agenda as we ate.

"Since this trip is to assess your ability in English," Sergej explained, "you'll be interviewed by two experts who will then issue a report to our leadership."

After the meal, Sergej bade me good-bye and left me to settle in to my new surroundings. I helped myself to some of the Georgian brandy I discovered in a credenza and watched a hockey game in distorted, blurry colors on the television. Finally able to relax, I fell asleep during the third period and woke up to a dark screen.

✛ ✛ ✛

The next day, I had back-to-back meetings with two English experts. The first to arrive at the apartment was an American-born woman who had somehow ended up in Moscow. She looked to be in her early fifties, with a slim figure and a sallow complexion. Her hair was a mixture of gray and faded blonde. She was pleasant, but her low energy, overall appearance, body language, and soft-spoken demeanor gave the impression that she had become weary of life. We conversed for about an hour in English.

After a break, a second examiner—a female professor of English from the famed Lomonsov University—arrived at the apartment. She was the exact opposite of the American examiner in every respect. In her midthirties, elegantly dressed and attractive, she spoke nearly flawless Queen's English and projected high energy and self-confidence. This was clearly not an ordinary college professor, and she knew why I was there.

"Dear comrade," she addressed me rather formally, "you have

certainly made excellent progress in learning the English language. However, your German accent is still very strong. I don't believe you will ever master the British dialect, and I doubt you will get close to a passable American accent either."

Her blunt assessment hit me like an ice-cold shower. I sat like a schoolboy being lectured by a stern teacher.

"Anyway," she continued, ignoring my discomfort, "learning the language is only one part of it. You must also learn how to *think* and *feel* like an American. Imagine living in their big houses and driving one of those huge cars. In order to be successful in the United States, you must think *big*. You must undergo a complete metamorphosis."

I was dazzled by the boldness of this statement, though it was hard to imagine myself bridging the wide canyon between my current humble circumstances and the future this woman painted. A rich undercover revolutionary in the United States? I felt like a little boy in a toy store with an unlimited expense account.

At the same time, I was determined to prove that this overbearing and condescending professor was dead wrong. I *would* learn American English, and I would learn to speak it *perfectly*.

That evening, several visitors arrived at the apartment—five men and the Russian professor from my interview. I sensed that these people were all high up in the KGB, especially when one of the men was introduced by his full three-part name, a sign of great respect in Russia.

The elderly Russian woman who fixed my meals had prepared a feast, and we all sat down at the table to enjoy it. After we settled in, the high-level KGB officer spoke directly to me in a voice of unquestioned authority.

"We have decided to send you to our main adversary, masquerading as a natural-born American."

I managed to keep a straight face, but inside, my excitement was growing. The United States! I nodded respectfully as I began to imagine great accomplishments and making a real difference in the world.

"This is an incredibly challenging task," the officer continued, "and will require much more preparation. For the next two years, you will live here in Moscow to receive your final training before the launch. This is in recognition of your talents and your excellent performance during training so far. Believe me, this is a very special assignment that can only be accomplished by a special individual. We don't send agents over like bananas." He nodded decisively and said, "Let's drink to that."

His "toast" was greeted with some cheers and laughter as everyone at the table emptied their chilled glasses of vodka in one gulp.

With the official part of the banquet out of the way, it was time to tackle the delicious array of food spread out before us. I was awestruck by the quantity and variety of items assembled—enough to give the sturdy wooden table a backache. And at the center of it all was a huge bottle of vodka in a bucket filled with dry ice.

For the next three hours, we ate and drank and smoked, and all the Russians at the table took their turn offering a toast. The soup and appetizers were followed by two main courses—a large whole fish and a beef stew. And there was plenty of fresh Russian bread available.

By the end of the banquet, everyone was in an excellent mood. Despite the massive amounts of alcohol consumed, nobody appeared drunk or slurred their speech. Perhaps it was the equally massive amounts of food we ate that slowed the absorption of the alcohol into our bloodstreams and kept us all relatively sober.

✦   ✦   ✦

Moscow was an unexpected new stopover on my uncharted journey. I was advancing up the ladder, earning my stripes, and would eventually be sent to America. This was so far beyond the dreams I'd had of becoming a professor of chemistry and living a respected life at the university, perhaps marrying and having children. My new path would follow an unknown route—perhaps like one of the heroic spies I grew up reading about. At the age of twenty-six, I had become convinced that I was meant to do something both very important and dangerous.

But I had some loose ends to take care of—one of which was Gerlinde.

Eight years after being unceremoniously discarded by Rosi, I had dared to open my heart again, and I had fallen in love. Gerlinde was everything I could wish for. She was beautiful, sexy, smart, and full of positive energy. But there was simply no place for her in my future life as an undercover agent in the United States of America.

Given Nikolai's reaction to the episode with Gabriele a year earlier, I had not told him anything about Gerlinde. This was one situation I would have to resolve on my own.

When I returned from Moscow to prepare for my move there, I realized I was at a point of no return. The switches had been set for the track of my life's journey. The KGB was grooming me to become an undercover agent in the United States of America—the number one enemy of the Soviet Union—and Gerlinde simply could not be a part of that.

I had about a month to prepare for the inevitable breakup. Our initial conversation about the topic was as painful as it was uncomfortable. I was half telling the truth and half lying to the woman I loved.

"Gerlinde," I began hesitantly, "I need to tell you about a great career opportunity I've been given."

Her eyes lit up and she leaned toward me in anticipation of the good news.

"I've been offered the position of deputy science attaché at the GDR embassy in Moscow."

"That's great!" she responded instinctively, but as the consequences of this appointment began to dawn on her, she asked plaintively, "But . . . what about *us*?"

I had rehearsed the answer many times in my mind, and now I forced it out.

"I've thought about this long and hard," I said, "and the timing is just really bad."

Her beautiful blue eyes were like lasers cutting into my heart. I looked down at my hands in order to stay on script.

"Our relationship hasn't really reached a point where I think we can talk about getting married . . ." I said.

She didn't respond to this, so I kept talking.

"And, you know, East Germans cannot just move to the Soviet Union without official permission and a job there. This is a two-year appointment."

"Okay," she said, as if considering whether she could handle a long-distance relationship. But I couldn't keep the charade going. I knew I wasn't coming back to Berlin after two years. My next stop would be somewhere in the United States.

"I'm sorry, Gerlinde, but I'm not ready for a lengthy, long-distance relationship with an uncertain future."

"So—so, this is it?"

"I can't think of another solution. It seems best if we both just move on."

Tears started streaming down Gerlinde's face, and I had a hard time holding back tears of my own. As if looking for a plausible excuse, I said, "You know, I thought hard about declining the offer—but it's just not an option. You say no to the Party only once," remembering the line my father had uttered many years before.

There was nothing more to say that evening, so I gave Gerlinde a gentle kiss on the forehead and left her apartment.

We continued seeing each other for the next three weeks, desperately clinging to a magical past that had no future. But on the night before my departure, it was time for a final good-bye.

When I entered her apartment, I saw her lying on the sofa staring blankly into an undefined point in space. The atmosphere was thick with an oppressive melancholy that settled like an immense weight on my chest. No more lighthearted laughter, no more teasing, no more kisses and hugs. This was good-bye forever. Gerlinde was wearing a red sweater and black tights, which revealed her attractive curves, but my focus was purely on bringing this scene to a quick end.

Without saying a word, I bent down and gave her a last soft kiss good-bye. Then I turned around, put my key to her apartment on the table, and walked out.

The heaviness of the moment squeezed my heart and muddled my thinking. But despite the numbness in my soul, I never lost sight of the final goal. I was on my way to bigger things, and now the last, most difficult obstacle had been overcome.

By the following day, final preparations for the trip had displaced all feelings of guilt or sadness. My mind was once again clear. The call to Moscow beckoned.

15

I ARRIVED IN THE SOVIET CAPITAL in mid-October 1975. Once again, Sergej met me at the airport and a chauffeured Volga limousine took us straight to my new living quarters in the Preobrazhenskoye district, about ten kilometers northeast of Red Square.

Sergej explained that the nearest Metro station, Elektrozavodskaya, was just a ten-minute walk across the Yauza River and that all parts of the city were readily accessible from there.

As we rode up the elevator to the third floor of a conventional, Soviet-style, concrete apartment building, I felt a wave of anticipation about taking over my very first, very own modern apartment.

But as Sergej put down my suitcase and showed me around, I caught sight of a tired-looking old lady in a shabby brown dress—a typical Russian babushka—stirring something vigorously on a gas-fired stove.

What on earth is that woman doing here?

Before I could ask Sergej, he explained the situation to me.

"This is Anna Sergejevna. She is the widow of a Red Army officer who was killed in World War II. You will be sharing the place with her and her son."

I kept my disappointment to myself as the woman poured us cups of tea and Sergej and I withdrew into my new room—not comfortable, but adequate for my needs—to discuss plans for the weeks and months ahead. Though I was excited about this new phase in my training, my mind momentarily drifted to Gerlinde and her tidy Berlin apartment.

Before Sergej left, he advised me to take as much time as possible to explore the city. "After all, this will be your operational stage for the foreseeable future."

The following day I set out to explore, armed with maps of the city and the subway system. Wearing slacks, a button-down shirt, and a jacket, I was dressed appropriately for the middle of October—or so I thought. But as the day wore on, I started feeling uncomfortably chilly. Was I coming down with some kind of flu?

As I continued to walk and shiver, I came across a large temperature display on the side of a building. It read minus 8 degrees Celsius (18 degrees Fahrenheit). Winter had arrived in Moscow, and it would keep a hammerlock on the city for the next six months.

I knew I was in Moscow to perfect my English, but as for any long-term plans, I was mostly kept in the dark. I would later learn that, in modern espionage, there are two distinct types of spies: legal residents, who operate under official cover—in a role such as a diplomat, embassy attaché, or a member of a trade mission—and illegals, who operate under fake identities, with no known connection to the country for which they are spying.

Legals have the advantage of diplomatic immunity. The worst that can happen to them is expulsion from the host country. But from an intelligence-gathering point of view, their ability to get close to secrets and secret-bearers is limited. Legal-resident agents often act as channels of communication between illegal agents and the Center and also provide monetary support.

Illegals have no diplomatic protection. If caught, they are subject to the full force of the law. The risk is offset by the potential reward of being able to move around the country freely and get close to unsuspecting targets.

From the moment I was introduced to the KGB, it was clear they were recruiting me to become an illegal. I wouldn't be deployed as a diplomat or a visiting professor. I would be sent in under the cover of a fake identity and fake citizenship.

What I didn't know was that the illegals program had been sputtering for many years and had suffered numerous failures. My recruitment was part of a renewed effort to establish a net of illegals in the United States.

+ + +

The Russian winter was definitely not what I was accustomed to in East Germany. The first snow arrived in late October and promptly stuck to the ground. It would not melt until sometime in April. With highs averaging 25 degrees Fahrenheit and lows around 15 degrees (and dips as low as minus 20), it was easy to understand how "General Winter" had been such a great ally to the Russians against the armies of Napoleon and Hitler.

The icy sidewalks soon turned into an ugly and dangerous mess, resembling a bumpy skating rink that made every step an adventure. The situation was particularly bad in high traffic areas, where a horrible habit of many Muscovites added saliva and mucus to the icy mix of mud and gravel.

To deal with the cold, I wore the hated long underwear I had ditched as soon as I was out from under my mother's clothing dictates. I also wore a fake-fur *chapka*, with flaps to cover my ears, and lined mittens on my hands. On extremely cold mornings, I put a scarf over my mouth to combat the icy, piercing wind and took shallow breaths, as Sergej had advised me, to avoid possible lung damage.

When it came to procuring food, I had to fend for myself. All Muscovites were in a daily struggle to find decent food, and it was even more difficult for a foreigner who barely spoke the language. My diet was quickly narrowed down to bread, canned fish, and mineral water—the only foods in ample supply—and an occasional restaurant meal. From my childhood and my years at the university, I was used to substandard food, but what really weighed on me was the lack of human company.

With the exception of my two weekly meetings with the English tutor and a handful of meetings with Sergej and various technical specialists, I was very lonely. Every day was work, work, work, and the highlight of my evenings was doing some light reading in English or straining to hear the weak reception of the *BBC Worldwide* program on the shortwave radio Sergej had provided.

How I wished to be back with Gerlinde! Even a day at my mother's apartment sounded good. But the last thing I would do in this situation was complain. Instead, I handwrote letters to my mother, assuring her that all was well.

During those first months, I lived the life of a prisoner—with no physical boundaries, but with severe mental and emotional constraints. Only my iron will, discipline, and sense of purpose helped me endure this bleak period and emerge with a fundamentally positive outlook about things to come.

✦ ✦ ✦

Perfecting my English and developing an American accent took a lot of work and a lot of time, including a twice-weekly, forty-five-minute trip across town to the home of Irina Pavlova, my American-born tutor, the same woman who had interviewed me on my first trip to Moscow. The first half hour of our two-hour lessons was dedicated to boring, but very useful, phonetics exercises designed to remove as much German from my accent as possible. The remainder of the two-hour session was spent in more or less free-form conversation with Irina. Outside of those Tuesday/Thursday sessions, not a day went by when I did not spend at least one hour memorizing new words to expand my vocabulary. Before I left Moscow, I had amassed a vocabulary of around 30,000 English words.

Irina was nice and wanted to be helpful, but her low energy and lack of enthusiasm made it a chore to engage with her in lengthy conversations. Still, it was my task to learn the language, and I took full ownership of it. Every evening, without fail, I spent an additional half hour listening to words on a phonetics tape and repeating them—listening and repeating, listening and repeating—ad nauseam. When it comes to basic life skills, repetition is the midwife of excellence. After continual practice of the most tedious exercises I have ever had to do, the results, though not entirely perfect, were very encouraging.

✦ ✦ ✦

Along with the spring thaw came an improvement in my living arrangements. When I finally gathered the courage to mention my challenging circumstances to Sergej, he apologized profusely and confessed that he had been wrong to assume that the babushka would cook for me. Apparently, someone had forgotten to tell *her*.

Within weeks, I was moved into a two-bedroom apartment, with a private bath, kitchen, and—to my great delight—a color television set. Measured by the standards of past accommodations, this was pure luxury. And with the opportunity to watch Russian cartoons, movies, and sporting events, I finally had an entertainment break from the intense world of training.

Sergej added another dash of color to my life by occasionally providing me a ticket to a sold-out premier concert or ballet performance, including an impossible-to-get ticket for the Bolshoi Ballet.

He also gave me tickets to an American theater troupe performance of Thornton Wilder's *Our Town* and the entertainment highlight of my entire time in Moscow: a sold-out performance by Roy Clark, who came to the Soviet Union as part of a cultural exchange. Clark's *Hee Haw* shtick was a rousing success with the Muscovites, and it took me back to my high school years, when I used to listen to British and American music via shortwave radio. Now here was one of my musical icons *in person*, and he was *good*! As an American-to-be, I applauded heartily.

In late May 1976, Sergej delivered a letter that my mother had sent to the post office box I used as a mailing address. I had recently written to her that I would not be coming back to East Germany for the summer as I had originally planned. Sergej and I agreed that a return to Germany at this point would only create difficulties—particularly the possibility of meeting old friends and acquaintances who might ask too many questions. I told my mother I would be vacationing with a group of other junior diplomats at a resort in Yalta, on the Black Sea.

I opened my mother's letter in Sergej's presence, and within thirty seconds I said, with alarm in my voice, "We have a problem."

"What?"

"My mother is coming to see me. She and her new husband have booked a trip to Moscow."

Sergej looked concerned and took a while to respond.

"How much time do we have?"

"They are coming in five weeks and staying for two days before going on to the Black Sea."

"Okay," Sergej responded, "we have two issues to deal with: your job as a diplomat and this apartment. Let me discuss this with the comrades."

Two days later, he came back with a solution. I would introduce Sergej as my new Russian friend, and with his help we would spend two days of intensive sightseeing to divert my mother's attention away from a possible desire to visit the East German embassy, the place where I pretended to work.

Because my apartment was a conspirational flat, my mother was not allowed to see it. Therefore, I would move to a hotel for the two days of her stay and simply explain that my apartment was being renovated.

When my mother and her new husband, Werner, arrived, the plan worked very well. With Sergej as our guide, we spent two days seeing some of the sights around Moscow. There was only one glitch: My mother wanted to commemorate her visit, and she had a bright idea.

"Werner," she said, "why don't you take a picture of me, Albrecht, and his friend on the streets of Moscow."

I saw a flash of fear in Sergej's eyes. Members of the KGB were not to be photographed by anyone other than their own families. However, if Sergej refused, it would look awkward or even suspicious. I could see the wheels turning in his head, and after a lengthy pause he agreed. And thus the only picture of me with a Soviet KGB agent was taken.

✝ ✝ ✝

One day, Sergej showed up at my new apartment with exciting news.

"Albrecht, tomorrow we are going to visit Lenin."

This pretty much took my breath away, and I stared at him in disbelief. To me, Vladimir Lenin was the most important person in history. He had taken the theories developed by Marx and Engels and put them into practice. Following one of Marx's most famous theses—"The philosophers have only interpreted the world in various ways; the point is to change it"—Lenin had created the promise of a great future for all mankind.

Lenin had led the Russian Revolution, built the Soviet Union, and laid the foundation for a world without the oppression and exploitation of capitalism. I was thoroughly convinced that, unlike Stalin and his murderous henchmen, Lenin was a pure revolutionary, who had suffered personally for his beliefs. Lenin was my hero, and we were going to pay our respects.

The next day, dressed in a suit and tie, I rode with Sergej in a Volga limousine that let us off at the edge of Red Square. I had passed the famous square many times before and had never failed to notice the endless line of visitors awaiting admission to Lenin's tomb. Today, the line stretched across the square, past the State Historical Museum, and turned left into the park adjacent to the western Kremlin wall. I expected to have to join the end of the line, but Sergei indicated that this would not be necessary.

"Follow me," he said, and we walked straight to the front entrance. When he flashed his credentials to the guard, we were promptly admitted.

The mausoleum was flooded in soft yellow light. I felt as if I were entering a holy place and about to see God on display. The others in line to pay their respects maintained a reverent silence as we all moved steadily toward the shrine. And then, there he was, my hero, reclining in a glass case, eyes closed.

As Sergej and I walked the slow circle around the casket, a sudden sense of disappointment fell over me. Was this really the dynamic Vladimir Lenin who had shaken the world? His five-foot-five-inch frame seemed even smaller in the low yellow light, and his embalmed skin looked like ancient, weathered parchment. After the short, silent walk around the casket, I wondered how these preserved remains could hold such an attraction for the masses.

On the drive back to Preobrazhenskoye, Sergej seemed in awe of the experience, and I said nothing to him about my disappointment. I still believed in Lenin and the cause, but given a choice between seeing Roy Clark or Lenin's tomb, I would not have hesitated to pick the live American entertainer over the embalmed revolutionary.

+ + +

The willingness to pound the pavement of one's operational city is one of the necessities of undercover life. Through all four seasons, I explored Moscow in detail, riding the Metro to the end of every line, searching out surveillance routes, and scouting potential dead-drop sites. Before my first year was over, I knew the city better than most native Muscovites. Along the way, I became familiar with the good (well-maintained and colorful historic buildings), the bad (shoddily constructed tenements of a more recent vintage), and the ugly (dilapidated older buildings with muddy backyards in the outlying sections of the city).

One of the best things I discovered was a marvel of modern engineering and construction that every Muscovite could take pride in: the impressive underground Metro system, which the London *Daily Telegraph* calls "the world's most beautiful metro" and "as much [an] underground art gallery as [a] transport network."[3] Each of the 150-plus stations has its own unique design, many with ornate mosaics, statues, or stained glass. Many platforms in the older stations look as if they've been pulled out of a palace somewhere. The more modern stations have a sleeker design, but in every case, only the best building materials were used. The architects and builders were given unlimited resources to construct a showpiece for Communism and its great leader, Joseph Stalin, and the Moscow Metro is an example of the greatness that can be achieved if a dictator spares no expense to build a monument to himself.

The operation of the Metro was just as impressive as its facilities. Running deep underground—and serving double duty as a bomb shelter—the Metro is not affected by the weather, and thus the trains always run on time. To get down to the platform from street level, I often had to ride for as long as two minutes on a fast-moving escalator. Once on the platform, there was never a long wait for the next train and the cars always had enough room to accommodate passengers. The doors opened and closed automatically, and a recorded female voice alerted the riders and announced the upcoming station. I heard that voice so many times that, decades later, I could still replay the Russian singsong in my head: "Attention, doors are closing. Next station . . ."

Other training subjects, not covered in Berlin, were added to the agenda in Moscow, including self-defense, analysis of American politics and policy, and visual observation. For three months, I worked with a personal trainer practicing the basics of tae kwon do. These were strictly self-defense moves meant to ward off an attack by criminals, not law enforcement, while in possession of materials or money that might fall into the wrong hands.

"It's time to improve your field operations training," Sergej told me at one of our meetings. "We have the best in the world right here, and Eugen, our senior surveillance trainer, is one of them."

"Okay," I responded with enthusiasm. I was ready for any new challenge. My English studies were taking up more than half my time in Moscow, and any other activity would be a welcome break from the routine.

When I met Eugen the next week, I found that he was only an inch or two north of five feet tall, but what he lacked in height he made up for in boundless energy. A mischievous twinkle in his eyes seemed to say, "Catch me if you can," and made him eminently likable. His cleverness bordered on the magical.

Soon after we were introduced, Eugen took me onto the streets of Moscow to teach me the intricacies of surveillance detection.

"You must use the city and its buildings to gain an advantage over someone who might be trying to follow you," he explained with a grin. "Deserted subway platforms, infrequently used bus lines, elevators in public buildings, escalators in department stores, and strategically placed telephone booths are some of those locations."

As we walked around the city and he explained the principles of detection to me, I began to see things from different angles and perspectives. Everything we did had to appear normal and not at all suspicious.

"The goal is to draw one or two members of the surveillance brigade close enough to get a good look at their faces," Eugen said. "If the same face shows up at another location, you have proof that you're being followed."

Eugen taught me how to devise a roughly three-hour crisscross trip through town, on foot and with public transportation.

"Plan your route in advance, and there must always be a plausible reason to go from point A to point B."

Every other month, I did a practice run to check my progress. I never knew when Sergej would drop by and announce, "Tomorrow morning, 9:00 a.m. sharp, you will check for surveillance."

On those mornings, I'd test one of my preplanned routes through the city. Sometimes I had a tail and other times not. On days when I was followed, they sent a team of eight to ten of the best trackers in the business. They used walkie-talkies to coordinate their efforts and would frequently switch the closest follower to allow that individual to change clothing, add a hat, put on a scarf, or change a jacket.

I learned very quickly that I had an excellent memory and could not be fooled easily. If I recognized a face I'd already seen, I knew without a doubt I was being followed. If that person was now wearing a different hat, a scarf, or a wig, it was a dead giveaway.

These test runs became a serious competition. Both the leader of the surveillance team and I had to file a report after each training exercise, and no one wanted to have to admit to failure. Although these exercises were all in friendly territory, they were incredibly stressful. From the moment I left my apartment, all my senses were on high alert.

It was harder to determine that I was *not* being followed. Caution is a spy's best friend; paranoia is his enemy.

One morning, I could feel it in my bones that I was being followed. Everywhere I went, I scanned the faces of the people around me.

Have I seen this person before?

What is she doing here at this deserted bus stop?

Hah! I remember that face, but she's is wearing a different hat and coat. You lost, young lady!

Is someone hiding behind that tree? Well, I can find out because there's a public restroom right next to it.

And so it went for three hours.

At one point, a man came up and asked me for a cigarette. I used the opportunity to scan my surroundings for any suspicious activities or familiar faces. Then I moved on. Later, at the debriefing session, I found out that the guy who bummed the cigarette was an agent. That bold fellow was the only one who ever tricked me.

"You've passed the test again," Eugen said after yet another practice run. "Final score: Dieter ten, surveillance team zero." I had beaten the best of the best, and Eugen promptly declared me one of his ace students.

He soon extended my training to include dead drops, which are a way for two agents to make an exchange (of a passport, money, or classified documents) by placing or retrieving an ordinary object—something that would not attract the attention of animals or humans (such as a rusty oil can, a piece of hollowed wood, or rock made from plaster of Paris)—at a predetermined location and time.

Eugen subscribed to the principle laid out by Edgar Allan Poe in his short story "The Purloined Letter" that the best place to hide something is in plain sight. I adopted this principle to some degree, but acknowledging Eugen's superior skills, I never went to his extremes.

"Today, follow closely and watch me very carefully," Eugen said at the outset of one of our training sessions.

He walked ahead and I followed, never taking my eyes off of him. After fifteen minutes, he stopped and turned around.

"Well, did you notice anything?"

"No, nothing," I said with confidence.

Eugen broke into a triumphant belly laugh.

"Come with me," he said.

We walked together back to a raised flower bed close to the sidewalk. I marveled as he pointed out a metal cartridge embedded in the soil, just deep enough for only a half-inch to be exposed.

"I used the art of distraction to catch your attention when we were walking," he said.

"But I watched you the entire time."

Eugen laughed again, thoroughly pleased that his sleight-of-hand trick had succeeded so well.

"As I passed the flower bed, I looked to my right—which made you look to the right for just a second as I made the drop."

I could not remember looking away from him at all, and I realized I needed more work before I could imitate such mastery.

+ + +

Operating under the generally accepted rules of conspiracy, agents almost never know the details of the decision-making process. I never knowingly met anyone who laid the groundwork for my undercover life. The agents and experts who came to my apartment gave me training or information, but they never let on if they had a larger role in planning my future.

Occasionally, a few agents who were stationed in New York City or Washington, DC, under diplomatic cover would return to the Soviet Union for a visit and stop by my apartment to say hello, drop off a book or magazine, and chat with me about life in America.

The most frequent of these guests was a bright, gregarious redhead named Alex, who came fully armed with a well-developed ego and a gift for self-promotion. When he first arrived at my door, he was proudly wearing a full-length orangish leather coat, which must have cost him a fortune in Western currency. He came in like a whirlwind and quickly let me know that he was an expert in all things American. I listened with rapt attention as he explained the differences and similarities between Russians and Americans.

"Americans are very similar to Russians in that they are very easy to get along with. Of course, they are also very selfish. All they think about is getting ahead in life. They lack what we have—a cause to fight for and sacrifice for. But they're great to be around."

When Alex finished his two-year stint at the United Nations, he moved back to Moscow and became a frequent guest at my apartment, second only to Sergej. One day, he briefed me on a central point of my mission: political intelligence.

"We need to get inside the heads of the decision makers," he said. "We need to understand what they are thinking and to what extremes they might go. Remember the Cuban Missile Crisis? If we'd had better intelligence, we could have managed that situation better."

"So what exactly do you want me to do?" I asked. "How can I come to understand these American decision makers?"

"First of all, you need to sharpen your analytical skills. I will provide you with a number of American publications, and I want you to write an analysis on a topic of my choice."

"No problem," I said. "But that is all secondhand information, filtered by the reporters who wrote the articles."

"That's true. And that's why we will need you to establish contacts with people who are connected to influential think tanks such as the Hudson Institute, the Columbia University Institute of Foreign Relations, and the Trilateral Commission. We are especially interested in Zbigniew Brzezinski, the national security advisor to President Carter."

"And how do I get close to these people?" I asked in disbelief.

"We are working on that one. Don't worry, you will be set up nicely."

His answer lifted my spirits tremendously. It was yet another sign that I would have the full weight of the mighty Soviet Union behind me.

Alex was an important figure in my life, but I had no idea what his official role was. Was he Sergej's boss? Was he ultimately responsible for my deployment and my mission? I had no way of knowing. There are no published organizational charts in the undercover world.

16

ALTHOUGH THERE WAS NO VISIBLE HIERARCHY among the KGB operatives I worked with, there was a sense that some agents had achieved the status of undercover "royalty." Near the end of the summer of 1976, Sergej showed up one day with some "very good news" to share with me. Our leaders had approved a proposal to introduce me to a couple who went by the names of Peter and Helen. The reverence with which Sergej spoke about Peter and Helen reminded me of the time he had handed me a tape recording of one of the most famous KGB spies, Colonel Rudolf Abel. It was as if he were entrusting me with a precious religious relic.

"Who are Peter and Helen?" I asked innocently.

Sergej leaned in as if to impart a deep secret. "Well, I can tell you that they are real Americans, and they have served our cause extremely well. Beyond that, please do not ask any more questions."

I looked forward to meeting this illustrious couple and to have another opportunity to talk with some real Americans. Sergej took me to the couple's apartment in the chic Arbat district. After he rang the bell and identified himself, he quickly turned to depart. "Aren't you staying?" I asked as the door opened.

"No, you go on in," he said with the same excited grin he had displayed when first telling me about Peter and Helen.

I turned back and saw a man who appeared to be in his seventies, with thinning gray hair and a dull, yellowish cast to his wrinkled face. But as soon as he opened his mouth, his voice projected the vitality of someone much younger, and in his handshake I felt the steely determination of a man who was not to be trifled with.

"Come on in, Comrade Bruno!" Peter said as he added a friendly slap on the back to his greeting. "Bruno" was the code name I had been given for the purposes of working with Peter and Helen.

When I stepped inside, I was amazed by the attractiveness of their place, which by Soviet standards was a luxury apartment. The interior, including the furniture, was much more refined than anything I had seen in Moscow.

When Helen came into the room and greeted me, she seemed just as strongly determined as her husband—if not more so. Her voice was very deep and raspy, likely the result of years of heavy smoking.

After the exchange of initial pleasantries, during which both Peter and Helen behaved like children in a toy store in their eagerness to converse with me, Helen said, "Would you like some tea? I would offer you some coffee, but they don't know what good coffee is around here."

This kicked off a short discussion about their longing for good coffee. Watching them banter, I enjoyed their lively personalities and the sound of American English. While Helen served tea and cookies, Peter engaged me in conversation.

"Bruno, we are very happy to be able to talk to somebody freely in English. This is also a time for us to pass the torch to the next generation—of which you are a part. We will help you as much as we can."

As I listened with great interest, Peter began sharing bits and pieces of seemingly unconnected information about his past.

"You know, Bruno, I played football for Mississippi State." This soon led to, "I tell you, the Spanish Civil War was hell—but at least I made a lot of friends there."

The more we talked, the more I began to ask questions—the guards of secrecy having been lowered very quickly.

"Did you meet Germans and Russians in the war?" I asked.

"I sure did. I was a member of the Fifteenth International Brigade. We fought a good fight, but in the end we had no chance against Franco, who was supported by Hitler and Mussolini."

"So how did you wind up here?" I asked the one question that would have made Sergej wince.

Peter let out a hearty laugh, "One day you may read about it, for now I can only tell you that Helen and I spent eight years in a British prison."

"Eight years?" Earlier, Peter had mentioned that he was sixty-six. The fact that he looked a decade older now made sense. No doubt the rigors of prison had added some years to his appearance. Moreover, his eyesight was failing, requiring him to use very strong reading glasses, and his arthritic, bony hands were the sign of a man who had aged before his time.

"Our friends got us out, you know. They will always get you out, you can bet on that." He gave me a knowing look, as if to assure me not to be afraid of going to prison. Over time, Peter would disclose more details about his past, but he and Helen never told the entire story.

Much later, I pieced together the truth. Peter and Helen Kroger were actually Morris and Lona Cohen, who had met and married in the United States. Morris had recruited Lona to join him in spying for the KGB, and they were instrumental in the theft of atomic secrets—he by recruiting and handling a number of young physicists, and she as a courier.

The exact role the couple played in the theft of the biggest secret of all time, and any relationship they may have had with Julius and Ethel Rosenberg—who were convicted and executed for sharing atomic secrets with the Soviets—is something that probably can be found only in the vaults of the KGB's archives.

In 1950, when the FBI was closing in on the atomic spies, Peter and Helen fled to Moscow before taking up residence in Poland to prepare for yet another mission. In 1954, they moved to England, posing as a couple from New Zealand, and set up shop as antique book dealers to cover for their underground activities. For almost seven years, they acted as radio operators for the spy ring led by Gordon Lonsdale, until all three were arrested in 1961. Eight years later, Peter and Helen were exchanged for a British national after serving only a portion of their twenty- and twenty-five-year sentences.

Among the illegals who operated on behalf of the KGB during those years, Peter and Helen Kroger were true standouts. Their undying belief in the Communist cause was the perfect foundation for their activities. They had none of the flaws that compromised many other illegals.

They didn't drink, they didn't party, they weren't in it for the money; instead, they were true soldiers of the revolution. And as far as I know, they held fast to their ideals to the very end, even through the collapse of the Soviet Union.

After that first day, I felt a similar reverence for this couple to what Sergej had expressed, even though I didn't yet know their full story. Also, I felt as if I had made two very good friends in what was essentially a friendless environment.

✦　✦　✦

The systematic and elaborate preparation for my eventual deployment continued into February 1977, when I spent two weeks with Peter in a two-bedroom apartment—just him and me. An elderly lady who came to the apartment in the mornings prepared meals for the entire day.

I expected to have the same kind of enjoyable interactions I was accustomed to in my weekly visits with Peter and Helen; but when he got away from his lovely wife, Peter turned into a cranky and rigid old man.

He immediately imposed a routine that began with getting out of bed at 6:00 a.m., an hour earlier than what I was used to. At 7:00, we walked for an hour in the biting February cold. The ground was slippery, and I often had to steady Peter to keep him from falling.

During the day, we spent much of our time in conversation about the United States, the Soviet Union, spy work, and the future of the world. But Peter was a hard taskmaster, sort of like the early Nikolai, and was quick to anger whenever I did something to displease him.

One day, as I looked out the apartment window at the demolition of a nearby building, I ruminated out loud, "I wonder if they will *ironball* this thing down."

This was an invented word and not in Peter's vocabulary.

"Don't you ever do that again!" he yelled.

I looked at him in shock at this unexpected outburst, but he was merely warming up to a full fury.

"If you are experimenting with a language you have not yet mastered," he roared, "you will be *dead meat!*"

My mouth hung open as he stormed into the other room.

My face grew hot and my heart began to race. I had never felt more afraid of anyone in my life—including my father. Was this the end of our relationship? Would we ever talk again? Would he report my transgression to headquarters?

I worried for about an hour, until Peter regained his composure and came out of the room. When he returned, he restated his point, but this time with calm logic. I apologized, and our relationship was whole again.

In spite of the rough moments, the two weeks we spent together were an overall success. The ability to hear and imitate a male speaker in the American vernacular improved my English pronunciation enormously. I felt ready for the next step.

If only I knew when and what that would be.

17

"HOW WOULD YOU LIKE TO GO to Canada for a while?" Sergej asked me one day in late March 1977. By that time, I had been training in Moscow for almost two years.

"Has the plan changed? Will I be deployed to Canada instead of the US?" For a moment I felt disappointed.

"Not at all," Sergej replied. "This is the final step in your preparation. We think that three months in Canada would be an excellent opportunity for you to practice your English and familiarize yourself with the culture and the way of life over there. After all, Canada is a lot like the US, only colder and with fewer people."

My spirits rose at the thought that we were finally making some progress.

"Great stuff," I said, jubilant at the prospect of my first extended trip to a Western country.

"Now I have to measure you. We need to get you a full set of West German clothes. You will be traveling on a West German passport."

Two weeks later, Sergej appeared at the apartment with a suitcase loaded with clothes and other items I would need for a long trip overseas—socks, underwear, shirts, sneakers, a denim jacket, and jeans. And so it happened that, at the age of twenty-eight, I became the proud owner of that most basic article of Western clothing: a pair of Levi's blue jeans.

Aside from the practice aspects of this trip, I had one important task assigned to me: the acquisition of a genuine American birth certificate.

Alex stopped by in his orange leather coat to give me instructions as we sat at the table in my apartment.

"Here we have this fellow, Henry van Randall, who was born in 1950 in California and died as a child. You will one day become Henry van Randall."

I nodded, listening carefully and thinking about the name Henry van Randall. I had never liked the name Albrecht, and Henry didn't sound too bad. Van Randall was even better. It had the air of nobility about it.

"What do I need to do?" I asked.

"You need to get his birth certificate. Memorize this information: place and date of birth and parents' names and birth dates. When you get to Montreal, you will apply for a certified copy of the birth certificate in the mail."

"Yes, but isn't it strange to ask for an American birth certificate to be mailed to a hotel in another country, even if it's Canada?" I asked. "Also, what business does a West German have asking for an American birth certificate?"

Alex smiled. "That's why I know you are going to be a good agent! You catch on to things quickly. I bet you can come up with a solution. Give it a try."

I thought for a moment and then started somewhat hesitantly.

"How about I find a small hotel with only a few rooms. I get to know the person who runs the place really well." I paused to further formulate my thoughts. "When I give the agency a return address, I can leave out the hotel name and then intercept the mail coming from California. I'll tell the hotel owners that I'm receiving mail on behalf of an American friend who will be joining me shortly. Do you think that might work?"

"Excellent!" Alex said. "That is exactly how we are going to catch that fish."

For the next few hours, we refined the plan for acquiring the birth certificate and went over other specifics of the trip to Canada.

"One more thing," Alex said as he prepared to leave. "That beard has to go."

"I know," I said with regret.

My height already made me stand out in a crowd, and the beard simply added another distinctive feature, which was undesirable for someone in my role.

The next morning, I went into the bathroom armed with scissors and a straightedge razor. As I watched scraps of hair fall into the sink, the process of shaving became symbolic for me. I realized that I was finally and officially saying good-bye to the playful aspects of my youth and joining the community of adults.

I stared at the clean-shaven face in the mirror and knew that my life was about to change.

✦ ✦ ✦

When the morning arrived for my departure to Canada, I switched into "execution mode," a technique I would use every time I had something very important or dangerous to do.

In execution mode, I emptied the clutter in my mind and focused with robot-like determination on how I would deal with whatever task lay ahead. I became tense, but not nervous. There was a distinct and important difference.

When Sergej appeared at the apartment, he seemed more serious than usual. This was, after all, the beginning of a big-time deployment of an important asset that he had helped to develop.

"I need your East German documents," he said.

I handed them over, and he handed me back a West German passport with my photograph on the inside. I looked it over and nodded my approval.

"From now until your return, you are Heiner from Hamburg," he said with a slight grin.

Next, Sergej scanned my luggage and examined my clothing for any leftover East German or Russian items I may have missed.

We rode to the airport in a limousine, and Sergej smuggled me into the departure hall via the now-familiar side door. As soon as I was on the other side, it struck me that for the very first time I was truly alone, a lone wolf ready to take on the enemy in enemy territory. I was on my first big adventure into the West.

Three hours after departure, the Aeroflot plane landed at Atatürk Airport in Istanbul, Turkey. The airport was heavily guarded by uniformed soldiers with submachine guns at the ready. Seeing the serious looks on their faces was a jolting reminder that I was traveling on a fake passport and could be arrested and imprisoned, if caught. The airport itself was old and outdated, and the arrival hall looked more like a large wooden shed than any kind of official building.

I went straight from the airport to my hotel, which was near the Bosporus Bridge. My only excursion amounted to walking across the bridge and setting foot in Asia, so I could say I had been on that continent. Then I walked back to the European side and straight back to my hotel. The next morning, I returned to the airport and bought a ticket for a flight to Geneva that was leaving that day.

When I landed in Geneva, I walked immediately to the Swissair counter.

"I need a round-trip ticket to Montreal leaving tomorrow," I told the attendant. Although I didn't know how long I would be in Canada, the return ticket was necessary to assure the Canadian authorities that I had no intention of overstaying my welcome in their country.

The Swissair flight arrived in Montreal early in the afternoon. As I entered the arrival hall, I had to force myself not to gawk with an open mouth. Like the airport in Geneva, this one was spacious, modern, clean, and functional—a marvelous facility. Moscow's Sheremetyevo was heads above Schönefeld in Berlin, but the airports in Geneva and Montreal were two classes above even that.

I sailed through customs and immigration without any problem. When the immigration officer asked about the purpose of my visit, I responded, "I just want to look around. Perhaps one day I may ask to be admitted to this country, but I don't really know."

According to my body clock, which was on European time, it was already late in the day, so I wasted no time in finding a moderately priced hotel.

As soon as I settled into my room, I indulged myself in the one treat I'd been eagerly anticipating for months, if not years—a live television program in North America. Finally, after four years of intensive study, here was the real thing. I was in heaven, and my travel fatigue dissipated at once. For the next few hours, for as long as I could keep my eyes open, I watched television—and it didn't matter what was on; all that mattered was that they were speaking American English.

When I awoke the next morning, the first thing I did was switch on the TV again. There I discovered *The Friendly Giant*, with Jerome the Giraffe and Rusty the Rooster, the main characters of a popular children's program aired by the Canadian Broadcasting Corporation.

The show was so good that I didn't want to leave the room, but hunger eventually climbed to the top of my priorities, so I got dressed and ventured into town. I walked slowly and deliberately, taking in every detail of my new surroundings.

It was early spring, so the trees had not yet sprouted leaves, and this was not the most glamorous section of Montreal, about two miles north of downtown, yet there was a sense of history and elegance in the air. The nicely kept buildings, clean streets, and well-dressed people made it a very attractive place indeed for this East German intruder. From now on, every day would be another step into an unknown world, a world that had to be conquered piece by piece, down to the smallest detail.

I decided to try a diner about five blocks from the hotel. The counter had several unoccupied stools, and I chose one near the door. I knew exactly what to order because I'd learned back in Moscow all about the standard American breakfast: ham and eggs over easy, whole wheat toast, a glass of milk, and a cup of coffee.

When the plate was set in front of me, my stomach growled in anticipation. Then I took a bite. And another. It was good—no, it was *excellent*, which was not a surprise considering the dreadful monotony of my diet in Russia. For my entire eight-week stay in Montreal, I ordered the same breakfast at the same place every day. Soon the owner, a young man originally from Greece, no longer even asked for my order. He just put the plate in front of me, and it was always incredibly delicious.

After finishing my first breakfast, I wasted no time returning to the hotel for more television. I was thoroughly delighted when the original version of *Sesame Street* (*Sesamstraße* in Germany) came on. After that, I watched a program called *Alice*, about a waitress in a diner much like the one where I'd eaten breakfast. When one of the waitresses came on, a lively character named Flo, I had to turn my ear and listen harder. Her Southern accent was a struggle to understand.

I had a similar problem while watching *Good Times*, a sitcom about an African American family in Chicago. The slang and inflection used by the characters—in particular the wisecracking J. J. Evans—made it clear that I still had a lot to learn about American English. I watched the entire show and barely understood the jokes and conversations.

Rounding out the morning schedule, I watched the holy grail of TV consumerism, *The Price Is Right*. I'd never seen anything like this—an elaborate TV game show where real people could win appliances, vacations, and even cash prizes. It was the epitome of American capitalist greed, but I couldn't help but be fascinated by it. The catchphrase, "Come on down!" barked by the inimitable Johnny Olson, is one of those phrases I can readily replay in my mind to this day. But after a half hour of vicariously "consuming" a trip to Jamaica, a new refrigerator, and the inevitable new car, I reluctantly turned off the TV. I had been sent to Canada to do some real work.

My first priority was to find a small hotel suitable for the task of procuring the Henry van Randall birth certificate. I needed a place where I could befriend the proprietors and intercept the arrival of the document when it was mailed to me under a different name.

I headed out to the streets and began my search. It didn't take long before I saw a small twelve-room, three-story establishment on Rue St. Hubert, not far from the intersection of Rue Sherbrooke E.

I pushed through the door and walked to the desk, where I met the middle-aged couple who managed the hotel. We talked amicably about the weather and room availability, and then I casually shifted to more personal kinds of questions. I learned that they were originally from Belgium and now lived in a basement apartment. This was a perfect setup for what I needed to accomplish. I paid one week's rent in advance and moved into a room on the top floor. I also told them that I was supposed to pick up some mail for a friend of mine named Henry in a few weeks.

At dinnertime, satisfied with my progress, I returned to the diner where I'd had breakfast. I ordered a small pizza and a bottle of Labatt's. When the waiter brought the beer, I asked for a bottle opener.

Apparently, the waiter thought I was joking, but he decided to play along. Picking up the bottle with an exaggerated flourish, he gave an elaborate demonstration of how to remove the cap by twisting it counterclockwise.

I was truly astonished for a moment—I had never seen a twist-off cap in my life—but I quickly recovered.

This episode underscored the wisdom of my handlers in sending me to Canada for a test run. Small details, such as not knowing about twist-off caps, could easily trip up an apprentice undercover agent and draw unwanted attention.

The next morning, I sat down and wrote a letter to the vital records department in the California county where Henry van Randall was born, requesting a certified copy of "my" birth certificate. I mailed the letter along with a self-addressed stamped envelope and a money order.

Now all I could do was wait for the birth certificate to arrive. In the meantime, I decided to explore the city of Montreal and work on the secondary tasks the Center had given me, which included collecting information about the attitude of Canadians toward the secessionist initiatives of the Parti Québécois and its leader, René Lévesque.

Because my time in Canada was a dress rehearsal for a more permanent assignment in the United States, I had to listen to shortwave transmissions from the Center once a week, find suitable dead-drop locations, perform periodic surveillance checks, meet people, and compose reports in secret writing on all my activities.

Every morning, after some intensive "research of language and culture"—also known as watching TV—I headed to the diner for my American breakfast. Sometimes I talked to other diners or the waiters as part of my ground-level research.

My search for surveillance check routes and dead-drop sites took me all over the city. As the spring temperatures arrived and the green leaves began to gingerly stick out their necks, Montreal was transformed into the most attractive city I had ever seen. I walked Rue St. Catherine up one side and down the other, enjoying the shops and cafes, until I stopped in front of large window in front of Simon's Department Store. I was drawn inside and looked at the incredible variety of high-quality goods, including oriental rugs, jewelry, furnishings, and clothes, a showcase of all that was available in the capitalist marketplace.

Though this exposure to affluence did nothing to weaken my belief in the Communist cause, deep down I couldn't wait to get my hands on some of the wares on display at Simon's.

Not far from my hotel, I found a small bar along Rue Saint-Denis and began to go there most evenings for a drink. Taking a seat at the bar, not too far from the door, I ordered a scotch on the rocks. As I sipped my drink, I'd talk to anyone who happened to sit near me. Soon all the regulars knew me as the restless German who was exploring the world in search of a place to eventually settle down.

One night, I heard a noisy conversation from the back room and recognized distinctly German accents. That was my cue to leave.

I paid my tab and was about to head for the door when one of my new Canadian friends called my name.

"Hey, Heiner! You have to meet these visitors."

I grinned and made my way over to the table where two Germans were drinking their beers. They gave me a hearty welcome and began talking about the differences between German and English profanities.

I knew I had to get out of there.

"I'm sorry, but I have a terrible headache," I said. "Please excuse me and enjoy your visit. It's a great city."

The Germans were disappointed because it's always nice to meet fellow citizens while traveling abroad, but I knew that once we moved past the initial greetings, they would ask where I was from, what I did for a living, and why I was here. I had to avoid betraying my ignorance of all things West German, particularly my "hometown" of Hamburg.

18

I FULLY EXPECTED TO RECEIVE the birth certificate in the mail within two weeks of mailing the application. Every three days or so, I stopped by the basement apartment of the Belgian caretakers and casually asked if there had been any mail for my friend Henry. The answer was always no.

At times, I wondered if they had become suspicious, opened the letter when it came, and notified the local authorities. But they always seemed happy to see me and not at all concerned about my inquiries—other than feeling sorry that nothing had arrived. We would often talk for an extended time, and my surveillance-detection runs always came up negative, so I was certain that no one was following me. To be extra careful, I set elaborate traps in my room to discover whether my belongings had been searched, but there was no indication that anyone ever came into my room. I remained cautious but never became paranoid.

When two weeks of waiting became three and then four—and still nothing—I decided I had to do something. Returning home without that important document was tantamount to failure, and failure was not an option for Albrecht Dittrich. Given the three-week communication cycle to Moscow and back, asking the Center for advice was also not an option.

I decided to force the issue by following up with a phone call to the office where I had sent the application. I practiced the call out loud in a secluded area of a nearby park. After numerous rehearsals, I took a deep breath, entered a phone booth, put in the four quarters required for an international call, and dialed the California number.

"Hello, this is Henry van Randall," I said in an exasperated tone when a deep male voice answered the phone. "I sent a request for a copy of my birth certificate to your office almost six weeks ago, and I have still not received the document. What is causing the delay?"

"Let me connect you to the vital records department," the clerk said.

After a one-minute wait, I deposited four more quarters to avoid losing the connection. When a female voice came through the receiver, I repeated my inquiry.

"Please hold while I check the records," she said.

I put more quarters into the phone, hoping the clerk couldn't hear the ping. A call from a phone booth might have alerted her that something was not quite right. When the woman returned to the line, she sounded apologetic. "You know, sir, I cannot find your application, but I promise we will expedite your request once we find it. Is there a number where we can reach you?"

Oops. I was not prepared for that question, but I recovered quickly and said, "I just moved into a new place and the phone is not yet connected. I'll call again next week if I don't receive the document."

I was now out of quarters and decided to give the matter one more emphatic push.

"Listen," I said rather forcefully, like I imagined an American would who was not well served by the government, "you have my money, and I want my birth certificate—it's as simple as that."

Before she could reply, I hung up and leaned my head against the cold window of the phone booth, feeling exhausted. My brain was on temporary lockdown.

I had two weeks before I planned to leave Montreal and visit the border cities of Sarnia and Windsor, Ontario. Four days before my planned departure, I went to the basement apartment to visit my Belgian friends again.

When I walked in, I saw a pile of mail on a shelf above the sofa where the couple usually sat. At the very top was a rather thick envelope. Could that be it? My heart started beating faster, and I wanted to grab the envelope and run up to my room. However, I managed to contain my excitement and avoid arousing any suspicion.

After thirty minutes of small talk, I casually inquired about any mail for Henry. The wife immediately retrieved the envelope I had seen and handed it to me. "I was hoping you'd stop by," she said. "I think this came yesterday."

My hands were sweating, and it felt like she was handing me a treasure map. I said good-bye as cheerfully and casually as usual—at least I hoped—and took the staircase up to my room.

Once inside, I locked the door, leaned against the jamb, and stared at the envelope, still doubting whether it could be real. But there it was: "Mr. Henry van Randall, Rue St. Hubert, Montreal, Canada."

I had done it. I had overcome all obstacles, and now I was holding the prize. The Center would be proud that I'd succeeded. This birth certificate unlocked the first step to my new identity.

I opened the envelope and pulled out the enclosed document. As I scanned the authentic, signed, and sealed birth certificate for Henry van Randall, every muscle in my body went tense, and my elation turned almost instantly to despair. Stamped across the page in big red letters was a single word that changed everything: *DECEASED*.

I felt like a lottery winner whose winning numbers turned out to be from the week before. After absorbing the initial shock, I stashed the document away and went for a long walk to clear my head. As I pounded the pavement, block after block, I thought about my phone call to California, the weeks of waiting, and the brief moment of satisfaction when I thought I had succeeded. I hadn't failed at anything in a very long time, but this was a clear failure, regardless of whose fault it was.

Soon, other thoughts came to mind. If a dead person requested a copy of his birth certificate, something shady was going on. Had the authorities in California notified law enforcement? Were they already on my tail? The Center had to be informed immediately. My existence in Canada had possibly been compromised.

I returned to my room, locked the door, and prepared to create a letter in secret writing.

First, I removed a mirror from the wall and cleaned it thoroughly with soap and water. I then awkwardly pulled out a piece of white paper from a regular writing pad so as not to leave any fingerprints on the sheet.

Setting the sheet of paper onto the mirror, I smoothed it out several times with the back of my hand to remove any impurities from the surface. I then proceeded to write an open text with a ballpoint pen. This text consisted of innocent banalities, as if I were writing to a friend. I always made a point of including a phrase such as "thank you for your recent letter" to make it appear that there was two-way communication.

Once that was done, I pulled out another sheet of paper and cleaned it on the mirror in a similar fashion. Now came the key component— a sheet of paper from a pad given to me by the Center. The first five pages were impregnated with a chemical that could be developed to make the secret writing visible. I placed that sheet between the blank sheet and the sheet with the open text.

Pulling out a No. 2 pencil, I wrote the message with even pressure, explaining my circumstances. I then placed the sheet with the open text and the secret writing in an ordinary envelope and sealed it using a moist rag to avoid leaving any trace of my saliva on the flap.

When I was done, I folded the piece of paper with the pencil writing on it, stood it up on the mirror, lit it with a match, and let it burn freely, a method I'd been taught to minimize smoke.

After completing the letter, I took to the streets for a three-hour surveillance-detection exercise. Once I was certain that no one was following me, I deposited the letter in a mailbox near the fake return address. Fake return addresses were typically large apartment buildings. If such a letter were ever returned, it would very likely just disappear.

By the time I returned to the apartment, every muscle in my body ached, and I dropped into bed without changing my clothes. The entire operation, from the time I opened the birth certificate to writing and delivering the letter, had taken six hours.

I needed sleep, but then again I had to get out of the hotel and Montreal as soon as possible. If law enforcement was chasing after me, getting out of town would be the best way of losing them.

The next morning, I packed up and left for Sarnia and then to Windsor, without any good-byes to the Belgian couple who managed the hotel. When my prepaid time expired, they would find I was already gone.

My failure to obtain a valid birth certificate weighed heavily on me.

When had I last failed at any goal or objective? I couldn't remember. It dragged me down and soured my mood. I was more disappointed about not achieving my objective than I was afraid of being tracked down.

I desperately wanted to return to Moscow with a success story, so I decided to test my ability to pass myself off as an American.

On my last night in Windsor, I headed downstairs to the bar at the Holiday Inn where I was staying. Having mentally prepared throughout the day to "be American," I sat down at the bar and ordered a drink with confidence and a touch of joviality. Soon I struck up a conversation with a Canadian citizen, the captain of a small commercial ship that carried freight across Lake Erie. We talked for more than an hour, and in my mind, phrases such as "I tell you what, the trip across the river is always worth it. Your beer is much better than ours" could only come from an American who hailed from Detroit or somewhere just across the border.

The conversation didn't seem to raise any doubts with the Canadian captain, and as I headed back to my room, I declared the experiment a success and believed the Center would as well.

With that final exercise behind me, I got ready for my return trip to Moscow via Montreal and Geneva.

19

MY DEBRIEFING THE DAY AFTER MY ARRIVAL in Moscow began with the failed birth certificate operation. Just to prove to my bosses that I was telling the unvarnished truth, I handed over the useless van Randall document.

Alex and Sergej both showed their disappointment, but at the same time they agreed that I was not at fault in this matter. When I told them about my success in impersonating an American, they cheered up considerably.

"Let's lie low for a while until we have a plan for your deployment," Alex advised. "We'd like for you to go back to Berlin, get in touch with Nikolai, and wait for instructions from the Center."

My old apartment on the Eitelstraße had been kept empty, so I moved right back into familiar surroundings, but the thick layer of dust that had settled on the furniture during my absence was a visible confirmation of something I had told Sergej a year before: I did not have a home anymore. Eitelstraße was a place to sleep until somebody in Moscow decided where to send me next.

Late one morning, about a week after I had settled back into my solitary life, there came a knock on the door. Very few people knew my address, and only the KGB knew I had returned to Berlin, so who could it possibly be? I jumped up from the sofa and turned off the television, which was playing—what else?—*Sesamstraße*.

When I opened the door, my heart stood still.

There was Gerlinde, in all her sparkling blonde-haired, blue-eyed glory.

"Do you still love me?" she said.

Instinctively, I gave her the only answer possible in that situation. "Yes."

I swept her inside the apartment and we hugged and kissed without concern for the implications of that six-word exchange.

Later, as we were talking about everything and nothing, Gerlinde surprised me.

"You didn't go to Moscow, did you?"

I stared at her, dumbfounded. "What makes you say that?"

"Well," she answered with a knowing smile, "you always carried English books and papers with you, never Russian."

That forced my hand.

"Listen, I did go to Moscow, but I never worked at the embassy. I can't tell you much more, but perhaps I'll be able to soon. "

Gerlinde looked me straight in the eye and said with unquestionable sincerity, "I sensed that you were involved in something top secret, but I didn't have the courage to bring it up. After you left, I tried to put you out of my mind. I dated other men. I wanted to pretend that you never existed. I have no idea what made me come here today after almost two years, but what I do know is that you're the only one for me. I will do whatever it takes to keep you. If necessary, I will wait, and I will wait for you a long time. Just don't leave me like that again."

My eyes teared up and I resolved to discuss the situation with Nikolai at the next opportunity.

That opportunity came two days later, when Nikolai came to the apartment to tell me that the Center had decided that I should study Portuguese and learn as much about Brazil as possible. It wasn't clear whether Brazil was my new target country or an intermediate stop on my way to the United States, but at that moment it didn't matter. Brazil was a fascinating country and a great second choice.

When the official briefing concluded, I asked Nikolai to stay for another minute.

"Listen," I said with great trepidation, remembering his reaction to the Gabriele episode. "I have a confession to make."

Nikolai looked at me impassively, and his eyes seemed to harden.

"I had a girlfriend two years ago. I never told her anything about what I was doing, and I broke up with her before I went to Moscow.

Two days ago, she showed up at my apartment out of the blue. Nikolai, I really love this woman. Is there any way she can be part of my life?"

Given our history, I was prepared for the worst, but Nikolai did not react with anger. Instead, he seemed to think for a moment and then said in a matter-of-fact tone, "I will discuss this with our comrades at the Center."

His response made two things clear to me: Nikolai was not the decision maker, and after four years of training I was now a valuable asset to the KGB rather than an unproven rookie. This made me hopeful that we could work something out.

Two weeks later, Nikolai came to our meeting with an answer from Moscow.

"Albrecht, we ran a background check on your girlfriend. She is cleared, and you may continue your relationship with her. There are several alternatives under consideration. If she qualifies, she may eventually be able to join you in the West. If not, we might arrange periodic visits—either here or in a third country—to keep the relationship alive."

I was ecstatic. I was going to have my cake and eat it too! I could proceed with the mission I had spent the last four years preparing for *and* have a lasting relationship with the woman I loved. I could not wait to share the good news with Gerlinde.

The next time I saw her, I gave her a lot more information about my situation.

"Would you have a problem if I told you that I work for the Soviet Union?" I asked.

"Not at all," she said. "I would even move there with you, if necessary."

"That is probably not going to happen," I explained. "Up until a month ago, I was pointed toward the United States, but things have changed. I don't know what's going to happen, but that's the reason I was carrying English books with me all the time."

And then I couldn't contain myself any longer; I had to show her. I started saying a few phrases in my best American English, and Gerlinde's jaw dropped.

"My goodness," she said when she had regained her composure. "What else can you do that I don't know about?"

I left that question unanswered. I had to be careful not to tell her too much about my unusual profession.

+ + +

My schedule over the next few months was light. Other than the Portuguese lessons and maintaining my technical skills, there wasn't much to do. Had it not been for Gerlinde, I easily could have slipped into depression. After all, I was twenty-eight years old and had accomplished essentially nothing. All I had done up to that point was study and train. If I had stayed at the university, I would've had my doctorate by now and would be sharing my knowledge of the wondrous world of chemicals with a new batch of students. I hinted at my growing impatience during conversations with Nikolai, who seemed to understand that I was eager for action.

In May 1978, the Center finally made the all-important decision. Nikolai informed me that Brazil was now out of the picture, and direct infiltration into the US was the plan of action. A month earlier, a resident agent had discovered the tombstone of a boy who had died just shy of his eleventh birthday and was buried at Mount Lebanon Cemetery in Adelphi, Maryland, on the outskirts of Washington, DC. According to the inscription, the deceased—Jack Barsky—was born on November 13, 1944, and passed away on September 7, 1955.

Armed with this information, the agent had obtained a death certificate, which he then used to request a certified copy of Jack Barsky's birth certificate, posing as the boy's father. That document was now stored at KGB headquarters in Moscow and designated for use by one Albrecht Dittrich.

20

IN JUNE, I LEFT FOR MOSCOW to do some final preparatory work for the launch. The focus was to create the cover story for Jack Barsky, whose identity I was about to assume.

So, how does one reconstruct the life story of a person who died when he was ten? Alex came to the apartment and we went to work. My "legend" was created piece by piece and with a lot of imagination.

"This is what we have so far from our friends who have been busy in Washington, DC, and New York City," Alex said as he pulled a thick binder from a briefcase he had brought with him.

Resident agents in the US had collected all kinds of information, like pieces of a puzzle that I would eventually put together. They located and took pictures of "way stations" for the fictional Jack Barsky—places he could have been during his life, such as an apartment building on the Upper West Side of New York City, and an elementary, middle, and high school. They suggested a factory where I could have worked— made all the more useful by the fact that it had since been torn down and no longer existed. As the final piece to the puzzle, they suggested the name of a farm in upstate New York where I could have worked for several years before reappearing in New York City.

It was now up to my imagination to weave a story around those basics.

"Let's simplify things and kill off my father," I suggested.

"What age?"

"When I was an infant. That way, I won't have to make up any memories."

"Good," Alex said, jotting down notes.

I leaned back against the wooden chair and continued with the story of my life as Jack Barsky. After my father's death, I was raised by my mother, with whom I had a very close relationship. She had been born and raised in Germany—conveniently, the real Mrs. Barsky's maiden name was Schwartz—so we spoke a lot of German around the house as I grew up.

"Excellent," Alex said, writing furiously to keep up with the tale I was spinning. "That will serve well as an explanation for any residual accent."

For childhood and school memories, I used many of my real experiences, as long as they seemed generic enough to translate across the Atlantic. I focused on a number of key friends and gave them Americanized names—Ronald for Reiner, Gary for Günter, and so on. I even took Rosi with me.

Since I did not have a valid high school diploma, and the unbreakable rule of my legalization was that we would use only authentic documents, it was necessary for me to have dropped out of high school. The immediate trigger for my dropping out was the death of my mother in a car accident during my senior year—a huge loss that sent me into a depressive tailspin from which it took years for me to recover. Her "death" also eliminated the need for any more memories or details about her. Eventually, I found a job at George Lueders and Company, a chemical firm that produced artificial flavorings. But when that company closed its doors, I decided to drop out of society altogether and went to work at the Miller dairy farm in New Berlin in upstate New York.

Four years later, with my mental and physical health restored, I was giving life another try and was about to resurface in Manhattan to start over.

I knew there would never be a situation in which I would have to reel off this much detail about my fake past, but the legend fulfilled its main purpose, which was to provide me with a psychological safety net. With time I would create a real history for myself in the US, reducing the importance of the legend as I would be able to divert attention from my early years by replacing old fiction with new facts.

"We got it," Alex said after hours of working on what we thought was a masterpiece of deception.

"Now I just have to cement this into my mind," I said.

"That's correct." Alex rose from the table, packed up his briefcase, and put his orange leather coat over his shoulder before departing into the night.

✦ ✦ ✦

With the reconstructed Jack Barsky in place, it was time to say good-bye to Gerlinde. This time, however, it would be in grand style.

The KGB flew Gerlinde to the city of Leningrad (now called St. Petersburg), and Sergej and I traveled by train from Moscow to meet her.

The hotel where we would stay was of prerevolutionary architecture and was one of the gems of the historic town center. Our room and other accommodations were outright luxurious. Sergej and I noticed many Western tourists around the hotel, and he warned me to keep a low profile and not to meet any of them.

Sergej served as our personal tour guide and interpreter, and he had a way of opening doors that would remain shut to foreign tourists and most Russians. We toured the awe-inspiring Winter Palace, the equally impressive Hermitage, and various other historic buildings in the downtown area. We also paid a visit to the Monument of the Heroic Defenders of Leningrad on Victory Square, a massive memorial to the more than one million victims of the two-and-a-half-year siege of the city by Hitler's army during World War II. Being at this site reminded me of the importance of my work and the vow I'd made long ago in Buchenwald. Hitler's fascism was gone, but the world would not find peace without Communism.

Our loaded agenda included other highlights, such as a performance of the world-class Leningrad Ballet. I looked at Gerlinde's face as she watched the performance in wonder, and for the briefest of moments I wondered how we would do apart from each other for such long periods of time.

When it was time for our last good-bye, Sergej and I took Gerlinde to the airport, and he discreetly left us alone for a few minutes before she departed. This time our good-byes were bittersweet—not just bit-ter as they had been three years before. I promised that we would meet again in two years' time.

✛ ✛ ✛

Back in Moscow, the preparations became more intense. I memorized the six-page legend down to the last detail and committed to memory the critically important, and very detailed, communication plan. This complex plan included radio frequencies and times of transmission, two addresses for sending secret letters, an initial dead-drop site in New York City, meeting spots in various cities en route to the US, signal spots, and instructions about the shape and meaning of the graphic signals to be placed in those locations.

The signals were simple shapes, such as a circle, a line, and a plus sign, among others. Each symbol had a different meaning: *come to meeting, container deposited, container retrieved,* or *radio transmis-sion received.* The most ominous signal was a red dot, which meant *danger—run!*

I was also given a special route in Brooklyn designed for surveillance detection. This route was laid out in such a way that a resident agent could observe me and any individuals who might be tailing me.

During one of Sergej's visits to check my progress, he said, "You know, if I had your talent for language, I'd go undercover too."

"You would?" It had never occurred to me to wonder what Sergej wished or wanted to do. He was just my easygoing handler, who was always generous and nice to be around.

"You're going to become the kind of person that all the girls dream about." He sighed, but there was a mischievous gleam in his eye.

"What are you talking about?"

"I was at a movie the other day, a spy movie, and I overheard two girls who were seated behind me. One of them said, 'I wish I could meet a guy like that.'"

This made me laugh. It was true that I was about to be launched as an actual spy—and the aura of that could not be denied. However, *undercover* meant I couldn't reveal my status to anyone.

"Well, if I follow the rules, which of course I will, I don't see how going undercover will benefit me in the same way it benefits James Bond."

We both laughed at this reality.

Finally, the pieces were in order and I was ready to go. I had no one else to say good-bye to. Gerlinde was the only person in East Germany who knew where I was going and what I would be doing. The cover story for my family and a few friends was that I had made yet another career change—this time back to science. I was joining the agency Interkosmos 77, an organization of the Warsaw Pact countries dedicated to the exploration of space under the leadership of the Soviet Union. To give this cover credibility, the KGB provided me with an official-looking document stating that I was drafted for a five-year stint at the Baikonur Cosmodrome in Kazakhstan, a closed facility accessible only with permission from the Soviet government. This location was chosen to prevent relatives, particularly my mother, from attempting to visit me at my new place of employment, like she'd done in Moscow. I mailed this document to my mother, explaining the new direction I was taking.

Next, I had to memorize the intricate details of a zigzag travel plan that started in Moscow and ended in New York City. These included specific airlines and flight numbers; meeting points and signal spots in Rome, Vienna, and Mexico City; and the names and biographical information of the fictitious individuals named in the three forged passports I would use en route.

"You have one last task," Sergej told me, arriving with a large stack of postcards and stationery.

"The letters," I said with a long sigh.

"The letters. You better get started." Sergej gave me a sympathetic look as I groaned. "You just gotta do it."

This was the most onerous task of them all. Because I could not just disappear for long periods of time without some sign of life, I had to write a series of postcards and letters to be sent to my mother and my brother at random intervals to keep them abreast of "current events." The letters were difficult to compose because all the content was pure fiction. I also had to give the impression that I had read—and was responding to—their correspondence with me, even though I had no way of knowing what they might actually write.

Of the many lies I told during my undercover career, these letters were the most difficult. After all, I was blatantly lying to my own mother.

In later years, to make the letters more believable, I switched to a typewriter, signed the typed letters in my own hand, and left space between the last typed sentence and the signature for someone at the Center to add a few sentences if they deemed it necessary. I also left a few blank signed pages, in case a lengthier response was necessary.

Completion of the letters brought to a close the almost five years of preparation for my undercover life in America. After one more painful and frustrating delay—a bad wisdom tooth that could have really caused problems if it had happened after I was deployed into foreign territory—I was psyched up and 100 percent focused on the mission and the future.

21

ON THE DAY BEFORE THE LAUNCH, Alex showed up at my apartment wearing an expression I hadn't seen on him before. He was typically so arrogant, and yet today he was almost solemn.

"Albrecht," he said. "Or should I call you Jack already?"

"Not yet. I'm still Heiner until I get to Rome."

He nodded with a slight grin and once again became serious.

"Listen. You have received the best training we could possibly give you. You are well prepared, and I have no doubt that you will succeed. But the key to your long-term success will be the acquisition of the genuine American documents we've already discussed."

I nodded. The plan was to start with a library card, which should be easy to acquire without much scrutiny, then move up the ladder to a driver's license, a Social Security card, and finally a US passport, in that order.

"If you return in two years with a genuine American passport, we will throw you a big party," he said.

"What's so special about the passport?" I asked.

"Think about it. With an American passport, you can travel almost anywhere and return to the US at will. Then let's say we send you to Switzerland. You could open a business there and make a ton of money. We can make that happen. Once you are wealthy, you can return to America and infiltrate the upper echelons of society. With wealth comes influence, and you could find ways to gain access to the movers and shakers and the political decision makers."

"Brilliant!" I exclaimed. This was the first time that anyone had spoken to me about a long-range plan. Clearly, my mission was designed to extend beyond just a few years in the States. And acquiring the necessary documents was the key to everything.

"So, think passport first," Alex said. "Then everything else you can do with regard to connecting with interesting people, or even collecting political intelligence, will just be the gravy."

As we discussed these things, the irony was not lost on me that I was to become a rich capitalist in order to bring down all the rich capitalists and create a world ruled by the working class.

After Alex left, I went back into execution mode. Emotionally, I was calm to the point of almost total numbness. I imagined that astronauts felt this way right before launching into space, or soldiers right before battle. I took a long walk through a nearby park and reflected on my past. Gradually, I stepped through the stages of my life that had brought me to this most critical point.

I thought about my family and friends but most importantly about Gerlinde. My tender love for her and the certainty that she would be waiting to eventually build a future together gave me great strength and solace.

✦ ✦ ✦

Sergej and a driver showed up at my apartment early the next morning. I had been up before sunrise after a rather restless night. Just as he had before my trip to Canada, Sergej checked my clothes and luggage for accidental giveaways from the East.

Then, out of the blue, he asked, "What's your name?"

"Heiner Müller," I answered promptly and without hesitation.

"Where do you live?"

"Hamburg."

On he went through a litany of questions that might be asked at various checkpoints.

The one checkpoint where nobody asked questions was passport control at the Moscow airport. As was our custom, I slipped into the departure hall via the side door. Sergej held the door open but stayed on the other side. We nodded to one another and I was on my way—officially deployed as an independent operator behind enemy lines.

The route I would take to the United States had been expertly devised to make it impossible to trace Jack Barsky, American born and bred, back to Moscow.

My first flight took me to Belgrade, the capital of Yugoslavia. During the three-hour flight, I sat like a zombie, unable to do even light reading.

I snapped out of it as soon as action was required. After retrieving my suitcase at the Belgrade airport, I boarded a bus to the railway terminal. There, I bought a ticket to Rome on a train scheduled to leave that evening. There were no first-class tickets available, so I regretfully purchased a seat in a regular compartment.

The temperature in Belgrade was still summerlike, so I spent the two-hour layover outside the terminal sitting on a bench, smoking cigarettes and staring into space. Before boarding the train, I bought an English paperback novel, which served me well when the other seven passengers in my compartment turned out to include some rather shady characters. I was exhausted, but I didn't dare close my eyes. My handlers in Moscow had warned me about pickpockets in Yugoslavia and Italy, and I was traveling with thousands of dollars in cash stuffed into various pockets—not to mention the all-important passport that I couldn't risk losing. As the hours dragged on, the paperback certainly helped to pass the time.

✦ ✦ ✦

Upon arrival in Rome, I booked a room at a nondescript hotel near the Vatican and headed out immediately to indicate my arrival in town by leaving a chalk mark on a lamppost in a designated location. Normally I would have followed a surveillance-detection route before such an action, but I didn't have a predefined route, and I was dog-tired after my overnight train ride. So, instead, I rather nervously broke the rules on the first day out on my own.

The next stage of the plan was to meet my contact the following evening to receive a "virgin" passport, without a stamp from Yugoslavia.

It was already getting dark when I left the hotel for the meeting. I couldn't help but feel nervous walking on poorly lit streets in a strange city, with almost $10,000 in cash. But I also didn't want to take the risk of leaving the money in my room. I walked from a busy area filled with the roar of cars and motorcycles to a quiet street where my steps echoed down the cobblestones. Finally, I approached the intersection near the north wall of the Vatican where the meeting was to take place.

My contact was right on time. We exchanged code phrases and quickly swapped passports. I returned to my hotel under a different name, walked briskly up the stairs to my room, and locked the door behind me. Before going to bed, I rehearsed the cover story that went with my new identity.

The next morning, I checked out early, took a taxi to the main train station, and bought a ticket to Vienna. This time, I managed to obtain a first class seat for the thirteen-hour trip, but even the relative comfort and safety of the first class cabin did little to ease my fears about losing my passport or offset my fatigue.

It was wet and stormy when I arrived in Vienna, and the weather made it impossible to check for surveillance before I placed the signal indicating that I had arrived in the city and was ready for a meeting the next day. Even the umbrella I had borrowed from the hotel could not protect me from the driving rain. But with everyone scurrying about with heads down to avoid the rain, nobody paid attention to the tall, dark figure who stopped under a lamppost along Hormayrgasse, quickly looked around, and placed a chalk mark on the pole.

I was afraid the signal might be washed away by the rain, but the next day my contact showed up right on time in front of a baby furniture store named Träum Schön (Sweet Dreams). It was an awkward exchange because the other man butchered the code words almost beyond recognition, but I walked away from the meeting with yet another identity. I was now William Dyson, a Canadian from the city of Toronto. I gave myself an extra day for rest and checked into a downtown hotel under the Dyson name for one night.

On the morning of my departure, I took a cab to the airport and bought a one-way ticket to Mexico City on Austrian Airlines. The flight left that afternoon, but when we arrived in Madrid, an airport strike delayed the flight for an extra day.

When I got off the plane in Mexico City, it felt as if someone had aimed a giant blow-dryer at my face and turned it on high. The contrast

ME WITH MY PARENTS, JUDITH AND KARL-HEINZ DITTRICH. EAST GERMANY WAS EXTREMELY IMPOVERISHED DURING MY CHILDHOOD—I DON'T KNOW HOW I MANAGED TO BE SUCH A CHUNKY BABY.

MY BROTHER HANS-GÜNTHER, ME, AND A FRIEND (L-R) NEAR OUR HOME IN BAD MUSKAU. WE OFTEN SPENT OUR DAYS RUNNING AROUND AND PRACTICING SHOTS WITH A BB GUN.

AT TWENTY-THREE, I WAS FILLED
WITH OPTIMISM AND HOPES FOR A
GRAND FUTURE.

ROSI, MY FIRST REAL LOVE.

MY MOTHER CELEBRATING HER FIFTIETH BIRTHDAY WITH HER SONS (HANS-GÜNTHER
IS ON THE LEFT). I HAD NO IDEA THAT THIS WOULD BE ONE OF THE LAST TIMES I EVER
SAW MY MOTHER.

WHEN I FIRST ARRIVED IN NEW YORK, I LIVED IN WOODSIDE, QUEENS. MY APARTMENT—
WHICH I DECORATED MYSELF—WAS SMALL, BUT IT WAS HOME.

MY SON GÜNTHER WITH
MY MOTHER, 1974. I WAS
ALREADY IN BERLIN AND
MISSED MANY SUCH
MOMENTS THAT A FATHER
SHOULD BE THERE TO
TREASURE.

DURING MY MOTHER'S TRIP TO MOSCOW, SHE PERSUADED SERGEJ AND ME TO TAKE A PHOTO WITH HER. UNBEKNOWNST TO HER, THIS WAS ABSOLUTELY PROHIBITED FOR KGB SPIES, BUT WE COULDN'T TALK HER OUT OF IT WITHOUT BLOWING OUR COVER.

HIDING IN PLAIN SIGHT: SIX YEARS AFTER MY ARRIVAL IN THE UNITED STATES, I MADE IT INTO THE PROFESSIONAL RANKS AS A COMPUTER PROGRAMMER AT METLIFE. MY COLLEAGUES WERE SMART AND FUNNY—AND I WAS SURPRISED TO FIND MYSELF MAKING REAL FRIENDS IN AMERICA.

Liebe Mutti!
Ich sende Dir heute die herzlichsten
Glückwünsche und die besten Wünsche
für Dein weiteres Leben anläßlich des
Internationalen Frauentages. Ich hoffe
vor allem, daß Du noch lange
so gut wie möglich gesund bleibst,
damit Dir das Leben noch viel
Freude bringt. Das hat sich jede
Frau in Deinem Alter verdient,
aber ich glaube, es gilt speziell
für Dich. Wenn wir auch oft öfter
anderer Meinung sind, so heißt
das noch lange nicht, daß ich
nicht voll hinter dieser Aussage stehe.
Alles Gute und viele Grüße Dein Alb...

ONE OF THE
PHONY LETTERS I HANDWROTE
FOR THE KGB TO SEND TO MY MOTHER
WHILE I WAS UNDERCOVER

ME WITH NEWBORN CHELSEA, 1987.
CUTE AS A BUTTON, SHE CHANGED MY LIFE
FOREVER THE MINUTE SHE WAS BORN.

TWO OF MY BEAUTIFUL CHILDREN, JESSIE AND
CHELSEA, AT OUR HOME IN MOUNT BETHEL.

LITTLE DID I KNOW THAT THE FBI HAD BOUGHT THE HOUSE NEXT DOOR TO ME IN MOUNT BETHEL, PA. THEY ASSIGNED TWO AGENTS TO LIVE THERE AND SPY ON EVERYTHING I DID. THIS IS JOE REILLY, THE MAN WHO ULTIMATELY APPREHENDED ME.

OCTOBER 2014: RETURNING TO BERLIN FOR THE FIRST TIME SINCE MY "DEATH." I WAS WORRIED ABOUT GETTING THROUGH CUSTOMS—AFTER ALL, THERE COULD HAVE BEEN AN ARREST WARRANT FOR ME.

REVISITING THE SITE OF THE FAILED DEAD-DROP OPERATION ON STATEN ISLAND. SOON AFTER THAT ATTEMPT, I DECIDED TO CUT MY TIES WITH THE KGB.

ME WITH MY TWO BEST FRIENDS FROM HIGH SCHOOL AND COLLEGE, GÜNTER (L) AND HELMUT (R). I DIDN'T KNOW AT THE TIME THAT THEY, TOO, HAD BEEN RECRUITED AND HAD WORKED FOR THE STASI, THE EAST GERMAN SECRET POLICE.

ALL OF MY ADULT CHILDREN WITH ME AT TEGEL AIRPORT IN BERLIN IN 2015. THIS WAS THE FIRST TIME ALL FIVE OF US HAD BEEN TOGETHER—IT WAS A VERY SPECIAL TIME. L-R: GÜNTHER, CHELSEA, ME, MATTHIAS, JESSIE.

IN APRIL 2015, I RETURNED TO JENA WITH MY CHILDREN AND A 60 MINUTES NEWS CREW. HERE, STEVE KROFT INTERVIEWS US NEAR THE RESTAURANT DIE SONNE, WHERE MY CAREER AS A SPY BEGAN. L-R: JESSIE, ME, CHELSEA, AND STEVE KROFT

MARRYING SHAWNA IN 2009

MY BEAUTIFUL WIFE WITH OUR NEWBORN DAUGHTER, TRINITY. THIS IS ONE OF MY FAVORITE PHOTOS—THE LOVE BETWEEN MOTHER AND CHILD IS SO EVIDENT.

SHAWNA, TRINITY, AND ME. TRINITY IS SPUNKY AND SWEET— ALL THE BEST PARTS OF HER MOTHER AND ME.

between the raw autumn weather in Vienna and the ninety-degree heat in Mexico was stunning.

With five days to kill in Mexico City, and not knowing a single word of Spanish, I took the time to catch my breath from all the travel and adjust to the time change before the big event: my entry into the United States of America. During my stay, I received one radiogram from the Center; but when I deciphered the code, it contained only well wishes. There were no additional instructions that could possibly be given at this point. I wrote a report about my trip in secret writing and mailed it to one of my convenience addresses, but then for the rest of the time, I slept and sat in the shade out by the pool.

After my short week in Mexico, I bought a ticket for an American Airlines flight to Toronto with a stopover in Chicago. For some reason, just before I left for the airport, I remembered Nikolai's strange routine. So I sat down and observed a moment of silence—a prayer that was not really a prayer. My American adventure was about to begin.

PART III

THE EMBEDDING
OF A SPY

22

AT 7:06 P.M. ON OCTOBER 8, 1978, William Dyson stepped off an American Airlines plane at O'Hare International Airport in Chicago and proceeded toward Customs and Immigration. At 10:00 a.m. on Tuesday, October 10, William Dyson vanished into thin air.

William Dyson is the only one of my fake identities I can clearly remember, because . . . well, it's memorable. Dyson was supposed to be a resident of Toronto, but he had never been there, and never would.

When I entered the customs area at O'Hare, I faced the most intense sixty minutes of my entire life. As I joined the long line for Immigration, my six-foot-three-inch frame rising above all the average-sized people around me, I felt as if I had a neon sign around my neck that said, "Watch Out for This Guy." To any bystander, I was just a lanky fellow with European features, piercing blue-green eyes, and dirt-blond hair, but I was carrying two items that would have raised suspicion from even the most junior customs officer. In my carry-on bag, I had a high-quality Blaupunkt shortwave radio, and the pockets of my burgundy leather blazer were bulging with wads of crisp $100 bills totaling about $7,000. On top of that, my light-blue Samsonite suitcase was only half full, with an unusual assortment of clothes for someone returning from a trip to Mexico.

I was prepared to explain everything about my unusual circumstances, and I had rehearsed it many times in my mind, but at the moment, I didn't want to have to explain anything.

I took a deep breath to calm my nerves, feeling certain that my thumping heartbeat and sweaty palms would be a dead giveaway. As the line inched forward, I was convinced that something about me would prompt the agent behind the counter to ask me to step out for some questions.

Then it was my turn, and the officer waved me toward his desk.

I stepped forward and handed him my passport.

"You live in Toronto?" he asked, looking at me and then back to the pages of the passport.

"Yes." I swallowed hard and hoped he didn't notice.

"Are you in Chicago for business or pleasure?"

"I just want to do some sightseeing before I head home," I said.

The immigration officer took one more look at me, stamped a page in my passport, and handed it back. "Enjoy your time in the Windy City," he said.

I walked forward, feeling almost ashamed for the near-panicky fear I'd felt during such a routine process.

Customs was even easier. I had filled out the form truthfully, stating that I had $7,000 in cash. Apparently, the amount did not raise any eyebrows. Neither did the jumbled-up contents of my suitcase when the customs agent opened it to look for contraband.

I was now officially inside the United States of America.

As soon as I was out of sight of customs, I set down my luggage with a huge sigh of relief and lit a cigarette. It was perhaps the most satisfying smoke of my life. As the tension in my mind and body eased, I suddenly felt exhausted. All I could think was, *I need to find a hotel. I need to get some rest.*

Suitcase in hand, I made my way out to the curb and boarded a bus with "Downtown" marked as its final destination.

✦ ✦ ✦

Once we entered the city, I spotted a sign for a Hilton hotel. Getting off the bus without hesitation, I walked into the lobby and approached the front desk.

"Good evening," I said to the young clerk who was standing there. "I need a room for the night."

"I'm sorry, but we're all sold out," she said in a tone that let me know she really wasn't sorry.

I stared at her in disappointment. "Really, you have nothing?"

She looked at her board again, and with some hesitation said, "Well, there is a room right next to the pool area. We sometimes rent it out as a last resort."

"I'll take it," I said without asking any more questions. I desperately needed some rest.

After registering as William Dyson and prepaying in cash, I followed the directions from the front desk clerk, walked to the end of a long hallway, and unlocked the door to my room. What I found was a normal hotel room, with one exception: The entire back wall was made of glass, which afforded a full view of the indoor swimming pool. This was not exactly the type of accommodation an aspiring undercover agent would find ideal for his first night behind enemy lines. I immediately pulled the curtains to cover the glass wall.

If this had been a movie, my next stop would have been the hotel bar for a martini—shaken, not stirred. But this was real life, and as I sat down on the bed to rest my weary feet, it suddenly hit me: I'm in America, and I'm truly on my own!

There was no lifeline to the other side of the Iron Curtain. All I had was a fake passport, a genuine US birth certificate, $7,000 in cash, and my wits.

I really needed a drink, so I opened the bottle of Johnny Walker Red I had acquired in the duty-free shop at the airport.

While slowly imbibing the scotch, I fiddled with the television remote and landed on an episode of *Gilligan's Island*—American pop culture at its best.

I woke up with a tremendous hangover the next morning, and after swallowing four aspirin, I gingerly proceeded to the hotel restaurant for my first-ever genuine American breakfast—ham and eggs over easy, of course, with toast and a side of home fries. My time in Canada had prepared me well, at least for the breakfast situation.

With my headache abating, I was ready to face the day. There was much to be done before I could depart for New York City, my final destination.

Back in my room, I searched the Yellow Pages for a hotel where I could find a room. Moving from city to city and hotel to hotel is a time-honored technique for spies to cover their tracks as much as possible.

If the elaborate preparation for my infiltration into the US had one gaping hole, it was my lack of information about Chicago. I had bought a city map at the airport, but I had no idea which areas of the city were safe and which were to be avoided. That ignorance could have cost me dearly.

I chose a hotel at random from the phone book and made a reservation by phone. I did not tip the doorman who hailed a cab for me, and only much later came to realize that this and other small cultural miscues could have easily left a trail that would alert a savvy investigator.

When I gave the cabdriver the address of the new hotel, he looked at me rather quizzically. I soon found out why. As I carted my suitcase to the hotel entrance, I realized I was the only white person on the street. The hotel was a well-worn, run-down multistory building, probably from the 1930s. On my way to the door, I caught a glimpse of what seemed to be elevated railroad tracks.

More warning bells went off in my mind as I entered the shabby, poorly lit lobby. The only furniture was a round table and four brownish easy chairs with a sheen that betrayed many years of use. The reception desk was tucked into a far corner behind a three-by-five-foot Plexiglas window that shielded the clerk from the public.

A German profanity popped spontaneously into my head, which was still a bit tender from the residual effects of the hangover.

The desk clerk was in the process of stubbing out a cigarette into a banged-up aluminum ashtray that was already overflowing with butts. When he finally looked up and saw me, he gave me the same quizzical look I had seen on the taxi driver's face.

"What can I do for you?"

At this point, my instinct was to get out and go somewhere else, but *where*? I had no idea where I was or where I should be. Making a split-second decision, which I would have to do many times in the coming months, I decided to proceed with the check-in.

Why not, I said to myself. *I've lived in worse places.*

"I called and reserved a room for two nights," I said in my best North American accent.

"Okay," the clerk replied.

I paid for the room and he gave me a key, directing me toward the elevator.

The room was just as shabby as the lobby—worn carpet, a creaky double bed with two small pillows and an ugly old bedspread, a shower with cracked tile and discolored caulking, and a faucet that dripped incessantly.

Quite fittingly, the black-and-white TV was connected to a rabbit ears antenna and had a coin-operated *on* switch. For a quarter, I could buy one hour of viewing pleasure.

As I took in my surroundings, I was suddenly shaken by a loud rumbling noise, followed by an earsplitting screech coming from the direction of the window. I opened the curtains and discovered the source of the noise—a metallic gray subway train that was rumbling along the elevated tracks I had seen on my way in to the hotel. The tracks were close enough that I could see the faces of the passengers behind the dirty tinted windows.

What more could I ask for than a pay-TV and an up-close-and-personal view of the "L"? Welcome to the South Side of Chicago! Though I didn't fully understand it at the time, I certainly realized later that this was the last place in town I wanted to be. If I had gotten mugged with all the cash I was carrying, I could have been stranded in Chicago with absolutely no backup plan.

That evening, I spent three quarters to watch TV and drank the remainder of the scotch to mitigate the noise of the "L" outside my window. Fortunately, the traffic became less frequent as the evening wore on.

The next morning, I did not need an alarm clock to get me up bright and early. The morning commute on the "L" began with a vengeance at 5:30 a.m. Even though I had prepaid for two nights, I decided that one night in that fine establishment was plenty. So after breakfast at a nearby diner, I set out on foot in the direction of the city center.

After a half-hour walk, I noticed that the neighborhood began to look a bit more upscale. When I chanced upon a small hotel with a well-maintained exterior, I decided to investigate. In stark contrast to the place where I had stayed the previous night, the lobby here was well lit, the seating area had comfortable looking furniture of recent vintage, and the reception desk was out in the open—no bulletproof glass.

I approached the clerk and inquired about availability. When she told me there were several rooms available, I made an important decision right on the spot and boldly registered as Jack Barsky. Luckily, the clerk did not ask me for ID. With visions of a nice, safe hotel room, I hurried back to the other hotel to collect my belongings. Before I checked out for good, I had one piece of business left to complete. It was time to commit murder.

I went into the bathroom and locked the door behind me, just to be sure and set about killing William Dyson by destroying his paper identity. Unfortunately, my five years of KGB training did not include instructions on how to destroy a passport, which proved to be more difficult than it might seem. Even the paper pages didn't want to burn. The passport picture resisted several attempts, before I finally just cut the charred photo into tiny pieces and flushed them down the toilet.

Then I tried to burn the plastic cover pages. Again and again, I tried to get them to burn, but they were definitely made from some sort of flame-resistant material. Every attempt resulted in an ugly molten mass and a suspicious acrid smell. Again, the only solution was to cut the plastic into small pieces and send them down the hatch into the Chicago sewer system.

The massacre took a full thirty minutes to complete, but in the end, William Dyson had been eliminated without a trace. I was now temporarily nameless.

To complete the metamorphosis, I cut into the back cover of the small notebook and removed the genuine copy of Jack Barsky's birth certificate.

I was now an American citizen with only a single piece of identification. It was a tenuous existence indeed. Quickly packing my bags, I applied a liberal dose of air freshener to the room (from my spy "tool-set") and walked out the door. When I finally settled in to my new room at the nicer hotel, the tension of the last forty-eight hours began to gradually melt away.

As I lay on the luxurious bed, staring at the ceiling, the enormity of my situation invaded my consciousness. I was truly a lone wolf in the Second City—alone, but not yet lonely. There was too much to do, too much to think about. The real adventure still lay ahead.

+ + +

When I awoke the next morning, feeling rested and refreshed after a peaceful night's sleep, I contemplated my next move. After breakfast at a diner just around the corner from my hotel, I decided that my first priority was to get some American clothes. Heading out into a beautiful autumn day, I strolled up and down the Magnificent Mile, gawking at all the window displays. Clearly, these stores were not for me. They were only for the rich capitalists, and I was not one of them—at least not yet.

Veering off Michigan Avenue, I stepped into what appeared to be a much more affordable men's clothing store and immediately fell prey to a team of two aggressive salesmen.

"Good afternoon, young man," the older one said in an ingratiating tone. "You strike me as a rather imposing figure that seems in desperate need of a new outfit or two."

I was surprised by his forceful approach, but I managed to respond, "Maybe. What do you have? I think I need a new suit."

If there had been a little man in my head advising me on the right moves to make, he would have screamed, "What? Are you really that stupid? What are you going to do with a suit? You're an unemployed and undocumented individual—get some more jeans!"

Unfortunately, there was no little man and no voice of reason. Instead, there was a greenhorn undercover agent walking out of that store with a gray flannel suit that came with a reversible vest and two sets of pants. One side of the vest, and the corresponding pair of pants, had a light-blue and gray checkerboard pattern. They were the ugliest pair of pants I had ever seen, but to me they looked so . . . American.

That suit would get very little wear, along with a sky-blue corduroy suit with very wide lapels that I also added to my wardrobe.

I did better at the next store, purchasing a short navy-blue leather coat with a removable flannel liner that would serve me well in colder weather. The salesperson assured me that the coat would keep me warm during the winter. "You know, this coat is made in Poland," he said, "and it gets *really* cold over there."

"Interesting," I said.

23

IF I CAN MAKE IT THERE, *I'll make it anywhere . . .*

I was not yet familiar with that line from the famous song "New York, New York," but I was determined to make it to the Big Apple and put myself in a position to gather useful information for the KGB.

I arrived in New York City on October 12, a magnificent Indian summer day with a cloudless, deep-blue sky overhead and a balmy breeze wafting through the streets. What a welcome contrast to the blistering Mexican heat and the gloomy, stormy European fall!

As soon as the Manhattan-bound bus left LaGuardia Airport, I craned my neck to catch a glimpse of the famous skyline. Finally, I would see with my own eyes what I had previously admired only in photographs. My heart started beating faster with anticipation, but as the bus emerged from the Queens Midtown Tunnel, I was rather disappointed. Compared to Moscow's expansive boulevards, the streets of Manhattan seemed narrow and constricted. I learned much later that the skyscrapers rising so close above the streets create an optical illusion that seems to squeeze the five lanes down into thin, black bands.

I hopped off the bus at Grand Central Station, taking a moment to gaze at the ornate interior architecture of this busy Manhattan train terminal. After a few moments, I came to my senses, stopped gawking, stashed my luggage in a locker, and set out on foot to look for a hotel.

To assist with my search for short-term lodging, the Center had given me the names and addresses of two extended-stay hotels on the East Side of Manhattan. After a full day of traveling, I was looking forward to settling into a nice, comfortable room with a color TV.

The first hotel was only eight blocks from Grand Central Station, just off Lexington Avenue. When I entered the well-lit lobby, I perked up. This was a very nice place, indeed! On my way to the reception desk, I passed a table where a party of elegantly dressed men and women were enjoying an afternoon drink.

"Do you have any rooms available?" I asked the attractive receptionist.

"As a matter of fact we do. Are you looking for daily, weekly, or monthly occupancy?"

"Monthly," I responded without hesitation.

"Well, you have a choice. At the low end, there is a room with a single queen-size bed. That rents for $1,800 a month."

Before I could let out a silent gasp, she chirped on, "But we happen to have one of the presidential suites available as well. Those suites feature a fully functional kitchen and a king-size bed. They're all on the top floor, with windows overlooking Lexington Avenue. That room is $2,900 a month. What is your preference?"

I hoped that my face didn't register the shock I was feeling, but it was clearly time to beat a hasty retreat and find something more affordable. At $1,800 a month, I would deplete my cash reserves within three months. Already, my bankroll had shrunk to just over $6,000.

I gave the receptionist the nicest smile I could muster and said, "Oh, I'm just inquiring. I won't be ready to move until next week. May I have your phone number so I can call when I've made my decision?"

With her business card in hand, I turned around and marched outside. The Center had certainly gotten that one wrong! How could anyone have thought that such an establishment would be suitable for my situation? Though I didn't expect any different results from the second hotel, which was about ten blocks away, I went there anyway just so I could check it off my list. When I found that their prices were similar, I decided to regroup at a regular hotel and give myself time to find a more workable long-term rental.

I found what looked to be a mid-priced hotel on Lexington Avenue and decided to make it my headquarters for the next two days. When the clerk told me they had rooms available, I told him I was ready to check in.

"ID please," he said absentmindedly as he pulled out a registration form.

I froze for just a moment before doing the only thing I could do in that situation—I pulled out the birth certificate from my jacket pocket and handed it to him.

"I'll be paying for the room in cash—in advance," I said.

The man looked at me curiously as he took the birth certificate from my hand, but he accepted it as my identification. The cash probably helped my cause quite a bit.

Next, he handed me a registration form and said, "Just fill this out and we're good to go."

I looked at the form, and the first thing I saw was a blank line for name and address. Again this was something the Center hadn't prepared me for. I didn't have an American address. The only thing I could come up with was William Dyson's address in Toronto. So I spent the first two nights in New York with a US birth certificate as my documentation and a Canadian mailing address. This was a rather uncomfortable situation and something I would have wanted to avoid even if I were still in training. But this was the real thing. I wasn't in training anymore.

+ + +

During my first night in New York, I was awakened again and again by the insistent hissing of the steam radiator in my room. Staring at the ceiling in the dark, I felt light-years away from everything and everyone I'd ever known. My grand and glorious assignment to infiltrate the United States didn't seem so grand and glorious at the moment after all. Right then, I realized that New York would offer as many challenges as opportunities and that my vision of a comfortable life in the US needed significant adjustment. But I knew this wasn't the time to mope or complain. Sacrifices had to be made, and my entire life of discipline and delayed gratification had prepared me well for the situation I was now in.

The next day, it didn't take long to find a monthly hotel that I could afford. After checking out a few places and realigning my expectations with reality, I found a room on the Upper West Side that rented for only $600 a month. The queen-size bed had several fist-size burn holes in the mattress, and the chair and table were the foldout picnic variety, but there was a chest of drawers and a nightstand to store my belongings, an electric cooktop, a small refrigerator, and an old color TV with rabbit ears. The most important feature was the private bath with a tub and shower.

+ + +

In the evening on my second day, I set the signal indicating my safe arrival. The signal spot, which was part of the communication plan I had been given, was a brilliant choice that even Eugen would have given an A.

The underpass at the 79th Street Boat Basin and Henry Hudson Parkway has a sidewalk that allows for pedestrian traffic. At the west entrance of the underpass, the sidewalk makes a 90-degree turn, creating a dead zone that made this operation as easy as a walk in the park.

This spot was also convenient for the resident agent, who could easily see the mark while driving by on his way to work—presumably at the United Nations.

The next day, I prepared a brief secret message to inform the Center about the details of my trip since I'd left Mexico. I made it a point to mention the bad hotel choices I had been given. This was the first chit I collected, in case I needed ammunition to balance what would surely be mistakes of my own.

Sergej's advice was ingrained in me now, so over the next several months, as long as the weather wasn't too bad, I set out to explore every nook and cranny of Manhattan—from the cavernous financial headquarters along Wall Street; to Chinatown, Little Italy, and Greenwich Village; to Broadway and the majestic Avenue of the Americas; to the richly decorated display windows on Fifth Avenue; and the 770 acres of Central Park. I quickly discovered that this city was *alive*—it had a heartbeat all its own, and that heartbeat never stopped. What a contrast to the grim utilitarian mood that permeated both East Berlin and Moscow.

I was particularly drawn to the area around the southern tip of Central Park, with its cavalcade of street artists, mimes, musical troupes, and pushcart vendors. I enjoyed the noise and the bustle and the thriving commerce in this little slice of capitalist America. Surely, I would soon discover the ugly underbelly of free enterprise as well.

On one of my walking excursions, I got another reminder of how ill-prepared I was for assimilating into America. In the Soviet Union, cigarettes were dirt cheap and readily available, so it wasn't uncommon to be approached on the street by a stranger asking for a smoke.

I was walking past Bryant Park on the Fifth Avenue side when a young man approached me and urgently whispered, "Smoke, smoke."

I reached into my pocket for a pack of cigarettes and politely offered him some.

"Here, take a couple . . ."

His reaction was altogether strange and inexplicable.

"Hey, if I want to play games, man, I'll call my little brother," he said with a sneer. "Don't play me for a fool!"

I had no idea what he was talking about, so I quickly walked away. Only later did I learn that Bryant Park was a hangout for small-time drug dealers and he was offering to sell me a few joints, not asking to bum a cigarette.

✦ ✦ ✦

Immediately upon moving into the hotel that would be my home for the foreseeable future, I established an observable pattern for the staff at the front desk. I wanted to give the impression that I had business in the city and avoid even the hint of suspicion that comes with the appearance of an erratic lifestyle.

So, Monday through Friday, regardless of the weather, I left the hotel no later than 8:30 in the morning and returned after 5:00 p.m. When the weather was good, I continued to explore the vast city and catalogued potential spots for future operational use. When winter arrived—thankfully much milder than the Moscow freeze—I spent time at the library, museums, or watching movies at one of the second-rate theaters, where two dollars could buy you three hours of American classic cinema, thereby adding bits and pieces to my knowledge of American pop culture.

When spring arrived, I often grabbed a towel and a book, and spent the day in Central Park. On one such afternoon, as I lay in the sunshine and stared up at the blue sky, I realized it was May 18, 1979—Albrecht Dittrich's thirtieth birthday. But this German, "Dittrich," was no more. The American flag high atop one of the buildings was a fluttering red-white-and-blue reminder that I was a stranger in a strange land.

Earlier in 1979, I had begun the process of acquiring genuine US documentation. The sketchy plan concocted by the spymasters in Moscow was brilliant in its conception but flawed in its details of execution.

The first step, obtaining a library card, was expected to be child's play. But when I visited a number of branches of the New York Public Library, the first thing I was asked—without fail—was to show some type of ID or a utility bill, to prove my address. Of course, I had neither one.

The need to have identification in order to obtain identification is a classic example of what Joseph Heller—whose signature book I had read with great pleasure—called a Catch-22. Was I really going to get stuck in neutral right at the beginning of this ambitious undertaking? And if I couldn't get a library card, what did that say about my prospects for one day getting close to Zbigniew Brzezinski?

To my disappointment, the Center had no advice for how to break the stalemate. I knew it was up to me to figure it out, and I certainly wasn't ready to give up yet. After several weeks spent scouring books and studying newspapers to find a possible solution for my dilemma, serendipity came to the rescue.

The American Museum of Natural History, on Central Park West, with its long hallways, wide staircases, and many cavernous rooms, had become one of my favorite places for surveillance detection. One day I noticed a flyer on the reception desk advertising museum membership. For a reasonable fee, I received a one-year membership entitling me to unlimited visits and discounts at special events. But the only thing that mattered to me was that the museum issued me a membership card with my name and address on it, no verification of identity or address required. This type of card seemed like a long shot as proof of address at a library, but it was worth a try. After all, I had been in the US for almost six months and had made zero progress toward the final goal of acquiring proper identification.

I chose the main Brooklyn branch of the public library system for my Hail Mary pass. After taking a deep breath to calm my nerves, I approached the desk and waited for the librarian to look up at me.

"May I help you?"

"I would like to get a library card. Here's my application."

She took the application and said, "We need proof of residence as well."

"Sure. I have my museum card." I handed it across the desk to her.

"Okay, give me a minute while I fill this out."

It took me a moment to realize that my application had been accepted. The plan was back on track!

Step 2 was getting a New York driver's license. I now had the minimum documentation required—a library card and a birth certificate—so all I had to do was pass the written and behind-the-wheel tests. The written test wasn't much of a challenge, but I didn't want to take a chance with the road test, so I took several driving lessons to refresh the basic skills I had acquired in Moscow.

The driving test turned out to be simple as well—almost trivial, in fact. Frankly, I would not allow anyone behind the wheel and out on the streets of the city based on the elementary skills required to pass that test. But, for me, it was all just as well. By May 1979, I was the proud owner of an official New York state driver's license. This was a great birthday present I gave myself and a huge step toward becoming a fully documented, and legal, US resident. After seven months of living in the shadows, I at least now had something that established me as a resident of New York City.

Step 3 of the process, obtaining a Social Security card, was the task I dreaded most because it required an in-person appearance at a Social Security office. I had no idea what to expect, so I prepared meticulously, with special focus on developing a plausible answer for why a thirty-four-year-old man didn't already have a Social Security card.

Though, in 1979, it was unusual for someone my age not to have a Social Security card, it was not inconceivable. Two groups were outside the jurisdiction of the Social Security Administration: employees of religious organizations and farm workers. The Center and I had chosen the farm option and consequently weaved it into my legend.

Two weeks before my appointment, I spent at least two hours every day rehearsing my cover story ad nauseam. I also practiced answers to possible interview questions out loud in a secluded section of Inwood Hill Park in the northern section of Manhattan.

On the day of the interview, I dressed in sandals, old jeans, and a slightly smudged T-shirt. I took other measures to create the impression of an ex-farmhand who had only recently arrived in the big city— I hadn't shaved for three days, and I didn't wash my hair that morning.

On the table in my hotel room, I had a houseplant and a bottle with motor oil. I ground my fingertips into the soil until my nails were filled with dirt. Then I used a rag to stain my hands with motor oil.

In the bathroom, I studied my face in the mirror and did not see a former farmworker. To remove the sharpness from my eyes, I rubbed them with soapy water until I could no longer stand the stinging pain. The red-eyed, unkempt, and unshaven face that now stared back at me gave me confidence that I had a good chance of pulling this off.

In fact, the ruse exceeded my wildest expectations. At the Social Security office, the nondescript middle-aged interviewer asked me four questions, to which I gave short, monotone answers.

"How is it that you don't have a Social Security card?"

"Never needed one."

"Why not?"

I shrugged. "I don't know. Just never did."

"Have you worked before?"

"Yes, of course."

"Where?"

"On a farm upstate."

APPROVED.

I was very proud of myself that day. I had overcome my fear and played my script to perfection.

Now I had a Social Security card.

Next up, an American passport.

24

AT THE BEGINNING OF MARCH, I had told the Center via secret writing that I was running out of money. Three weeks later, they informed me in one of their routine weekly shortwave radiograms of a proposed dead-drop operation on a Sunday in April. When I decrypted the code, the details regarding place and time emerged. The site was in Kissena Park in Flushing.

The week before the planned operation, I went to that part of Queens to find the site and identify the two signal spots. I had no problem finding the drop site, but I was terribly disappointed with the location. Eugen would have given this one an F. It was right out in the open, in a park where there was certain to be a lot of foot traffic on a Sunday in April.

It was too late to call off the operation, and I really did need the money, so I made plans to follow through on schedule.

On the following Sunday, I left the hotel at 11:00 a.m, armed with a black plastic shopping bag and a piece of white chalk. The first order of the day was to check for surveillance.

From the hotel, I took the subway to Times Square, checked out the movie displays, walked to Macy's, went up the escalator, checked out the goods on display, turned around, went down the elevator, changed my mind, and went back up. Then I left the store, took a crosstown bus to Grand Central Station, bought a train ticket for later, walked to Saks Fifth Avenue, went up the elevator and down the escalator, then up the escalator and down the elevator. Next, I took a train to 86th Street and followed the same routine inside Gimbel's.

This went on and on, for three hours, until I had determined that nobody was following me.

At about two o'clock, I boarded the #7 train to Flushing. I reached the Flushing Main Street station early, so I had a quick snack at a Chinese restaurant to kill time. At exactly 3:05 p.m, I began my purposeful walk toward the signal site near Kissena Park. At exactly 3:15, I saw a vertical chalk mark on a lamp pole. The container had been placed. Within two minutes, I was at the drop site where the container was supposed to be.

Because the whole area was out in the open, I was very nervous. I had completed my own surveillance detection, but what if the resident agent had been followed and didn't know it? What if the FBI was lurking somewhere nearby, armed with a camera to catch me in the act?

From a distance, I spotted the dented oilcan lying next to a drainage grate at the edge of the park. For the last fifty steps, my legs felt as if they were filled with lead. I finally reached the drop site, looked around briefly, and snatched up the container, dropping it quickly into the plastic bag.

Before returning to the hotel, I surveyed the park and made my way to another lamppost. Leaning over casually, I struck the pole with the chalk, making a horizontal line to indicate that I had retrieved the container. Then I wasted no time leaving the area.

Back at the hotel, I pulled out the oilcan and turned it over, trying to figure out how to open it. The agent had done a great job of securing the goods inside the can. Finally, I used a knife to pry off the lid of the can and found three more layers of packing inside: a wire mesh, duct tape, and a clear plastic bag. After a half hour of poking, prying, and cutting with a pair of scissors, I finally succeeded in extricating the prize: a neatly pressed stack of freshly printed one hundred dollar bills, totaling a whopping $10,000.

After putting four hundred dollars into my wallet, I attached the remainder to the back of the refrigerator with a magnet, a spot that the cleaning staff was unlikely to ever go near.

✦ ✦ ✦

Eleven months had now passed since my arrival, and I still had no idea what kind of work I might be able to find. I had no job history in the

US, no marketable manual skills, and Albrecht Dittrich's academic credentials were of no use to Jack Barsky.

For months, I studied the want ads in several newspapers. I also researched the two jobs the Center had suggested: longshoreman or taxi driver. Neither one seemed a viable option for me. Longshoremen belonged to an exclusive union that typically admitted only the well-connected into their ranks. Taxi drivers had to work long hours to make a living, and the frequent stories in the news about cabbies being robbed and assaulted by street thugs convinced me to reject this option. I finally concluded that the only unskilled job that was readily available to someone like me was that of a messenger working for minimum wage.

Early one Monday morning, in August 1979, with a newspaper ad in hand, I showed up at the offices of Swift Messenger Service on West 46th Street, a midtown location between Fifth and Sixth Avenues. The office was a storefront with a picture window facing the street. A dispatcher sat behind a desk at the back, and a few colorful characters were seated on wooden benches that lined the two side walls of the room.

Though it was barely 9:00 a.m, the place was already busy. As I walked up to the desk, people were constantly coming and going—picking up packages and dropping them off.

When I reached the desk, I waited for the dispatcher to have a free moment.

"Good morning," I said when my turn came. "I read your ad in yesterday's *Daily News*." I waved the newspaper to punctuate my statement.

The man looked me up and down and paused for a moment.

"Do you have a bike?" he asked.

"I can get one."

"Okay then, show up tomorrow at 8:30 sharp with your bike and a shoulder bag. And don't forget to bring one of those Kryptonite U-locks—bikes get stolen all the time. Oh, by the way, my name is Jay, and I'm the chief dispatcher here. See you tomorrow."

As I walked out of the office, I was still pondering the situation. During my wanderings around Manhattan, I had often noticed the antics of some of the cyclists in city traffic. They rode on sidewalks, weaved in and out of traffic, and traveled the wrong way on one-way streets, all the while frantically blowing on whistles to announce their presence.

This was going to be one heck of a dangerous job!

I wondered if I could really do it. Even more to the point, *should* I do it? Should I risk life and limb and my assignment? I remembered the first time I had ridden a bike as a young boy and how I had plowed into a neighbor who had once referred to me as an awkward sad sack. He had become a victim of his own prophecy.

But they say that riding a bike is a skill one never forgets, and in the absence of a reasonable alternative for employment, I decided to give it a try. I found a bike shop on Eighth Avenue and bought a brand-new black ten-speed, a U-Lock, a whistle, and a messenger's shoulder bag, for a grand total of $155.

The next morning, I took my bike down the elevator and very cautiously began my first bike ride in the big city, down Broadway to 46th Street and across town to the Swift office.

When I arrived shortly before 8:30, Jay seemed genuinely happy to see me.

"Let me tell you how this works—it's not brain surgery." He rose from the desk and pointed to a table full of packages. Each package had a rectangular piece of paper on top. Jay removed one of these slips and said, "This here is a ticket. Every package has a ticket associated with it. There are three sections: customer information, pickup address, and delivery address. We fill out all the tickets here in the office. All you need to do is get a signature from the person you deliver the package to."

"Sounds easy enough," I said eagerly.

But Jay wasn't finished yet. "When I started in this job, I changed things to make us more efficient. Most of our customers are right in this area, so I have foot messengers pick up the packages, assemble them in groups by delivery area, and then we give them to the bike guys to deliver. This is much faster than our competitors' one-off method, and it's also good for you—you get to do more deliveries. We pay you a 50 percent commission, which at current rates is $1.75 per ticket."

I perked up. A dollar-seventy-five per delivery? This could be good! In 1979, the minimum wage was $2.90 an hour, and I figured I could easily average more than two deliveries an hour making local drops around town.

"Finally," Jay said, "we need a bike man at our 52nd Street office. I'll give Al a call to tell him you're going to be over there shortly. Here's the address." He handed me a slip of paper, and I was on my way.

Because I didn't want to break the law on my very first day by going against traffic, I walked my bike over to Sixth Avenue and rode to the 52nd Street office, just off Madison Avenue.

When I walked in the door, a slim African American man, with glistening jet-black hair combed straight back, was barking out orders to the messengers. I soon learned that Al, the chief dispatcher, was a kind and patient man behind his harsh and strident demeanor. But it required a certain toughness to manage the variety of shady characters who worked as messengers, several of whom were only a step away from the gutter.

"You must be Jack," Al said as soon as he saw me. "We desperately need a bike man. Our last guy, Pete, did not show up today, and he did not call. Probably drugs—I saw this coming. There's just too much turnover with these bike guys."

Al looked me over and asked, "How well do you know Manhattan?"

"Very well," I answered truthfully. After all, I had explored almost the entire island on foot.

"We shall see." Al pointed to a pile of six packages and letters and said, "These are all for the Upper West Side. Deliver them and come straight back."

I stowed my freight in the messenger bag, threw it over my left shoulder, and joined the hustle and bustle of Manhattan traffic on my very first day of work as Jack Barsky, the American.

It being my first day, I rode very carefully, and it took me two hours to deliver all six packages. Still, when I returned to the office around noon, Al seemed pleased.

"Not bad. Here's another pile—these are all East Side."

By now it was lunchtime, and I was hungry and thirsty under the hot Manhattan sun. But stopping for an hour to eat and rest seemed like a bad idea. After all, there was work to be done and money to be made. So I worked right through the hunger, as I would for my entire time as a bike messenger.

At the end of the day, I counted eighteen tickets with my name on them. When I did the math, I turned a mental somersault. Eighteen times $1.75, and working five days a week, meant I'd make $157.50 a week. That was more than a dollar an hour above minimum wage.

I felt like I'd hit the jackpot. This was a livable wage, and with that income to supplement my stash from the Center, I would be able to rent an apartment and finally get out of that dreadful hotel.

When I arrived at the hotel that night, I was hungry, thirsty, dirty, and tired. But I was anything but miserable. I kicked off my shoes and tossed my empty messenger bag on the table, feeling ecstatic after my first day on the job.

✦ ✦ ✦

After a month as a messenger, and with four paychecks deposited into a brand-new bank account, I started looking for an apartment. Like others who hailed from out of town and "had just jumped off a potato truck" I fell for a classic New York City scam. The *pied-à-terre* studio apartment on the Upper East Side that was advertised in the Sunday section of the *Daily News* seemed like a perfect fit.

After touring the marvelous apartment, I asked again if the advertised rent was correct. It seemed too affordable. My excitement grew when the agent confirmed the price. I had to have this place. It was the first slice of the good life in America, and it finally seemed to be within reach. In fact, it was almost too good to be true.

"This place will go fast," the agent said. "I've already shown it to a few people who are trying to get it. But a $300 cash deposit will lock it in for you."

I told him I had to get the money from the bank, and I hurried to my hotel room to retrieve the cash from my "bank," the hiding place behind the fridge. I then rushed back uptown and handed over three freshly minted hundred dollar bills to make sure that no one else would beat me to the prize.

The next day, when I tried reaching the agency by phone, I couldn't make a connection. When I went to the place the following weekend, it was empty. A few weeks later, the mystery was solved when I saw a local TV report about a group of scam artists who had used the very same apartment to collect thousands of dollars in cash "deposits" from gullible victims. Because I had plenty of cash reserves, the $300 loss didn't hurt me as much as missing out on that apartment. I chalked it up to inexperience and learned a valuable lesson about capitalism: *If it sounds too good to be true, it probably is.*

✦ ✦ ✦

After searching for an apartment for weeks, I finally came to terms with the reality that Manhattan was not an option for me. To expand my search, I randomly picked a subway line—the #7 train, which connects Times Square with Flushing, Queens—and got off in Woodside at the 61st Street express station.

In the early 1980s, that section of Queens was a safe and clean lower-middle-class neighborhood in the midst of a transition from Irish/German to multiethnic. The real estate agent, who was just around the corner from the train station, wasted no time in showing me exactly what I was looking for—a small, fully furnished one-bedroom apartment in a four-family house on 39th Avenue, a five-minute walk from the subway station.

The landlord, an immigrant from Colombia, lived in one of the upstairs apartments with his wife and mother. My apartment was on the ground floor in the back, with windows facing a fenced-in yard. The dinette adjacent to the small kitchen was shielded completely from the window, providing me with a safe space where I could conduct my intelligence-related activities without having to worry about prying eyes from the outside.

Leaving the seedy hotel on the West Side and moving into an apartment was another big milestone in my efforts to fully establish myself in the United States. Not only was I joining the mainstream, with a steady income and a place of my own to live, but I was also able to enjoy some creature comforts.

So, how does a German starved for a home-cooked meal celebrate after moving into his first apartment in the US? Boiled potatoes, sausages, and butter. There was still a bit of homesickness in me after all.

✦ ✦ ✦

The Center congratulated me on my achievements and advised me to continue in the bike messenger job for another nine months before embarking on the final step of my legalization—applying for a passport. Nine more months would take me right on through winter and up until the next summer—which meant the full gamut of New York weather. As satisfying as a good day on the bike could be, my handlers in the KGB did not quite understand how demanding, and sometimes even demeaning, this job was.

On a typical weekday, my alarm went off at 7:00 a.m. On days when it was raining or snowing, I really did not want to get up. But I would remind myself that if I didn't show up in bad weather, they might not want me back when the sun came out. Besides, it was important to build a consistent work history so that whatever came next in the evolution of my undercover role, I could show potential employers that I could hold a job.

After hastily eating my cereal, I would layer on my work clothes for rainy weather: jeans, a flannel shirt, nylon jacket, rubber boots, and the final layer of protection: a yellow rubber rain suit, with pants and a jacket.

Next, I'd sling the waterproof messenger bag over my shoulder, roll my bike into the street, and climb awkwardly onto the saddle. The twenty-minute ride to Manhattan would take at least thirty minutes on those days, and the driving rain often hit me right in the face.

Al always gave me a great route, but even six deliveries in this weather would take me all morning. And though most people were happy to receive their packages, they were not necessarily happy to see me, dripping wet, step into their office or their home.

I'll never forget the time I was picking up an envelope at Ronald Lauder's residence on Park Avenue to deliver to the Estée Lauder offices on Fifth Avenue. When I stepped off the elevator, I was dazzled by all the pastel colors and the white carpet. That is, until the receptionist shrieked, "Do not come in here!"

She hurried over and very carefully removed the envelope from my outstretched, dripping hand, trying to avoid any contact with the dirty man from the street.

On another occasion, when I was making a delivery in the Garment district, the young receptionist who saw me walk in turned around and yelled to the back, "Christine, the messenger boy is here."

I wanted to scream, *Lady, you don't have a clue who you just called a messenger boy!*

Right then, I really yearned to be back in Germany, standing in a warm, dry lecture hall, teaching chemistry or math—or anything, for that matter. This spy stuff was not living up to its marquee billing.

Occasionally, a special package made the job more interesting. In addition to several pickups and deliveries at Ronald Lauder's luxurious home, I once took some carpet samples to the residence of Jacqueline Onassis. On another occasion, I made a lunch delivery from the famous Russian Tea Room to Dustin Hoffman's hospital room. (The Tea Room was Hoffman's favorite restaurant, but they didn't deliver.) But for all my time as a bike messenger, that's as close as I got to moving and shaking with the upper crust of American society.

Even though the messenger job wasn't exactly a great platform from which to conduct intelligence work, hanging out with the motley crew at the messenger office allowed me to gradually and safely integrate into American culture. The office was a safe haven where I was in the company of men at the fringes of society, who had no interest in finding out who I was, where I'd come from, or where I was going.

✦ ✦ ✦

Despite my careful and defensive approach to New York traffic, I could not escape the fate of every bike messenger who works the job for any length of time: accidents.

I was involved in two serious accidents, and the first one almost ended my undercover operation altogether. In that instance, I crashed into a deep pothole in the middle of Madison Avenue, totaling my bike and escaping by inches from being run over by a truck.

The second accident was not life-threatening, but it had more serious, long-term consequences. I was sailing through an intersection on a green light when a beat-up old Buick made a left turn without looking for oncoming traffic. I crashed hard and immediately felt a sharp pain in my right shoulder.

After the police arrived and laid the blame squarely on the driver, I locked up my damaged bike and walked to the emergency room at nearby Cabrini Medical Center. The diagnosis was a dislocated right clavicle, as well as damaged ligaments and muscles at the back of my shoulder. Because I had no medical insurance, the doctor advised against expensive surgery of the kind that would typically be done only on high-performance athletes. He immobilized my right arm with a sling and advised me that I was likely to contract arthritis in that permanently dislocated joint later in life.

As I walked out of the hospital, still dazed from the experience, I had the sudden urge to light up a cigarette. So after six months of hard-fought abstinence, I joined the ranks of backslidden smokers.

For the next three weeks, I could not ride a bicycle, and being right-handed, I could not communicate with the Center through secret writing. Once I was able to explain the reason for my silence, it established a precedent for the comrades at the Center and helped them understand that there would be times when I would be nonresponsive for a valid reason. This unplanned silence, and the subsequent trust generated by the explanation, would later help me in ways I could not have imagined at the time.

25

ON A SUNNY MONDAY in the middle of June 1980, I was on my way to Manhattan via subway. I had taken the day off to take care of "a personal matter." That personal matter was the quest for the crown jewel of my American documentation: a genuine US passport.

This application was critically important to my future, and I followed the instructions from Moscow to a tee. We had practiced filling out the application to make sure I wouldn't make an inadvertent mistake.

As instructed, I went to the New York passport agency in Rockefeller Center armed with a completed application, two passport pictures, my driver's license, and the Jack Barsky birth certificate. There were others ahead of me in line, so I took my place at the end and waited.

I felt relaxed, thinking that this process would be a mere formality, a piece of cake. After all, I had two other foundational documents that established my identity as Jack Barsky.

After waiting for fifteen minutes, I was waved over by one of the agents, a balding, bespectacled, middle-aged bureaucrat.

"Good morning," he said in a perfunctory tone.

"Good morning," I replied casually. By now I was familiar with how to respond in such situations.

I handed over my documents and the pictures and took a half step to the side, waiting patiently while the agent perused my application. It seemed he was taking a long time going over the paperwork. Finally, he reached into a drawer and pulled out a piece of paper. As he handed it to me, he said matter-of-factly, "There are some questions concerning your identity. Please fill out this supplementary questionnaire and come back to me."

I was stunned, but I managed to react with a natural-sounding response. "Do I have to go back to the end of the line?"

"No," he answered politely. "You may come straight to my window."

I withdrew to the back of the large room and started filling out the questionnaire: name, address, birth date and place . . . and then I read, "What is the name of the high school you attended?"

I immediately knew that it made no sense to read any further. Any answers I might concoct could not be verified, and handing in the questionnaire with bogus answers to a government official could easily trigger a more thorough investigation.

I had to act quickly and decisively. Without giving it much thought, I strode briskly back to the agent's window, planted myself next to the woman to whom the agent was now speaking, and blurted out with feigned indignity, "I don't need to deal with this BS."

Reaching across the counter, I grabbed my documents and pictures, which the agent had set off to the side, and walked out of the office as quickly as I could. As I hurriedly descended the stairs to the ground floor, I was half expecting a security guard to try to stop me. Once I reached the street, I blended in with the tourist crowd in Rockefeller Plaza and made my way back to the subway.

As I walked south on Fifth Avenue, I realized I had escaped a dangerous situation by the skin of my teeth. But this was clearly not a moment of pride and triumph. This was the most important assignment I'd been given to make me fully American and launch me into the life of a rich capitalist who could do some real damage to the enemy, and I had just failed the final exam.

I went back to my apartment and drowned my sorrows in a bottle of wine.

The following Saturday, I reported the event in a secret letter to the Center and asked to make arrangements for the planned trip back to the Center and to East Germany.

✦   ✦   ✦

The passport debacle had a lasting effect on me. For the first time in almost two years, I felt deeply lonely. The shock of my failure unlocked a back door into my heart, and the cold, unfeeling Jack gave way to the German Albrecht, who desperately wanted to be home among friends and reunited with the woman he loved.

The two months I had to wait before the trip could be arranged felt like another two years.

Finally, in the middle of August, I received travel money and a passport via a dead drop. I told my boss at the messenger office that I wanted to take a rather lengthy vacation. I had no idea if I would ever see him again.

About a week prior to my planned departure, I went on a shopping trip in Manhattan and spent some of my hard-earned messenger money on expensive gifts for Gerlinde—a pearl necklace, a pair of wedding bands, and several articles of clothing acquired at Bergdorf Goodman and Saks Fifth Avenue. With respect to consumer goods, I had developed the same contradictory attitude as most of my KGB colleagues who had exposure to the West. We all loved and desired the products of the system we were working hard to destroy.

Just before leaving my apartment en route to LaGuardia Airport, I retrieved the fake passport from its hiding place and left my American documents hidden in my apartment. Thus began my circuitous trip to Berlin, via Chicago, Vienna, and Moscow. As soon as I fastened my seat belt on the plane to Chicago, my stress level diminished greatly. Albrecht Dittrich was going home.

✦   ✦   ✦

When I reached Vienna, it felt like I was already home again. It was such a relief to speak in my native language for the first time in more than two years.

I set the signal indicating my arrival and went to the meeting place the next afternoon.

This time, the recognition protocol proved to be unnecessary. To my surprise, my contact was a young agent named Arkadi, whom I had met a couple of times in Moscow. I didn't know quite how to respond when I saw this old comrade, so I waited for his cue.

"Hello, Dieter. It's good to see you again," he said warmly. "Let's go have a cup of coffee."

Apparently, he was not worried about being followed by Western intelligence agents, because we sat down at a nearby café for coffee and a piece of Black Forest cake. It was delicious.

Between bites, Arkadi said, "The comrades at the Center are eagerly awaiting your return, and Gerlinde is waiting in Berlin."

For those few words, I would have gladly given up all the cake and coffee in the world!

Arkadi then told me that Sergej had been transferred to Berlin, but that another agent would pick me up at the airport. After giving me detailed instructions for the flight to Moscow, he stood up to leave. As he stepped away from the table, he swept up the newspaper I had been carrying, which contained the passport I had traveled on. After he was gone, I pocketed the manila envelope he had left on the tabletop, which held my passport and new identity for the trip to Russia.

✦　✦　✦

As the Aeroflot plane made its final approach into Moscow and I recognized the strip of forest I had flown over several times before, my sense of anticipation grew. I was one step closer to home. My new handler, Mikhail, was waiting for me at the gate.

We went to the apartment where I would be staying, and after a light meal he handed me the mail that had been sent by Gerlinde and my mother during my absence.

I could not wait to read Gerlinde's letters. As soon as Mikhail closed the door behind him, I devoured them one by one. When I was through, I read the letters from my mother, but with some reluctance. Every line she'd written was a poignant reminder that I was guilty of lying to her.

For the next two days, I met with agents at the Center to fill them in on the details of the past two years. In spite of my failure to obtain a passport, my infiltration was declared a success because I had established a foothold in the United States and could still become an important asset to the KGB. We would discuss a new strategy for how to make use of my position after my vacation in East Germany.

When I entered the arrival hall at Schönefeld Airport in Berlin, I immediately saw Sergej walking toward me with a giant grin on his face.

"What's this I hear about you working in Berlin now?" I said as he gave me a hard slap on the back.

"Ja, my years of learning German finally paid off," he said. "The work here is also more interesting, but you know we can't talk about that."

"I understand you have maintained contact with Gerlinde. How is she?" I asked.

"She's a beautiful and brave woman. You are lucky to have somebody like that waiting for you at home."

Sergej smuggled me through customs, and we drove to my old apartment on Eitelstraße. Gerlinde was still at work, but I went over to her place on the chance that she might have left work early that day.

After a full hour on the sidewalk in front of her house—pacing, sitting, waiting anxiously—I finally spotted her in the distance, elegant as ever in a black skirt and green leather jacket.

When she saw me, she ran toward me as fast as her high heels would allow, and we fell into each other's arms.

"Albrecht, is it really you?"

Inside her apartment, she talked happily about the details of her life in Berlin. She didn't ask about my work, and I volunteered little. She knew this visit was only temporary and that it would still be a long time before we could truly start a life together.

"I brought gifts," I said with a great deal of pride and satisfaction. I unpacked the presents and laid them out in front of her. She gasped, and her face flushed with excitement when she saw the wedding bands.

The next day, Sergej provided me with a "company car" and directions to a secluded Party retreat in southern Germany, about forty kilometers from the border of Czechoslovakia. There wasn't much to do in the little town of Plauen, but for a young couple in love who had not seen each other for two years, sightseeing was not at the top of our to-do list. For the next two weeks, we enjoyed the wonderful home-cooked German food prepared by the resident caretakers and spent time in the garden or in our room reading and talking and getting reacquainted. Knowing that I would soon be back in New York, I wanted to soak up as much of my homeland and my beloved Gerlinde as I could.

One afternoon, as we were sitting on a bench in the garden, Gerlinde brought up the future.

"So, Albrecht, be honest, how long will you be gone?"

This was the kind of question that made me very uncomfortable. Deep inside, the mission came first, but I didn't want to be too blunt about this.

"I should be back for another visit in two years, and I have been told that the entire assignment is likely to end after ten years. And then I will be all yours."

I hesitated for a moment before adding the necessary disclaimer.

"Of course, you know how serious this is. I could also wind up in jail, in which case the future becomes very uncertain."

"I understand," Gerlinde said, "and I support you one hundred percent. For me, it is either you or nobody. But I would love to have a child with you."

I was surprised but also happy that she felt this way. "But would you be okay with raising a child without the father present?" I asked.

"Oh yes," she said with determination, as if she had already thought it all through. "My parents would play an important role, and my brother is in Berlin now. I want something of you with me while you're gone."

We agreed that having a child together would be wonderful, and I think she hoped it might actually happen during this short time we had together.

A week or so later, we returned to Berlin, and on September 27, 1980, we were married in a civil ceremony in Prenzlauer Berg. Gerlinde's younger brother was the only witness. The next day, I threw a few belongings into my suitcase, removed the wedding band from my finger, and said good-bye to Gerlinde for another two years.

"You know I'm doing this for a very important cause," I said. "We just need to be patient."

Gerlinde had tears in her eyes, but they betrayed sadness, not despair. We both believed that one day we would no longer have to say good-bye.

✦   ✦   ✦

By the time I returned to Moscow, the key decision for my future had been made. As a well-trained and somewhat battle-tested agent, fluent in American English, I could have been given any number of short- or medium-term assignments. But, as I expected, the foundation I had established in New York City was deemed too valuable to discard, even though the timeline before any useful intelligence could be gathered would be much longer than originally planned.

The Center had decided that I should get an American college degree, in order to establish myself in a profession where I might be more likely to make valuable contacts.

"Columbia University would be a good place to study," Alex said.

"Sure," I said. "But how do we establish my credentials? A high school dropout bike messenger doesn't just walk into an Ivy League education."

"Yes, you are right, of course," Alex said with a moan. "I just allowed myself to dream for a moment. Let's shoot for a degree in economics from the City University then. While you are there, you should get to know and report on as many students as you can. They may become the decision makers of the future. The earlier they are recruited the better."

With that decision fleshed out in more detail, my last two days in Moscow were filled with the drudgery of prewriting letters to my mother and brother, and the customary send-off banquet.

I returned to New York through Vienna and Chicago. As soon as I arrived at my apartment in Queens, I destroyed my travel passport and retrieved my American documents from their hiding place. With memories of Germany and Gerlinde locked tightly away in the most remote section of my brain, Jack Barsky reported for duty as a bike messenger the following morning.

26

ONE SATURDAY IN LATE NOVEMBER, I went to my favorite hangout, the TGI Friday's at 75th and Broadway, a holdover from my days living on the West Side of Manhattan. I was sipping a drink and smoking a cigarette while gazing idly at the mirrored wall behind the bar when suddenly my eyes caught the reflection of a beautiful woman, who was seated immediately to my right and appeared to be looking straight at me. I turned and smiled, and soon we were engaged in a lively conversation.

Luz Maria was a great conversationalist, and I found her mild Spanish accent extraordinarily charming. She said she was in New York with her mother for some shopping and entertainment. She pointed to a well-dressed, dark-haired woman who was seated on the other side of her and talking very intensely to someone else.

"What country are you from?" I asked. I had to start with something.

"Well, originally we are from Chile. But when the country was caught in the struggle between Allende and Pinochet, we left. I wound up in Spain, and my mother lives with her husband in Washington, DC."

She leaned over and whispered with innocent, girlish charm into my ear. "He's Belgian and a little weird. I don't like him much at all."

The spy in me took note of Luz Maria's leftward leanings and her mother's apparent wealth. They were staying at a very expensive hotel on Central Park South.

At that point, her mother interrupted our conversation. Apparently, they were about to meet someone at the hotel. But before she left, Luz Maria paused for a moment and said, "Why don't you join us tomorrow night for dinner? Say around seven?"

I was delighted to accept.

The next evening, I joined Luz Maria, her mother, and a young Filipino musical genius named Glenn Sales, whose training as a pianist in the US was being sponsored by Luz's mother. The conversation around the table was delightful, and too soon it was time to say good-bye. At that moment I felt as if we were leaving a huge loose end floating in the air.

✤   ✤   ✤

At the beginning of December, the Center informed me via shortwave transmission that Gerlinde had gotten her wish and was now pregnant. I was thrilled, but I had no one to share the news with. I was going to be a father, but like everything else in the life of Albrecht Dittrich, I had to keep it all locked inside.

The first six months of 1981 passed uneventfully until June 25, which was a Thursday, the night of my weekly radio transmission from the Center. At the end of a forty-five minute decryption process to decode the latest instructions from Moscow, my eyes widened as the final message emerged letter by letter: CONGRATULATIONS ON THE BIRTH OF YOUR SON, MATTHIAS, BORN 17 JUNE. MOTHER AND CHILD IN GOOD HEALTH.

I jumped up from my chair and turned two consecutive somersaults on the carpet in the hallway. What Gerlinde and I had only dared to dream about in September had actually happened. I was so excited that I almost forgot to destroy the paper with the message.

I needed to let Gerlinde know how happy I was, and I decided to take extraordinary measures. On certain occasions, I had so much information to transmit that there was not enough space in a letter or even two. In those cases, I would write out the message, photograph the sheets of paper, and pass along the exposed, but undeveloped, film cartridge via a dead-drop operation. I had recently prepared a lengthy update about the political climate in America and had also identified three new dead-drop sites, which I needed to describe. At the end of my report, I included a congratulatory note and a sweet love letter to Gerlinde.

With that done, I locked up the Albrecht drawer in my brain and slipped back fully into the persona of Jack Barsky.

✦ ✦ ✦

Two months later, Luz Maria came to Washington, DC, for a visit. She called and invited me to a black-tie musical soiree at her mother's house, given in honor of the Austrian cultural attaché and featuring Glenn Sales.

I had three days to acquire an appropriate outfit. Instead of renting a tuxedo, I went to Barneys, one of the finest outfitters in New York City. This time, I knew what to buy—no more checkered "American" pants. Instead, I chose a pin-striped, navy blue Armani suit. The suit with a double-breasted jacket, a white dress shirt, a light blue tie, and cuff links, set me back about $750. But for that one evening, it was worth it. I never looked better.

On Saturday morning, I took the Eastern Air Lines shuttle to Washington National Airport and checked into a hotel not far from the US Capitol.

When I arrived at Luz's mother's colonial-style house in the suburbs of Washington, DC, I caught a glimpse of the marvelous lifestyle of the American upper class. Each room was painted in a different rich, royal color. Chair rails, ornate crown moldings, strategically placed old-style paintings, and handcrafted antique furniture created an atmosphere I had previously experienced only in museums and century-old castles. As soon as I entered the living room, my eyes were drawn to a magnificent ebony grand piano.

As Glenn Sales took his place at the keyboard and played a number of pieces by various romantic composers, it all felt like pure magic.

With time, I became more comfortable and was even able to exchange some pleasantries—in English—with the Austrian guest of honor, and I realized that I could fit in with this crowd! When people asked me about my profession, I told them I was an independent accountant, a lie I could not have sustained for any length of time.

When the evening was done, I was forced to walk away from a great opportunity to connect with a group of people who might ultimately have yielded some interesting results for my comrades in Moscow. It wasn't time yet, even though the thought of mingling with the diplomatic crowd in the nation's capital made my mouth water. But as a bike messenger? Forget it!

I returned to New York on Sunday evening, and the next morning I put on my yellow rain suit and mounted my bike for another wet day on the streets of Manhattan—painfully aware of the chasm between my fairy-tale weekend and the grimy reality of the workweek.

When Luz Maria had told me of her plans to move to the United States within a year, my pulse rate accelerated. Although I wasn't thinking of the long-term consequences of her being in America, I was content to think that I would at least see her again.

I decided I would try to surprise her the next time we met, so I spent the next several months studying Spanish, with the same dedication I had devoted to learning English. Within the year, my command of the language was good enough that I could read Spanish language novels, including the linguistically complex *Cien Años de Soledad* (*One Hundred Years of Solitude*) by Gabriel García Márquez.

A few months after the Washington, DC, soirée, I found a letter in the mail from Luz Maria. I opened it quickly and paced the floor while reading her words. She had met someone in Spain and now planned to stay with him in anticipation of marriage. She thanked me for our time together and wished me well.

I sat at the table and read the letter again. Though somewhat abashed for all the months I had spent studying Spanish, I also felt relieved. Jack Barsky needed to remain focused, and a beautiful woman could be my downfall.

27

I HAD NOT LOST SIGHT of the primary task ahead of me: earning a college degree. My research convinced me that the only viable options were public schools. Their open admission policy guaranteed that somebody with only a high school equivalency diploma would be accepted. (I had taken the GED test and received my certificate in December 1979.) Public colleges also had reasonable tuition, making them affordable even to a lowly bike messenger.

In preparation for my enrollment, I earned twenty credits via the federal College Level Examination Program. The goal was for me to finish my degree as quickly as possible so that I could join the professional ranks while I was still young enough to be hired. I was accepted at Baruch College, a part of the City University of New York, and showed up for my first day of class in September 1981.

In order to maintain my financial cover, I continued my job as a messenger. I took classes in the morning and reported for bike duty in the afternoon. With this demanding schedule, my ability to socialize outside of school or engage in intelligence-gathering activities was reduced to a bare minimum.

It was a strange feeling to return to academia as a freshman after leaving eight years earlier as a professor. The average student at Baruch was about a dozen years my junior, but I began to develop friendships with some of my classmates—including a set of identical triplets who had been separated at birth and had found each other by accident at the age of nineteen. They were now enrolled together at Baruch.

Another new friendship was with a remarkable young immigrant from Hong Kong, with whom I shared at least one thing in common: We both had a laser-like focus on becoming successful in American society.

In calculus, he and I competed for the best grades, and our contest ended in a tie when we both scored 99 percent. But if you consider that I had *taught* calculus at the college level ten years earlier, you might say my friend was the true winner.

I also remember sitting next to him in political science and noticing how many passages he had highlighted in yellow in his textbook. When I told him that by highlighting so much of the page he was essentially highlighting nothing, his response was astounding: "Those are all the words I don't understand."

I could relate well to his challenge, and I volunteered to help him soften his accent by leading him through some phonetic exercises similar to the ones I had used when studying English in Moscow.

Not surprisingly, my friend went on to study at Columbia Law School and became a member of the *Columbia Law Review* in his first semester, so he was well on his way to making an impact on the world. When I met him again years later, he told me that he had chosen me as the subject for one of the essays required for his application to Columbia. I never saw the essay, but it wasn't hard to guess that its main thrust was how an American had welcomed this Chinese newcomer to his country with open arms. The irony, for me, was delicious.

✦ ✦ ✦

While walking between classes one day in early 1982, I saw a bulletin board notice for a current affairs group meeting, and I signed up immediately.

Led by history professor Selma Berrol, the group of about twenty students met on Wednesdays at lunchtime to discuss current world affairs and American politics. For purposes of these discussions, I positioned myself on the left of the political spectrum, with some sympathy for the Western European brand of socialism, but firmly anti-Communist.

Over the next couple of years, this group provided great insight for my reports to the Center about the mood of the country—particularly in 1983, when President Ronald Reagan's Strategic Defense Initiative (SDI) and the downing of Korean Air Lines Flight 007 by a Soviet fighter jet reignited tensions between the US and the Soviet Union that had largely diminished during the period of détente in the 1970s. There was widespread concern in our group that Reagan might push the world to the brink of nuclear war with his aggressive approach to international diplomacy.

Only one person in the group, a guy named Fred, sided with Reagan. Fred was ultraconservative, and the rest of us would chuckle or roll our eyes when he started on one of his rants.

"I'm telling you, the Russians are deathly afraid of Ronald Reagan. We need to show them that we are serious. Historically, appeasement has never worked, and it will not work today. And if the Russians try to keep up with us in this race, they will simply go bankrupt."

In his own way, Fred actually expressed historical truth before it became evident.

During my years at Baruch I sent profiles of about twenty students to the Center. Those profiles included basic personal data such as their name, address, contact information, physical description, character traits, political leanings, and possible angles for recruitment. The Center was always on the lookout for sources of secret information.

There was quite a variety of recruitment angles: money, addictions, information that would make a person vulnerable to extortion, and radical political leanings, left or right. From that perspective, Fred was a promising lead. Many a right-wing radical had given information to the Soviets under a "false flag," thinking they were working with a Western ally, such as Israel, when in fact their contact was a KGB operative.

✦ ✦ ✦

In the summer of 1982, after one full year of college, my two-year stint was up again. It was time for a second return trip to debrief in Moscow and see Gerlinde in Berlin. I couldn't wait to finally meet my son, who was now a year old.

The stopover prior to Moscow was in Rome. When I arrived there,

I made contact with the resident agent to exchange passports and then went to a travel agency to book my flight to Russia on Aeroflot.

"I'm sorry," the travel agent told me in English. "There is a baggage handlers strike and all Aeroflot flights have been canceled until further notice. She pointed out that Alitalia still had flights going to Moscow.

I paused to think about this alternative. I had been instructed to always use Aeroflot in and out of Moscow. I decided to wait a few days.

To relieve my anxiety, I forced myself out of the hotel, but I was not in the mood for tourism. All I wanted to do was see my wife and son, and every day in Rome stole a day from my time in Berlin. I had to be back in New York in time for the start of the fall semester.

After five days of waiting, and no end in sight for the strike, I decided I was entitled to break the rule. I booked a flight on Alitalia, set the "departed country" sign, and flew to Moscow.

When I got off the plane, Mikhail was waiting for me, and he was visibly upset.

"You should not have done that," he said. "The passport you just used is now worthless. Do you know how much time and effort it takes to create a working passport?"

I apologized profusely but said, "I had to improvise. I only have a five-week window before reporting back to college, and I've already lost a week."

Mikhail accepted my apology but added sternly, "I want to be very clear. From now on, you will follow our travel instructions to the letter."

It was the only time Mikhail ever spoke to me in that manner, and it was a warning to remember.

✦ ✦ ✦

After my customary three-day debriefing session, I flew to Berlin, where Sergej was waiting for me at the airport. He put me to shame by giving me a big plush teddy bear as a present for Matthias, something I had not thought about.

With the help of the KGB, Gerlinde had moved into a larger, four-room apartment in the Friedrichshagen section of Berlin. When she answered the door, I looked past her to see Matthias, who was standing rather shyly in a remote corner of the hallway. As I showed him the teddy bear, he ran away and hid behind his mother, clinging to her skirt.

When Sergej called him, he reappeared and allowed Sergej to pick him up.

I stood there with the teddy bear, feeling like the outsider I was.

Gerlinde half-apologized for the awkward scene. "Matthias is very sensitive, and it takes a while for him to get used to strangers. And you know, you are a stranger to him."

Though her words were spoken in love, they stung like needles, reminding me that I was an absentee father.

This time, we did not travel far for our vacation trip. The KGB put us up in a guesthouse on the Müggelsee, the largest lake in Berlin. With Matthias in the mix, the marital dynamic had changed significantly. I was no longer the center of attention for Gerlinde. The little one had taken the number one spot.

Like his father, Matthias was a light sleeper, and he caught a cold on the first day. The following nights were anything but restful, in stark contrast to the many nights I had spent with Gerlinde in the past.

Well, fatherhood has its price, I thought as I tried to adjust to the new situation. Every morning I got up at 6:00 a.m, warmed a bottle of milk for Matthias, and took him for a stroll in his carriage.

After three and a half weeks with my family, it was time to go back to Moscow. I left with mixed emotions. I was still very much in love with Gerlinde, but our time together had been chaotic. I tried to bond with Matthias, but three weeks was not enough time to establish a meaningful connection with a one-year-old who had no idea who I was.

✦ ✦ ✦

During my preparation meetings with Alex in Moscow, I was reminded repeatedly of the need to meet and report on interesting human targets.

"We need you to produce more valuable contacts," he said.

Rather than try to explain the limitations imposed by my circumstances in the US, I promised to do a better job.

Alex also suggested that I do everything possible to finish college in the next two years.

"We need you on Wall Street. We need you to make contact with decision makers. And as you look for your first job out of college, try to stay away from the larger companies. They may conduct a more thorough background check."

This time, my itinerary had me flying to Vienna, taking a train to Paris, and from there catching a flight to Washington, DC. I spent my day in Paris sightseeing and finally got to see the famous places I had only read about during my years as a student: Notre Dame, the Arc de Triomphe, Montmartre, Les Tuileries, and the Louvre. The only sight that didn't live up to my imagination was the surprisingly diminutive *Mona Lisa*.

The following day, I made my way to Charles de Gaulle Airport, where I got an unpleasant surprise. When I stepped up to the Air France counter and requested a ticket for the flight number I had been given by the Center—not wanting to repeat my transgression from Rome—the young desk agent smiled politely, turned to her left, and announced for all to hear, "Concorde!"

Though ordinarily the sound of this word pronounced in a Parisian accent would be music to my ears, in this context it had the effect of fingernails scratching on a blackboard. Here I was, traveling with a false passport and almost $10,000 in my pockets, paying $1,700 in cash to fly on a plane that catered mostly to the well-off elite.

The needle of my risk meter entered the red zone. A cash-paying customer on this type of flight could easily have triggered closer scrutiny from either the French or the American authorities. Luckily, no one seemed to pay any attention to me, but in my first letter to the Center after returning in the US, I complained strongly about this obvious mistake. I never received an explanation, but I felt I had at least regained the high ground after being chided about the Rome incident.

The Concorde took off from de Gaulle on a dark, rainy evening, and three and a half hours later we landed at Washington Dulles International in bright sunshine, having outpaced the earth's rotation. The flight itself was nothing special. There was a large display at the front of the cabin showing our speed expressed in Mach (where Mach 1 equals the speed of sound). When the meter went from .99 to 1.00, indicating that we had broken through the sound barrier, nothing happened inside the plane's cabin. The sonic boom was audible only from below.

I took a bus back to New York and rode the subway to my apartment. After what amounted to a whirlwind trip across Europe and back, I was glad to be home in Woodside. For the first time, I realized that I felt more comfortable in the country that I was spying on than I did in my native land. My trips to Berlin from this time forward would feel more like visits than going home.

28

I KNEW THAT PART OF MY VALUE to the KGB was simply my presence in the United States. In December 1983, I was instructed via shortwave radio to fly to Los Angeles, take a bus to San Bernardino, and try to locate a certain Nikolai Khokhlov, who was believed to be working at the San Bernardino branch of California State University. If I could locate this man, the Center wanted me to send his home and workplace addresses. "But under no circumstances should you make contact with this person," they warned.

One advantage of being an illegal was that I could travel freely anywhere in the country, whereas legal agents, working under diplomatic cover, were restricted to a limited radius around their officially recognized office.

My window for completing this task was pretty tight because I had to be back at school in time for final exams, which were scheduled for the third week of December. I flew into LAX and took a bus to San Bernardino. On the bus ride, I enjoyed a most beautiful smog-enhanced sunset.

The next morning, I set out on foot from my hotel room to visit the university campus, which was on the outskirts of town. The five-mile walk along streets without sidewalks made me somewhat uncomfortable. It appeared that nobody walked in California, even if the destination was only a block away.

When I arrived at the campus, I decided to just walk up and down the hallways of the office buildings, looking for some sign of Mr. Khokhlov. Of course, I had a cover story if anybody asked me what I was doing on campus—I was there to explore the possibility of moving to California to continue my studies.

It didn't take long for me to find a sign reading, "Professor Khokhlov—Psychology" on one of the doors.

I was standing about ten feet from the door when it suddenly swung open and a man walked out. Mr. Khokhlov himself? Our eyes met, but I didn't know for certain that it was him. I quickly made a U-turn and walked away.

Khokhlov's home address was listed in the local phone book. I visited the single-family house in the suburbs to confirm it. Having finished my task well ahead of schedule, I spent the next two days sunbathing in a nearby park. It felt odd to work on my tan in the middle of December. Even more bizarre for a German who now lived in the northeastern United States was the Christmas atmosphere at the downtown Carousel Mall. In the center of the mall was a large artificial Christmas tree decorated with fake snow and gaudy ornaments. Nearby, a young woman dressed as an elf took pictures of children who sat on the lap of a man portraying Santa Claus. All the while, a steady chorus of cloying Christmas music played on the public address system.

About two months after I returned to New York, I saw a televised interview with Mr. Khokhlov, during which he was identified as a Soviet defector. The man I had seen in California was indeed Nikolai Khokhlov. Given that he had been sentenced to death in absentia by the Soviet Union, and that he had survived a poisoning attempt in 1957, his appearance on TV seemed to be a rather bold move. Had he known that the KGB had sent an undercover agent to confirm his whereabouts just a few weeks before, he might have been a bit more circumspect. Much later, I was glad to learn that Mr. Khokhlov lived to the ripe old age of eighty-five.

✦   ✦   ✦

One of the classes required for a bachelor's degree in business administration was Introduction to Data Processing. When I wrote my first lines of code in FORTRAN, fed them into the card reader, and saw the results printed out faster than you can say "computer program," I was hooked. This emerging technology appealed tremendously to my affinity for raw binary logic.

So I changed my major from economics to computer systems. Rather than ask for permission, I simply informed the Center, justifying the switch by asserting that it would be easier to find a job in data processing.

My time at Baruch flew by, and soon my graduation date was on the horizon. I did my best to fit in and keep a low profile, but no matter how hard I tried, there were times when I just couldn't escape who I was. Albrecht Dittrich was a highly competitive student, and Jack Barsky inherited that trait. When I finished my first semester at Baruch with an A average, I bragged to a group of fellow students, "I think I just might ace the whole thing."

Three years later, my prediction came true. But what hadn't occurred to me, until it was too late, was that a 4.0 average can also be spelled with thirteen letters: *v-a-l-e-d-i-c-t-o-r-i-a-n*.

Near the end of my final semester, I received an invitation to the dean's office to discuss my role in the graduation ceremony, where it was customary for the valedictorian to give a speech.

This was anything but good news. I realized that the somewhat unusual case of a "40-year-old" valedictorian at a well-known New York college might catch the attention of an enterprising journalist or at least someone from the college paper. If my unauthorized public appearance came to the attention of my bosses in Moscow, I could reasonably expect some sort of punishment.

"I don't want to do this," I told the dean. "I am older than most students—why not give it to a young kid who deserves it and would get great satisfaction out of this honor?"

My protestations hit a granite wall. "We have to go by the rules," the dean explained, "and the rules say that the valedictorian is selected strictly based on grade point average. You are the only one in your class with a 4.0. The salutatorian has a 3.94."

I tried another tack: "Listen, I have never spoken before an audience, and the Felt Forum is such a big place. I would be scared to death."

The dean now forced my hand with a clever trick: "If you are that afraid, how about if you write the speech and let someone else read it?"

Agreeing to such a proposal would be a cowardly act. That wasn't me. Ultimately, I couldn't turn away from the challenge. So I gave in, and on a sultry day in July 1984, I stepped to the podium at the Felt Forum in Madison Square Garden, dressed in a cheap dark-blue nylon gown and a constantly shifting nylon cap, and delivered a fully memorized five-minute speech to an audience of approximately four thousand people.

The irony of a KGB agent delivering the valedictory at an American business school did not escape me. In my speech, I tried to marry my romantic notions of a worker's brotherhood with the hard-core business lessons taught at the school. I wanted to remind the audience that making money was important, but so was being kind to others. My last phrase still rings in my head: ". . . where a smile is worth just as much as a dollar."

That speech was not pure fiction. It reflected a genuine shift in how I viewed the world in those days. I had gradually softened my stance from hardcore communism to a fuzzy vision of capitalism with a human face. Perhaps socialism was the answer after all. I knew I would never discuss any of this transition with my comrades in Moscow, or even with Gerlinde. It took me years to admit it to myself.

I walked off the stage to the sound of applause—mostly polite and perfunctory, I'm sure—relieved to have it all over with. What was really important that day was that I had achieved the Center's goal to become a graduate of an American university.

✛ ✛ ✛

During my final semester, in the spring of 1984, I had interviewed with several companies that sent recruiters to Baruch. Of the half-dozen companies I spoke with, only one showed any interest in a forty-year-old computer programmer with a perfect grade point average, and that company was MetLife.

As a messenger, I had made deliveries to the MetLife Building at 1 Madison Avenue. But when I entered the massive, marble-decorated lobby for an in-person interview, I hoped I could one day refer to this place as "the office."

After briefing me about company benefits, rules, and procedures, the human resources representative took me to the nineteenth floor for a meeting with two MetLife managers, Mark and Eileen. Right from the start, Mark challenged me with a question: "So why do you want to be a programmer?"

I was well prepared and pulled out from my briefcase a thick printout of a COBOL program I had written. I placed it on the table and proudly proclaimed, "I'm a programmer already!"

The two managers complimented me on the clarity and organization of my code, but Eileen added, "Real life is a lot bigger and more complicated than this college stuff. You'll see for yourself."

That sounded like an indirect offer, and indeed it was. Three days later, I received a letter in the mail offering me a position as a junior programmer, with a starting annual salary of $21,500. When I called HR to accept the offer, I asked them to delay the start date until early September. What I neglected to mention was that I first had to make a trip to the other side of the Iron Curtain.

This time, I traveled back via Stockholm and took an overnight ferry to Leningrad (now St. Petersburg). Mikhail was already waiting for me, and we traveled to Moscow together by train.

✛ ✛ ✛

My five weeks in Moscow and Berlin followed the established routine for such visits, but I wasn't looking forward to my meeting with Alex. What if he had found out that I had given the commencement address at one of the biggest schools in New York City?

But those first anxious moments passed quickly when Alex congratulated me on the new job and didn't even criticize me for choosing a large insurance company. He expressed the hope that I would take advantage of this new platform as a professional to get to know more interesting people.

It was now clear that the Center had developed an implicit trust in me. They were not observing me from a distance or double-checking the information I provided. This knowledge would play a big role in two major decisions I would later make.

Reflecting on my years as a spy, I have come to the conclusion that trust is the only viable foundation for a successful undercover operation.

If the Center could not trust an agent (as when Stalin ignored the warnings from Richard Sorge—the KGB's most important asset in Japan prior to World War II—of the impending invasion of the Soviet Union by the Nazis in 1941), they were better off not having an agent in place. And if an agent couldn't trust his handlers, he would become ineffective or stop operating altogether.

In the end, I was the one who would breach that trust.

My arrival in Berlin was the most exciting part of the entire visit. Sergej had once again bailed me out by finding a present for me to give to Matthias. This time it was a remote control car made in West Germany.

When I entered the apartment, my now three-year-old son hid behind his mother before sticking out his head and saying, "Ich bin ein Löwe" ("I am a Lion"). But his shyness and my natural reticence did not allow for a real greeting between father and son. I didn't want it to be this way, but I didn't know how to bridge the gap between us.

Gerlinde rose from the sofa, and we embraced. After giving her a gentle kiss, I went straight to the main event, unpacking the dresses and other articles of clothing I had brought for her from some of the most expensive stores in Manhattan. Items of this quality were not even available in West Berlin, let alone East Berlin. After applying some of the cosmetics I brought and putting on the gold necklace and bracelet, Gerlinde looked like a wealthy movie star.

Matthias was in awe. "Mutti, you are so pretty!" he exclaimed. Turning to me, he said, "Thanks for these things, Onkel."

That stung. He had just called me *uncle*, an endearing term used by German children to address friendly strangers.

Behind the scenes, Onkel's influence had contributed to a major improvement in Gerlinde's standard of living. Because the KGB gave her my salary, she had been able to stop working and dedicate her time to bringing up Matthias. The previous summer, the KGB had arranged for a vacation in Sochi, on the Black Sea. Gerlinde and Matthias had spent two weeks at a luxury resort, where they were catered to by a cook, a translator, and a dedicated chauffeur.

Gerlinde's new apartment was well furnished, including a color TV, a piano, and even a telephone. Telephones were in such short supply that they were granted only to important individuals.

The most prestigious new status symbol was a high-end car, a Lada sedan. Sergej had pulled some powerful strings to move us to the top of the fifteen-year waiting list. The Lada, produced in the Soviet Union under a licensing agreement with Fiat, was the most upscale vehicle available to East German citizens.

Now we could drive ourselves, rather than depend on a "company car," when we made the trip to Gerlinde's parents in Rehna, a country town two hours northwest of Berlin. I was a bit hesitant to visit them because I was afraid of a barrage of uncomfortable questions. But Gerlinde allayed my fears.

"Albrecht, don't worry about my parents. They are not nosy, and to them, you are simply a highly successful fat cat who is taking very good care of their daughter. That is all they want to know."

After a week in Rehna and a few more days in Berlin, it was once again time to return to Moscow on my way back to New York. On this visit, I could feel that the emotional connection with Gerlinde had become rather shallow. With our separate lives and such brief opportunities to reconnect, we didn't seem to feel the same passionate love of six or eight years ago. With a large dose of wishful thinking, I pushed all my thoughts about our relationship out into the future.

One day, I'll be back for good, and then we can reignite the flame.

I also failed to gain much traction with Matthias. He had learned to call me "Vati," but he probably didn't know what that meant. He had no frame of reference. I played games with him that fathers of three-year-olds would play, but there were no hugs or kisses or other expressions of love. One day, after we had kicked the soccer ball for an hour, I sat down on a park bench and Matthias came up to me and nestled in my lap. This felt rather awkward to me, and I didn't know how to respond. I was following in my father's footsteps, and I didn't know how to change it. With such a short time together, I felt there was nothing I could do.

✦ ✦ ✦

Back in Moscow, Alex lectured me about the relationship between the US and the USSR. When he spoke about the role of President Reagan, his voice took on a sense of urgency.

222 ＄ DEEP UNDERCOVER

"Albrecht, this is the first time since we tried to deploy the missiles to Cuba that the world is getting close to a nuclear exchange. The Reagan Doctrine is upsetting the balance that was guaranteed by the concept of mutually assured destruction. He's playing with fire, and I tell you, this talk about the apocalyptic end times by some of the pastors of the churches Reagan and his followers are associated with scares the daylights out of me. What if Reagan thinks that he is an instrument of God and has the urge to push the button to start the final destruction of the planet? If at all possible, get close to somebody who has an understanding of Reagan's mind."

I found it interesting that the fears Alex expressed were just as Fred, the ultraconservative from the current affairs group at Baruch, had predicted. But Alex had no idea. Getting close to someone in the Reagan Administration, for a junior programmer at a New York insurance company, was a tall order indeed!

This fear of President Reagan stemmed from a fundamental lack of understanding of the American political system. First of all, the president of the United States is not the all-powerful strongman that so many Communist leaders in the Soviet Union assumed he was. Also, a better understanding of the Christian faith would have provided the Communists with some assurance that Reagan did not see himself as an instrument of God whose job it was to accelerate the coming of the end of the world. On the contrary, Reagan's goal was to rid the world of the nuclear threat. It is my personal belief that the Russians' irrational fear of President Reagan contributed significantly to the eventual fall of the Soviet Union—an event that was not yet foreseeable in 1984.

29

AFTER RETURNING TO THE US, I started my professional career on the first Tuesday of September 1984. The concept of "business casual" had not yet been adopted by the insurance industry. So, prior to my trip to Europe, I had bought three suits, half a dozen dress shirts and ties, and a pair of Bally shoes.

For a former bike messenger, who had not yet cashed his first paycheck, I was overdressed, but this was not enough of a misstep to raise the curiosity of my new bosses and coworkers.

The insurance industry was on the eve of a radical transformation, fueled by information technology and aided by automation. In the past, armies of claims adjusters, sitting behind desks in neatly arranged rows, had toiled away, analyzing, approving, or rejecting claims. Now they were about to be replaced by a much smaller number of knowledge workers who delegated the routine aspects of data processing to the computers.

When I joined the company, the floor layout still reflected the paper-based tradition. I shared a desk with a fellow named Felix, a middle-aged senior programmer with dark, curly hair and a sharp nose. To my surprise, he spoke with a Russian accent.

"Are you Russian?" I asked.

"No, I am Ukrainian, and I hate everything Russian."

That was a strong answer, but very much reflective of the historic hostility between the two nations.

"So how do you like working here?" I asked.

Felix looked up from his stack of computer printouts and answered with a smirk. "Sometimes I feel like a slave. They work you hard, and when things go wrong at night, they have no problem waking you up. Get ready for a rough ride."

He was certainly not a happy camper.

Later, I sat down in the terminal room to sign on to my account for the first time. The man to my right turned and smiled. "Hi, my name is Joe. Welcome to MetLife!"

Joe was a well-groomed, perfectly dressed gentleman. His black hair and dark eyes reflected his southern European ancestry, but he spoke without an accent.

After telling him my name, I repeated the question I'd asked Felix. "So what is it like to work here?"

"Oh, this is a great place. We're working on the biggest medical claims system in the country, and we have all the resources needed to do a good job. And they treat us so well."

"But what about the night calls?" I asked.

"That comes with the territory," Joe responded with an ear-to-ear grin.

Joe turned out to be of Sicilian descent. He and Felix were among quite a number of immigrants and first-generation Americans on the team of about fifty information technology professionals—a reflection that computer work was the fastest avenue to success for smart people from other parts of the world.

There was Gerard, a Cuban, and one of the smartest individuals I've ever met; Savely, an equally smart Jewish refugee from the Soviet Union; Olga, a former Russian schoolteacher; Bob, a highly capable immigrant from Hong Kong; Rufus, from the small island of Saint Kitts in the Caribbean; and José, a Spaniard who was as smart as he was droll. And then, of course, there was an East German Soviet spy masquerading as a full-blooded American. The only real American in the gang I socialized with was Patrick, who is still a good friend today.

One day, I was sitting next to Joe, typing some computer commands into the mainframe, when the far door was flung open and a short fellow with disheveled hair and wire-frame glasses walked in. He picked up an ashtray full of butts, threw it on the floor with a curse, and stormed back out.

"Who was that?" I asked Joe.

"Don't mind him. That's just Ron, acting out. He is a bit odd, but boy, his code is out of this world."

This was my kind of crowd—intelligent, full of energy, and just a little odd. The terminal room, where we had access to the mainframe, had an atmosphere of camaraderie, and friendly insults flew back and forth to break the tension. On my second day, Joe looked at me, smiled, and said, "That's a very nice tie you have on. How many polyesters gave their lives to make that one?"

I quickly embraced the culture and soon was able to trade insults with the best of them. Within six months, I had mastered the learning curve and was able to produce functioning programs. I loved the opportunity to create something from nothing by stringing together logical thought.

It didn't take long for me to see a wide gap between the Communist saga of the exploited worker in a capitalist society and the reality as I experienced it. For some reason, insurance companies were always near the top of the list of capitalist villains in Communist propaganda. But I never felt I was being exploited. Instead, I was quite comfortable in my job, everyone treated me well, and the paternalistic culture of the traditional mutual insurance company was very appealing to my statist roots. The chinks in my ideological armor began to grow into wide-open cracks, and I sensed that it would be difficult to walk away from this job when the time came.

✤ ✤ ✤

While my job at MetLife was both demanding and fulfilling, it had another interesting effect on me as well. Slowly—and barely perceptibly to me—it began to turn my value system upside down. At first, it was more of an attitude shift than anything else. Instead of feeling that the demands of my job interfered with my intelligence-gathering activities, it seemed that the intelligence activities interfered with my job and my life as an American.

On Thursday nights when the radiograms exceeded two hundred groups in length, I stayed up until the wee hours of the morning deciphering the messages. On top of that, creating and mailing letters with secret writing every two or three weeks had also become a burden. Having to write the open letters was tedious enough, but it took an additional hour to create the invisible writing on the message to be mailed, and then there was all the cleanup—all working papers had to be destroyed. Finally, the rules stipulated that I go on a three-hour route to check for surveillance before dropping the letter in a mailbox in the vicinity of the fictitious return address.

Another burden was the requirement that I submit an expense report every two months. The KGB was very meticulous in their desire to account for all expenses. They paid for my car and my rent, plus all my medical and travel expenses, and 50 percent of my auto expenses. They also continued to pay me a monthly salary of $600. With the salary I earned at my job, there was no longer a need for an infusion of extra cash. As a result, the balance in my account with the KGB swelled to more than $60,000.

With the demands of my daytime job and nighttime intelligence work, I felt I had no choice but to prudently cut some corners. I started writing my secret letters on Sunday afternoons and holding them overnight (against the rules). And then I skipped the surveillance check and deposited the letters in the mail chute at one of the older office buildings that had such a facility. I perfected a system to ensure there was no chance that anyone could have seen me make the mail drop, even if I was under surveillance.

Another shortcut was the elimination of the routine monthly check for surveillance. I decided that two signals in my apartment would be sufficient to alert me to the possibility of being under investigation.

The first hot spot was a drawer in my living room chest, which I left open exactly 4 mm. That gap was measurable only from below and it would be invisible in a routine inspection. It was highly unlikely that even a well-trained operative would spot this trap.

The second sensor was a hair that I glued very lightly to the underside of another drawer. One would have to know where to look to find that hair. If the drawer was opened, the hair would come unglued and drop down.

Some of my corner cutting was the result of an increasing—and possibly false—sense of security. My rationale was that I wasn't engaged in any activity that would have triggered a law enforcement investigation.

Without a doubt, my most vulnerable moments were the dead-drop operations. With these, I still took more elaborate precautionary measures. But, even then, I was looking for ways to reduce the time the operation took. For example, I devised what I thought was a brilliant method of shaking a tail. I loaded my bicycle into the trunk of my car and drove to a park at the outer edge of the city. Then I rode the bike to a street on the other side of the park, locked the bike near a train station, and continued onto the subway. This combination of moves, which was also part of my emergency escape plan, made it next to impossible for anyone to follow me.

Despite the constraints imposed by my "above cover" life, I managed to produce some value for the Soviets. In addition to portraying at least one new contact per letter to the Center, I continued to provide reports on "the mood of the American public." I imagine they used this type of report to flesh out the briefings they gave to various decision makers.

✦   ✦   ✦

One spring day, I arrived at my apartment and froze when I opened the door. Inside, I saw clear evidence that someone had been there. Cautiously, I walked inside and surveyed the damage. My belongings were strewn all over the floor, my clothes were tossed on the bed, and some drawers had been removed from a chest with their contents poured out on the floor.

When I went back into the living room, I realized that my new state-of-the-art stereo system was gone. As I continued to check the apartment, I realized that the thieves had entered through the living room window, which faced a fenced-in backyard. All signs pointed to a hurried search for valuables and a quick getaway. They hadn't found my hidden cash or the expensive tennis bracelet I was going to take to Gerlinde, but of course both my markers had been disturbed.

There was always the possibility that the break-in was staged to cover up a search by the FBI. But a footprint left by one of the intruders and a half-eaten cup of yogurt that was spilled on the carpet led me to believe that it was a real burglary.

Not taking any chances, I left the apartment immediately for a three-hour surveillance-detection run. But nobody was following me, so I slept safe and sound that night. When I reported the break-in to the Center, I noted that I saw no reason for concern.

But Moscow wasn't so easily convinced.

30

WITH SIX MONTHS TO GO until Albrecht Dittrich's next planned visit to his wife and son in Germany, Jack Barsky, living by himself in New York City, felt deeply lonely. My cover identity would never quite be complete as long as I had to stop short of building deep and lasting relationships. When all my colleagues talked about their wives, children, homes, and plans for the future, I had nothing to contribute. After more than seven years of living alone in America, what I really longed for was friendship and connection.

I met Penelope via a personals ad I placed in the *Village Voice*. After a first chat on the phone, we decided to meet. I suggested Tony Roma's, a popular steak and ribs place in Greenwich Village.

Because it was winter in New York City, she was bundled up in a heavy coat with a scarf and hat. When she removed these outer garments and took off her glasses, it was as if a beautiful butterfly had emerged from its cocoon. I was definitely smitten.

We spent two hours eating and talking, and even though I made the mistake of ordering barbecued ribs—never order ribs on a first date; they're just too messy—I enjoyed her company immensely.

"I've been in this country for only three years," she said with a soft, melodious accent that I couldn't place.

"So where are you from?" I mumbled around a mouthful of ribs.

"Guyana," she said. "Do you know where that is?"

I had a vague notion that several places in South America were called Guyana, but not wanting to admit my ignorance, I simply nodded.

At that point she opened up. "You know, people in my country are very, very poor. My father is a well-known journalist, and we should have had a good life. But even a journalist's income is not sufficient to feed twelve mouths."

"Twelve children?" I said, wiping barbecue sauce from my hands with a cloth napkin. Penelope's story seemed disconnected from the beautiful woman sitting across the table from me.

"My mother actually had fifteen children, but three of them died when they were very young. I was the second oldest, and I was only seventeen when my father left us."

"He left your mother with twelve children? How did you all survive?"

"It was extremely difficult. There were days when we all went to bed hungry." Clearly, the memory was still painful.

"How did you get here?" I asked.

"When I turned eighteen, I became a flight attendant for Guyana Airways. Now I work as a nurse's aide and live with a friend in Brooklyn."

After dinner, we talked further as I walked her to the subway station. When we parted, she gave me a light kiss on the cheek. It was sweet and gentle but also intoxicating. I called her the following day and asked to see her again. We soon started seeing each other regularly, mostly on Saturdays, to take in a movie or share a meal.

It wasn't long before Penelope was spending many Saturday nights at my place. That presented a minor problem because every three or four weeks I needed the weekend to create my reports for the Center. But Penelope never once questioned my excuses for why we couldn't see each other—indeed, she was the perfect date for someone in my situation.

By now I had lived in the US for almost eight years, and I had immersed myself in American culture; yet I was still ignorant about many aspects of American life. Ironically, one of those areas was illegal immigration. Thus, I was perfectly unprepared for the day when Penelope asked me a very strange question.

"Can we still see each other, even if I get married to another man?"

"What? You want to get married and still date me? That doesn't make any sense."

What ensued was an education—from one illegal to another—about what it was like to live in the shadows of the law (but, of course, without the support of a powerful intelligence agency).

"As an employee of Guyana Airways, I was in the US on a tourist visa," Penelope explained. "On one of those trips, I simply did not return home but went to live with my friend Margaret in Brooklyn instead. She helped me get a job as a nurse's aide, and I saved enough money—two thousand dollars, in all—to pay an American citizen to marry me. According to the arrangement, we would get married and he would apply for my citizenship, and then we would go our separate ways. That is the quickest way to become an American."

"It is?"

"Yes."

"And so you are married?"

"Well, I got married, but the guy never applied for a green card on my behalf. Instead, he disappeared with my money, and I got a divorce. Now I have saved up the money again, and I'm looking for another man who might be willing to marry me for a fee."

I shook my head in disbelief, yet I also felt bad for Penelope. She was trying to better her life by doing the same thing I had done—acquiring American documentation by whatever means possible.

"How do you know that the next guy won't cheat you like the first one did?"

"I don't know. I just have to trust."

"Okay, look, don't do anything yet. Let me do some research."

Over the next several weeks, I went to the library and studied immigration law and procedures. I also asked one of my colleagues at work who had married a woman from overseas about his experience with the authorities. At the end of my analysis, I determined that I could safely do this favor for Penelope. I had solid US documents, I had a good job, and I didn't see how the KGB could find out. I had already determined that they trusted me and never checked on me.

One evening in May 1986, I shared the good news with Penelope over dinner: I would marry her and file for her citizenship papers, after which we would divorce and go our separate ways. Perhaps she had told me her story in the hope that I would respond the way I did, but ultimately the decision to marry her was mine, a decision that was driven by what I call my "damsel-in-distress syndrome."

Even today, whenever I see a little girl or a young woman in trouble in some way, my instinctive reaction is to want to be the knight in shining armor. And that is how, at roughly the same time I was making preparations for my next reunion with Gerlinde and Matthias, I also promised to marry an illegal immigrant for the purpose of obtaining documentation on her behalf.

✦   ✦   ✦

My next trip to Moscow was scheduled for the summer of 1986. I had saved enough vacation days at MetLife for exactly one month of absence. After subtracting my travel time and the days I would be at the Center, I had two weeks left to spend with Gerlinde and Matthias.

Fortunately, the connection through Helsinki, Finland, went like clockwork, and only three days after leaving New York, I was sitting with Alex and Eugen in Moscow for my usual debriefing session.

"Tell me about the break-in," Alex said. "Is there any chance the FBI is onto you?"

The two men peppered me with detailed questions about everything in my life that might indicate I was under investigation. I had not expected that isolated incident to blow up into something like this. The powers that be within the KGB were even considering pulling the plug on my American assignment right then and there to avoid the risk of an arrest and an international incident.

I thought their concerns were overblown, but as they weighed the alternatives, I saw a glimmer of a chance to complete my assignment and go home to permanently join my family in Berlin. Gerlinde and Matthias had been without husband and father long enough.

And yet, as I reflected on my circumstances, I felt that I had some unfinished business—that I hadn't yet delivered what the KGB had sent me to New York to accomplish. With no hard evidence that I had come to the attention of the FBI, or that my cover had been compromised, it seemed a shame to close down the operation when I was successfully embedded in the US. What was missing was the piece that would allow me to pursue the original plan to infiltrate the upper levels of American society: the elusive US passport. Circumstances were different now—I had a professional job and a job history, and getting a passport might not be that difficult after all. I was eager to finish my assignment with a success that would wipe out what had been arguably my biggest failure.

After I dangled the bait in front of Alex, he took the idea to his superiors, and the decision was made to send me back to New York for another two-year stint.

✦ ✦ ✦

When I arrived in Berlin for the latest round of hello-and-good-bye with Gerlinde and Matthias, there was more tension in the air than there had ever been during our more than ten-year relationship.

"So when are you finally keeping your promise to stay with me and Matthias?" Gerlinde screamed at me when I told her about the two-year extension. When I gave her the tennis bracelet, she tossed it onto the table and said, "Diamonds are wonderful, but I have enough of this stuff now. I want *you*!"

I put my head down in silence as guilt welled up within me. At that moment, I was painfully aware that it was my *ambition*—not my revolutionary zeal—that was driving me, and now that ambition had gained the upper hand over Gerlinde's desires. Nevertheless, I responded, "Two more years, darling, two more years. They will go by in no time, believe me."

We spent the remainder of my time in Berlin like an ordinary family with some time off from work. We took a boat ride on the Spree River, visited the zoo twice, and drove to the woods outside Berlin to pick mushrooms. My farewell meal was wild mushrooms fried in butter with mashed potatoes.

Matthias was now five years old, and he was a bright young boy and very conversational. But I could never shake my feelings of awkwardness around him. Perhaps it was my guilt about being a derelict father. I felt like such a stranger in both of their lives now—and I was. By the end of the trip, I seriously wondered why Gerlinde wanted me full time at all.

✦ ✦ ✦

By the time I got back to Moscow, Alex and the others seemed reenergized by our joint decision to make another run for it. We had three days to prepare me for my return to New York, and those three days were as intense as I could imagine.

The second encryption algorithm I had used during the past four years had outlived its usefulness and had to be replaced. There was no time to memorize a new algorithm, so instead I received a small notepad (called a one-time pad) with 100 sheets containing groups of five digits for use in the encryption process. Those digits were made visible by developing the sheet of paper with an iodine solution applied carefully with a cotton swab.

I also received two unusual requests for specific tasks. For the first time, I was introduced to someone from a different section of the KGB: industrial espionage.

This fellow shared with me quite openly that the Soviet economy was not in good shape. He cited the arms race triggered by Ronald Reagan's "Star Wars" program and the war in Afghanistan as the primary reasons for the economic slump.

"We need an infusion of modern technology," he said. "This is imperative to the future." Because I worked in information technology, he pleaded with me to collect whatever I could get my hands on, software or hardware, that might be useful to the Soviets.

The second request was unusual, in that it was the first and only time I was given the option to say no to a request, but it also seemed very important.

"We want you to drive up to Keene, New Hampshire," Alex said, "and identify a dead-drop location where a large container can safely be deposited. That's all I can tell you."

The task itself sounded rather simple and innocent, but the reason for the request and the nature of what would be dropped were cloaked in utter secrecy. My assumption was that they wanted to use me as a middleman between the Center and an important asset who could not risk having direct interaction with a resident agent. This middleman option highlighted one more benefit of having an anonymous illegal embedded in the US.

Shortly after my return to New York, I drove the 400-mile round trip to Keene and located a suitable spot behind a large rock on Route 12A about two miles from the intersection with Route 9. I described the location to the Center via secret writing, but the drop operation never took place.

Based on the timing, and the unusual sensitivity with which the Center handled this request, I believe this operation was intended to transfer materials from either Robert Hanssen or Aldrich Ames—two high-value assets to the KGB who had to be protected as much as possible from even indirect contact with Soviet resident agents.

Both of these agents caused tremendous damage to the interests of the United States and were responsible for the deaths of a number of American spies in the Soviet Union. Hanssen worked for the FBI, and Ames was an employee of the CIA. Both were eventually caught and are now serving life sentences without possibility of parole.

✦ ✦ ✦

I left Moscow in excellent standing with the higher-ups in the KGB. During the farewell meeting, a senior official asked if I had a special wish for my future in Germany. I cautiously hinted that I would love to live in a single-family house, similar to the one I had grown up in. His response was quite encouraging.

"I think that can be arranged," he said with a wry smile. Using a Russian idiom that implied some sort of trickery, he added, "We'll do some creative accounting."

He also gave me a glimpse of the Center's plans for my future.

"First you will have fun relaxing with your family, but soon you will get bored. Your son will bring home bad grades, and you will get antsy and hungry for action. But trust me, we will find something exciting for you."

As it happened, Matthias never brought home a bad grade. He inherited my propensity for math and science, and today he has a doctorate in physical chemistry. (But I suppose we can cut the KGB officer some slack for not fully grasping the power of the Dittrich gene pool!) At the time, everything he said to me was encouraging, and as I left the meeting I was thinking, *Perhaps I could make the GDR my real home once again.*

Back at my job at MetLife, I soon earned my third promotion. It was good to be back with my buddies in IT, and it struck me how much I genuinely liked these guys.

To cover for my monthlong trip to Moscow and Berlin, I had told Penelope I was going on an extensive, cross-country bike trip. Nevertheless, she had been afraid she would never see me again, and she cried when I returned. She reminded me that she was betting her entire future on our relationship.

A few weeks later, I found out just how big of a bet that was.

One day, late in October, as Penelope and I were lounging around my apartment, she blurted out a confession.

"Jack, I am pregnant."

"What! Are you sure?"

"Very sure," she said. "I had a pregnancy test done by a doctor. And I don't care about your opinion in this matter; I'm going to keep this baby."

Not only was I an undercover spy, but now I was going to become an undercover father, as well.

At that moment, my clever plan for a clean breakup after Penelope received her green card went up in smoke. For several moments, I couldn't think, couldn't feel, and couldn't respond. I wanted to help her and I enjoyed being with her, but I knew I didn't love her.

As the magnitude of her announcement began to ripple through my brain, I knew I had to prepare her for the inevitable separation that would come when I returned to Germany in two years.

"Okay, this is hard for me to take," I said with intentional harshness, "but I respect your decision, and I always keep my promises. So I will go through with the marriage, and I will support you and the baby to the extent possible. But I don't see us as a real family, and I cannot see myself as an active father to the child."

My hurtful words had the desired effect, and Penelope cried long and hard. To my shame, I created a poisonous environment that would ultimately lead to the destruction of a marriage that never should have been.

✛ ✛ ✛

A wedding is usually a joyous event in a young couple's life. But given our circumstances, my wedding to Penelope—with no friends, no celebration, no dreams—felt like just another task to complete before the end of the day.

The ceremony was conducted at the Queens County Courthouse on December 10, 1986. Penelope's housemate, Margaret, served as our witness. After a modest meal together at a nearby diner, the three of us went our separate ways.

Two weeks later, we were ready to start the green card application process. To file for permanent residency of a spouse, couples had to appear in person at an office of the Immigration and Naturalization Service. On the last Monday of December—one of those dark, cold, and damp mornings when fall, winter, and spring fought to a miserable three-way tie—I met Penelope at 6:00 a.m. in front of the INS building, and we joined a line that had already grown to considerable length. We stood beside each other, barely speaking, as we waited for the doors to open.

By nine o'clock, the line had wrapped around the entire block. We squeezed into the large waiting hall inside the building as it filled to capacity. When the room was full, the doors were closed and anyone who had joined the line too late was told to come back another day.

After another three-hour wait inside the building, we were finally called to a counter where the clerk collected and reviewed our application and the accompanying documents.

A month later, we received an invitation for the dreaded interview, which was designed to ferret out fake marriages like ours. These interviews often played out like an episode of *The Newlywed Game*, where couples were separated and asked the same questions. The difference was that here, at the INS, it wasn't funny or entertaining when the answers didn't match.

But while questions such as "What does your living room look like?" or "What is your spouse's favorite food?" could easily trip up the inexperienced, I believed that with proper preparation we could easily pass the test. So Penelope and I had met several times to practice for the ordeal.

As it turned out, none of that was necessary. As we were ushered into the office, I saw the female interviewer take a knowing sideways glance at Penelope, whose well-rounded belly clearly showed she was pregnant. After that, it only took a minute for the woman to shuffle some papers, check a few boxes on the forms, and wish us luck. Penelope was elated, and I was happy that I had beaten the system again.

✦ ✦ ✦

Soon after my return to MetLife, I began to look for technology that I could obtain for the KGB. After many evenings of "overtime," in which I sorted through numerous unprotected electronic libraries, I found the perfect candidate, a highly popular industrial software package. The next night I stayed late again and printed out sixty pages of code. Back at my apartment, I photographed the individual pages and then sent them on to Moscow via a dead-drop operation on Staten Island. Whether Soviet engineers were ever able to make use of the code is unclear. It was a raw hexadecimal version without documentation. It would have to be reverse engineered, a tedious but doable task, in order to make it useful.

By 1987, the regular Thursday night shortwave transmission had become more of a nuisance than anything else—especially when I went to the trouble of decrypting a message only to find a birthday greeting or some proclamation about a Soviet holiday.

So when I saw the word *Congratulations* at the beginning of a message one night, I felt anger welling up inside me. I did not need to waste my time on yet another bit of rah-rah.

But as I decoded the rest of the message, my eyes grew bigger and bigger:

```
CONGRATULATIONS, COMRADE, IN RECOGNITION FOR YOUR
ACHIEVEMENTS AND YOUR DEDICATION TO THE REVOLUTIONARY
CAUSE, THE CENTRAL COMMITTEE OF THE COMMUNIST PARTY
OF THE SOVIET UNION HAS AWARDED YOU THE ORDER OF THE
RED BANNER AND A BONUS OF $10,000.
```

I stared at the words in disbelief. After never receiving as much as a letter of commendation, I was now being awarded the second highest decoration of the Soviet Union? This was an enormous honor, and it boded well for my future.

I knew that Sergej would have delivered the medal to Gerlinde, and I wondered how she had responded.

One day, I will be able to tell my mother, I thought. *When she finally understands what I've been doing, perhaps she will forgive me for all the secrets and lies over so many years.*

31

ONE BENEFIT OF MY MARRIAGE to Penelope was that she was covered by my health insurance from MetLife, which meant that most of the expenses associated with childbirth were covered. Like any expectant father, I often accompanied her to the prenatal exams. Because the hospital where she planned to deliver was only ten minutes from my apartment, I invited her to stay at my place when she was a few days from her due date.

Summer made an early entrance in 1987, and by the last weekend of May, the outside temperatures hovered around ninety degrees. Without air-conditioning or ceiling fans, my apartment was not a comfortable place for someone close to giving birth.

By the following Monday morning, my patience with Penelope's moaning and complaining about false alarms had worn thin. So when she told me that her water might have broken—but she wasn't sure— I decided to take charge. "Get up and get dressed. I'm driving you to the hospital right now."

The ten-minute drive to Elmhurst felt like an eternity. No other high-pressure situation during my undercover existence could measure up to the tension I felt while driving Penelope to the hospital. When we arrived at St. John's, I parked the car near the entrance, left the hazard lights on, and accompanied Penelope to admissions.

As we walked up the steps, I saw a trail of blood trickling down one of her legs. This caught the eye of an alert nurse, and Penelope was rushed to a birthing room—the admissions paperwork could wait.

I raced back outside to move the car to a legal parking spot in the neighborhood, and it took me about twenty minutes to get back to the hospital. I went upstairs to the maternity ward and joined a handful of nervous expectant fathers for what I thought would be a long wait. But I had barely settled into one of the vinyl-covered seats when a nurse popped into the waiting room and said joyfully, "Mr. Barsky, you have a girl!"

This now was my third child. I wasn't man enough to be there for Edeltraud when she gave birth to Günter, and I wasn't able to be with Gerlinde when Matthias came into the world, but this time I was able to see my newborn daughter soon after her birth.

A nurse guided me through seemingly endless hospital corridors to a room containing several clear bassinets, and I saw my daughter for the first time.

"Chelsea," I said out loud as I leaned closer and saw her tiny fingers and toes.

The medical staff had decided to put the otherwise healthy nine-pound baby girl in an incubator as a precaution because of the early water break. I felt sorry for the lonely little pink creature who was deprived of her mother's touch. Little did I know that the day would come when this seemingly helpless baby would radically change my life and teach me the power of true love.

After two days in the incubator, Chelsea was reunited with Penelope, and the next day both mother and daughter were released from the hospital. I picked them up, and as I carried the bassinet with the precious cargo through the hallways of the hospital, something strange stirred inside me. This was my daughter! One day she would grow up and perhaps look a little like me and be a little like me.

I chased away this unwelcome emotion. My primary responsibility was to the KGB, and my real life was back in Berlin waiting for me. I would care for this baby and her mother as much as possible, but the unchanged plan was to set up Penelope to fend for herself. After all, there were millions of single mothers in the world, and she would learn to manage just fine.

With my income from work, I was able to afford my own apartment as well as a furnished apartment in Queens for Penelope and Chelsea. I would make sure there was always food, baby formula, and other needed supplies, and I would go with them for doctor's visits. What I didn't know was how I would care for them once I was gone.

For the next nine months, Penelope lived alone with her baby, fully dependent on a fake husband for support and with little hope for a secure and happy future. During the week, her only companions were Chelsea and a color TV. On weekends when I wasn't busy with work for the Center, I often drove over and took the two of them to a nearby park. But for the most part, I was so wrapped up in my work for MetLife and the KGB that it never occurred to me to wonder how it must have felt for Penelope to endure that kind of seclusion. That experience left another big gash in our marriage of convenience.

✛ ✛ ✛

It didn't take long for Chelsea to shed the look of a newborn. Every time I paid a visit, I noticed something new. Her large dark-brown eyes were her first distinguishable feature, before she began growing a full head of curly jet-black hair. Her toothless smile stirred something in my heart I had never felt before. But what sealed my affection for her was the day I entered her room and found her standing in her crib, holding on to the rail. As soon as she saw me, her entire face lit up with the most radiant smile I had ever seen. Without any words, the message was clear: "I love you, Dad."

Love tiptoed up on me—at first almost imperceptibly, but in the end, undeniably. And this love was unconditional. It came from deep within me and wasn't linked to or rooted in desire. It was pure and powerful. All I wanted to do was take care of this little one and protect her, expecting nothing in return.

Along with all this love grew an equally strong emotion: *guilt*.

Like a torturing demon that never left my side—when I awoke, when I was at work, when I was doing my KGB activities, and when I closed my eyes to sleep—this guilt hounded me with the one question I couldn't answer: *How are you going to take care of this helpless baby?*

Guilt is a hard emotion for anybody, but the fact that I felt it at all showed that I was becoming a different person. The wall of protection I had built around my heart—the impenetrable armor that had allowed me to walk away from numerous human connections with only a tinge of remorse—was beginning to crumble, and I had no idea how to stop the process.

When Chelsea was nine months old, the landlord in Queens told Penelope that she had to vacate her apartment. After a two-week search for a reasonably priced alternative yielded no results, serendipity once again came to the rescue. Our real estate agent showed us a spacious two-bedroom apartment on the second floor of a two-family home in Ozone Park.

There have been many occasions in my life when the word *serendipity* seems the most appropriate descriptor. I used to think it was accidental dumb luck, but I've come to believe that it was actually the hand of God working in the background of my life to open doors I didn't even know existed and lead me onto a path that only He could know and foresee.

As I inspected the apartment, it occurred to me that the layout made it suitable for the three of us to live together. There was a small study at the far end of a long hallway that would allow me to continue my operational activities—primarily radio reception and secret writing—without being disrupted or discovered. After mulling it over for a day, I talked to Penelope about it and signed the lease for us to live together.

When we moved into that apartment in April 1988, I made it very clear that I was never to be disturbed when I was working in the study.

"I'm working on some intricate computer code that could one day be sold for a lot of money," I told Penelope, and she never once knocked on the door while I was holed up in that room.

Out of our new togetherness, the seeds of a somewhat normal family life began to sprout. There were more walks in the park and more opportunities for Mom and Dad to spend time together with their always smiling baby. There was a first birthday party and Chelsea's first tentative steps. And there was a visit to my office, where all the ladies shrieked with delight at the sight of my beautiful little girl, with her dark, curly hair and big, curious eyes.

One day, while Penelope was waiting for me in the lobby at One Madison Avenue, she put Chelsea on a table near one of the elevator banks. At one point, a woman approached slowly with a curious look on her face, and when she came close enough to see, she let out a startled cry.

"Oh my! I thought this was a doll!"

These times when people made a fuss over Chelsea made me swell with pride. After all, this was *my* child.

Summer came and went, and by autumn 1988, it was already a few weeks past the agreed-upon end date of my ten-year assignment in the United States. I wasn't sure why there was a delay, but I didn't broach the subject in my communications. My mind was like that of the haunted creature in the famous series of expressionist paintings by Edvard Munch called *Der Schrei der Natur*—more commonly known as *The Scream*. Like me, the tortured soul in those paintings is covering his ears as if to avoid the persistent question of an ever-present demon.

How are you going to take care of this helpless baby?

My demon also had an ally—time—which was moving relentlessly forward and would ultimately force an answer to the unanswerable question.

Confessing my sin to the KGB was out of the question. It would only trigger a punishment of unpredictable severity. All I could do was wait and hope that a solution would miraculously appear.

PART IV

THE DEATH
OF A SPY

32

IN EARLY DECEMBER 1988, the clock finally ran out for me.

As I translated a shortwave radiogram from digits into letters, the message began to sound more and more ominous.

```
PREPARE FOR URGENT DEPARTURE. WE HAVE REASON TO
BELIEVE THAT YOUR COVER HAS BEEN BLOWN. YOU ARE IN
SEVERE DANGER. LISTEN ON THIS FREQUENCY EVERY DAY TO
RECEIVE FURTHER INSTRUCTIONS. CONFIRM RECEIPT OF THIS
MESSAGE WITH SIGNAL AT REGULAR SIGNAL LOCATION. THIS
IS AN ORDER.
```

I left my little study and softly closed the door behind me so as not to disturb Penelope and Chelsea, who were already asleep. I heard Chelsea stir, but luckily she did not wake up. I leaned against the wall, drained of all energy, creativity, and drive.

I had no idea what to do next. So I stalled and did not set the signal. As a result, the Center could only assume I had not received the message.

Exactly one week later, the radiogram from the prior week was repeated verbatim. Again I ignored it, while furiously searching my mind for a solution to this dilemma. By now, the comrades at the Center would be trying to make sense of the situation. There were all kinds of possible reasons for my silence. Maybe I had fallen ill or been injured, as had happened a few years earlier. Maybe the shortwave signal had degraded to a point where it was no longer audible. Maybe I had accidentally destroyed the pad used to decipher the messages.

Or worst of all, maybe I had already been arrested and was under interrogation.

After another week passed, the Center escalated the emergency drill. On Monday morning, I spotted the danger signal on my way to work. A resident agent had placed a large red dot on a metal support beam for the elevated tracks at 80th and Hudson, which they knew I passed every day. The meaning of this signal was unequivocal: *Leave the country immediately, using the predetermined emergency route.*

The meaning of *immediately* was quite literal. When I saw the warning, I was supposed to grab enough money for a trip to Toronto, retrieve a set of emergency documents—including a Canadian birth certificate and driver's license—and cross the border as soon as possible. I was then to travel to Toronto, where I would contact the Soviet embassy, and the comrades there would make arrangements for my exfiltration.

On one of my early forays into the boroughs of New York City, I had stashed my emergency documents in a safe, long-term outdoor hiding place in the Bronx. But instead of following orders and retrieving my travel kit, I ignored the screaming red dot and continued on my commute to work.

The Center finally decided on a last desperate measure. A week after the first appearance of the red dot, a resident agent approached me on the subway platform and whispered an ominous phrase that would rattle around in my head for a long time: "You must come home or else you are dead."

I was stunned but not panicked. After looking around and ascertaining that nobody could have overheard this brief encounter, I got on my train as usual and went to work. I didn't get much done that day, however, as my mind wrestled with a million thoughts.

One thing was clear: I couldn't stall any longer. The KGB now knew that I knew, and I was forced to choose. I must either obey the order to return home with a reasonable explanation for my temporary silence or find a way to ignore the order and stay in the United States.

Applying logic and weighing the consequences of either decision, I wrote down my thoughts.

IF ALBRECHT GOES HOME . . .	IF JACK STAYS IN NEW YORK . . .
Rejoin my German family and live my life in peace and safety.	Take on a double risk—either of going to jail because my cover had been blown or of being kidnapped or assassinated by the KGB.
Be a hero in my own country and enjoy the rewards the KGB had promised, including a single-family house in the suburbs.	Assuming I wasn't caught or killed, continue to live the life of a programmer residing in a modest apartment with Penelope and Chelsea.
Reconnect with old friends.	Retain my new friends and my very satisfying job as a computer programmer.
Find the peace that would come with a fully legal existence in my homeland.	Lead a peaceful, quasi-legal existence for the rest of my life.
Rejoin a system and a party whose viability and validity I had begun to question.	Enjoy the freedom the United States grants its citizens.
Never see Chelsea again.	Never see Gerlinde and Matthias again.
Lose the ability to support Chelsea. (Considering that her mother has only four years of formal schooling, Chelsea may grow up in poverty.)	Not be able to support Matthias directly. (This concern was somewhat mitigated by the knowledge that he was supported by a functioning family structure and that the GDR generally did not let children slip through the cracks.)

For any reasonable man motivated by self-preservation, the equation was severely tilted in favor of returning home. However, I was not the same coldhearted, mission-focused individual I had been in the past, who would choose only the most logical and self-serving option.

During my time with Chelsea, I had discovered my heart. It was as if she made me human, perhaps more human than I'd ever been. When I looked at her face, so innocent and pure, so trusting and dependent, there didn't seem to be a choice at all. Though staying in the US was utterly risky and completely foolish, somehow this sweet little child's mere existence put the equation in balance.

I still hadn't made a final decision by the following Thursday, when I deciphered the weekly radiogram. The Center was calling me for a dead-drop operation the very next day.

The location for the operation was Clove Lakes Park on Staten Island. After retrieving the container with a passport and travel money, I was to immediately leave the US and make contact with a KGB representative in Toronto.

It was around 11:00 p.m. when I finished deciphering the radiogram. Chelsea and Penelope were already fast asleep. I kissed them both lightly on the cheek, still uncertain about what I would decide to do. After getting very little rest that night, I left early the next morning before the two of them awoke. Though I was committed to complete the drop operation, I was not yet committed to leave the country. Once I retrieved the travel documents, though, I would have to choose.

I drove my car to the Hunters Point Avenue station of the #7 subway line and took the subway to work, arriving shortly before 8:00 a.m. For the next four hours, I stared at the flickering green display of my computer screen, unable to do any real work. At lunchtime, I excused myself under the pretense of a splitting headache. I then took the Queens-bound #7 train, retrieved my car, and drove to Staten Island. The drop operation was scheduled at 3:15 sharp, as usual.

As I walked through the heavily wooded park, I had every reason to believe the operation would be routine. It was a cold late-autumn weekday and the park was essentially deserted. The location, which I had selected and transmitted to the Center, was one of my favorites, with a drop site next to the roots of a large fallen tree about 300 feet from the edge of the park to the right of a narrow, winding walkway.

As I approached the area, the "container deposited" sign was clearly visible on the designated lamp pole. When I reached the fallen tree with my plastic shopping bag at the ready, I expected to see an old oilcan nearby. But at first glance, I saw nothing.

Maintaining the casual posture of a man on a stroll in the park, I looked around more thoroughly.

Still nothing.

After a minute or two, the truth began to sink in: There was no container.

This can't be!

In my confusion, I widened the search perimeter, but to no avail—there was no container to be found.

During my ten years as an active agent, I had conducted six dead-drop operations and six meetings—and every one of them went like clockwork. There was no reason for this time to be any different. The drop site was easy to find and identify, the signal had been set—I checked it again—but the drop had not been made.

I couldn't imagine that a passerby had seen my contact drop the oil can and picked it up, or that my contact had faked the operation and kept the money for himself. Both explanations seemed highly unlikely, if not nearly impossible.

Without the travel documents, I couldn't execute the departure plan. I think, subconsciously, that was exactly what I was hoping for—that someone or something would make the decision for me. Was it luck, or something more?

Of course, I had the option of asking the Center for a repeat, but as I drove back to my apartment, the final decision took shape: I was going to take the risk and stay behind.

All of a sudden, the anxiety I had carried in my heart for weeks—the worry of leaving my young daughter to an uncertain future and never being able to see her again—gave way to an inner peace I hadn't felt in months.

✤ ✤ ✤

Making the decision to stay was one thing, but how could I make a clean break from the KGB? They weren't going to let a rogue agent just walk away.

Defection was not an option. By now, I had already betrayed my mother and brother, as well as Gerlinde and Matthias. I didn't want to make things worse by betraying my country and my friends who still lived there. I was also concerned that the American authorities might put me in jail, deport Penelope, and make Chelsea a ward of the state.

But what could I tell the KGB that would minimize the chances of retaliation against Gerlinde and Matthias—as well as keep me safe here in the US?

The idea struck me like a bolt of lightning. During one of my meetings with Alex in Moscow, he had mentioned the AIDS epidemic that had ravaged certain sectors of the American population, and he had seen it as a clear sign of the decay of capitalist society. "We just need to be very careful not to let the virus in here," he said. "I hope we will soon have a test to screen out infected would-be visitors."

AIDS—*that's it!*

At that time, an AIDS diagnosis was the equivalent of a death sentence. The Soviets wouldn't want me back if I was infected, and in time they would assume I had passed away.

I walked around for days thinking it through. Could it really work? It had to.

I penned a letter using secret writing, telling the KGB that I could not return to Moscow because I had been diagnosed with AIDS three months earlier. To make my story as credible as possible, I traced my infection back to a woman I had dated and profiled in the past. I claimed she had caught the disease from a drug addict ex-boyfriend. I assured the Center that I would not commit treason by contacting the US authorities, that my focus was on getting whatever treatment I could, but the prognosis was not good. Finally, I asked them to tell Gerlinde the bad news and give her the savings of approximately $60,000 that had accumulated in my account.

For days, I monitored the shortwave frequency every night, and every night there was action on the airwaves. I made no attempt to write down the message or decode it, but I knew what it said.

"Come home or you are dead."

"Come home or you are dead."

"Come home or you are dead."

Then one day the voice went silent. No more mesmerizing dits and dahs in the ether. The Center had apparently received my letter.

With amazement, I realized that this was the end. Everything I had worked for had now been abandoned—all for the love of a father for his daughter. Even more amazing to me was that I knew it was the right choice.

Many years later, I found out that the big lie had worked exactly as intended. I had stumbled onto what was likely the only viable exit strategy—and I had succeeded in deceiving the mighty KGB.

My established reputation for complete honesty must have played a role in their decision not to pursue me; they had swallowed my story hook, line, and sinker. During a final contact with Gerlinde, Sergej had handed her the $60,000 bankroll—what a fortune for an East German in 1988!—and told her I had died from AIDS.

✦ ✦ ✦

For several weeks after the radio transmissions went silent, I remained in execution mode. I burned the contact paper used for secret writing and destroyed the pads with the encryption numbers. As a precaution to avoid any "accidents," I began to alter the pattern of my daily routine—changing the times when I would leave the house in the morning and return at night, and varying the route I took by alternating between two subway stations that were near my apartment.

No one could have ever guessed what was happening beneath the surface in my life—especially my little girl. Whenever Chelsea saw me, she reached up her arms with complete trust and affection. She could say a few words by now, and the things she pointed out made me see the world with new eyes. Her unquestioning love for me both astounded and assured me that the risk I had taken was justified.

Several weeks after the final radio transmission, I drove to a parking spot near the 59th Street Bridge and took the Blaupunkt shortwave receiver from the trunk of my car. Walking out to the middle of the bridge and seeing that no one was around, I dropped the radio into the East River. The sight of that radio disappearing into the murky waters is still etched in my memory as the final act of my separation from the KGB. By destroying the radio, I silenced the voice of my former masters forever.

✦ ✦ ✦

The spring melt of 1989 symbolically captured the inner thaw I experienced as the fear and tension of the past winter gave way to feelings of peace and security. The zigzag routes to and from work were abandoned, and Chelsea's second birthday party wasn't overshadowed by any anxiety about the future.

In November 1989, I witnessed the fall of the Berlin Wall on television. And as the Germans broke down the barrier dividing East and West Berlin, stories of suffering and separation imposed by the Communist regime began to emerge. They were stories I hadn't heard before.

I watched it all from my adopted homeland with the emotions of a distant observer. My interest in politics and international relations had been replaced by a focus on my young family and the goal we had to establish ourselves as members of the American middle class.

As far as the KGB and Gerlinde were concerned, Albrecht Dittrich was dead. And the American Jack Barsky had no connection to that once divided country across the ocean.

33

WITH THE DECISION MADE and the uncertainty gone about my future, I became a normal person. There were no more late-night "computer coding sessions" on Thursdays or occasional all-day absences on Saturdays. My life now revolved around work and home.

My job became even more demanding—and rewarding. In May, I received another promotion, which came with significantly more responsibility. I was now in charge of about a thousand overnight program runs that adjudicated medical claims, created checks, and printed statements for more than one million policy holders. When things went wrong, regardless of the time, I would get a call from the computer operators—which often disrupted the sleep of our entire family. I frequently complained to Penelope about these calls, and like a true partner she decided to do something about it.

One morning, I showed up at the office as usual, but when I got off the elevator on the nineteenth floor, a welcoming committee was waiting for me in the hallway—including the vice president of our department, who was clearly fuming.

"Jack, where have you been?" he said. "The overnight processing stopped, statements and checks are not going out—but even worse, there are five hundred claims adjusters across the country twiddling their thumbs waiting for the system to come back up. I have been getting phone calls from executives all the way up the chain. You had better have a good explanation."

I stared at him in shock. "I did not get a single call last night," I said. "And believe me, I always hear the phone. I'm a very light sleeper."

"Just get to work and fix this problem right away. And when you get home, make arrangements to get your phone fixed. This can't happen again."

I fixed the computer glitch, and at lunchtime I called home. When I asked Penelope if she knew anything about the problem with the phone, she said, "You're always complaining about it waking us up at night. I simply took it off the hook so we could get a good night's sleep."

When I got home that night, I made it clear that middle-of-the-night phone calls were a necessary part of my job. "That's one of the reasons they pay us so well. We just have to grin and bear it."

Soon after this event, Penelope received her green card and started her first full-time job. She had taken a word processing course and was hired by a real estate development company in Manhattan. Now that we were both working full-time, we joined the ranks of American parents who had to make child care arrangements. We found a kind, elderly Italian woman who lived only a block away from our apartment, and MetLife's management was extremely accommodating in allowing me the flexibility I needed to make the arrangement work. Penelope dropped off Chelsea on her way to work in the morning, and I started my workday at 7:00 a.m. so that I could pick up Chelsea on my way home at 4:00 p.m.

This gave us about two hours of exclusive "daddy time" before Penelope got home. When the weather was good, I took Chelsea to the local McDonalds playground, and when we were forced inside, I read her picture books such as *Don't Forget the Oatmeal!*, featuring Bert and Ernie from *Sesame Street*. Chelsea's favorite toy was a set of wooden blocks, and she loved to watch me assemble rickety structures that she would gleefully collapse with the touch of her hand.

Her thick dark hair often got tangled, and Penelope didn't always have the patience to deal with the mess. Chelsea would end up crying out in pain when her mother tried to brush out the snarls.

"Come sit here, little princess, and I'll take care of it," I'd say when the tangles got too bad. I would remove the knots strand by strand, minimizing the pain by holding onto the tufts of hair as close to the scalp as possible. This together time, and the ways in which I was able to care for Chelsea, really cemented our daddy-daughter bond.

Around the time that the Berlin Wall came down, I made another decision that reflected my determination to build a life in America.

Taking Penelope aside one day, I said, "I've been thinking about us and the future. Would you consider having another child?"

Penelope was delighted, and we embarked on that journey the very same night.

Another sign that I was settling into an American middle-class lifestyle was my enrollment in the company's 401(k) plan, which all of a sudden made a lot of sense. I also began to pay more attention to the lunchtime discussions about houses and mortgages. Penelope and I, two illegal immigrants living in the US as quasi-legals, were ready to pursue one of the key elements of the American dream: a single-family home in the suburbs.

✦ ✦ ✦

As I fully embraced my American existence, I eradicated all things German from my mind. Any thoughts about Germany and the people I had left behind would only torture my conscience, so I stashed all my memories away and tried to move forward as if my mother, my brother, Gerlinde, and even Matthias had never existed. It was as if, with Albrecht's death, they, too, were no more. In truth, I did not speculate about the effects that my sudden disappearance may have had on those left behind or the reaction of my handlers and connections in the KGB. Even if I wanted to, there was no way to contact my mother without risking myself and my new family.

Meanwhile, a sense of urgency accelerated our house hunt as we headed into the summer of 1990.

One Saturday afternoon, Chelsea insisted that we take her outside to play. Neither I nor Penelope had time at the moment, and letting Chelsea go outside by herself was not an option.

A few minutes after I had given Chelsea a decisive *no*, I was startled by the sound of shattering glass. The little tyke had tried to take things into her own hands—or rather, her own feet—by kicking in the glass door that separated our upstairs apartment from the downstairs.

Fortunately, she was not hurt, but she had given us a clear message, as only a two-and-a-half-year-old can: "I want freedom!"

Another reason to expedite our search was the fact that Penelope was now pregnant again. Chelsea was thrilled at the prospect of a little brother or sister, but even more so by the news a few weeks later that we had finally purchased our first home. For the next several days, she marched around the apartment singing songs about the castle she was moving into, where she could run "upstairs and downstairs, and downstairs and upstairs."

One month after Chelsea's third birthday, we gave her the best present ever—a castle with stairs. On a very hot day during the first week of July, we loaded our modest belongings onto a move-it-yourself van and drove to our new home in Washingtonville, New York, about sixty miles north of New York City.

For both Penelope and me, this house was far beyond what we had ever dared to imagine in our dreams. And even the heavens seemed delighted. On the day we moved in, a huge rainbow decorated the sky right above our home.

With my job continuing to go well, I earned enough money for Penelope to be a stay-at-home mom to Chelsea and the new baby, who was soon to arrive. Though suburban life suited us well, the two-hour commute to the city was pure torture. I was now part of the great American trade-off, sacrificing my time in exchange for better and cheaper housing.

I was also able to replace my old run-down Honda with a brand-new Toyota Camry. This reliable new vehicle came in handy on the evening of September 30, 1990, when Penelope turned to me and said, "I think I'm having contractions."

Based on our experience with Chelsea, Penelope and I wasted no time in getting out the door. After throwing some clothes on Chelsea, the three of us raced into the night on a wet, leaf-covered country road.

When we arrived at Goshen Hospital, Penelope was immediately admitted to the delivery room. Because children were not allowed and we had no one to watch Chelsea, she and I took seats in the waiting room.

But we didn't have to wait long. True to form, Penelope delivered the baby within a half hour of our arrival, and soon the nurse was announcing for all to hear, "Mr. Barsky, you have a son!"

With Jessie's arrival, we were now the perfect American family—with a daughter, a son, and a house in the suburbs. My life, which until only recently had been filled with plans and reports, secrets and subterfuge, had slowed down to a safe and comfortable pace.

But no matter how much I wanted to control my own destiny, I could not. While I was settling into my new life in New York, a retired KGB archivist by the name of Vasili Mitrokhin was preparing a huge stash of notes he had collected over the years. From out of the crumbling remains of the Soviet Union, he was ready to share this information with the West. Among the many secrets contained in those notes was a name I had come to call my own: Jack Barsky.

34

IN LATE 1991, the news of upcoming changes shook up the normally tranquil atmosphere in the offices of MetLife. One day, my manager, Mark, asked me to join him in a small conference room. As soon as he closed the door, he began talking in a hushed, almost conspiratorial voice.

"Listen, Jack, the company has made a decision to move our entire department to New Jersey."

My jaw dropped. "Man, I just bought a house up north. There's no way I can commute to New Jersey."

Mark smiled and said, "We know that. We have identified you as one of a handful of key employees who will get full relocation assistance. We want you to come with us."

So off we went on our second house-hunting adventure in eighteen months, this time in eastern Pennsylvania. After a disappointing first day driving all around the area with a real estate agent, we were on our way home when a house we passed caught Penelope's attention.

"Look, it has a 'For Sale' sign, and it looks really nice," Penelope said, grabbing my arm.

"Okay, we can come back next week to look at it."

The following Saturday, we went to see the house. As soon as we walked inside, any thoughts I had of considering the pros and cons went out the window.

"I want this house," Penelope announced without further ado.

"But the price seems high, and there's not much landscaping."

"I don't care. This is the house I want."

Penelope's declaration became the first and last word on the matter, and exactly two years after moving into our first house, we moved out and made our way to rural Mount Bethel, Pennsylvania. When I say *rural*, I mean we had only one neighbor within earshot, and the nearest place to buy something was a gas station two miles away. But the house had all the features of Penelope's dream home, and the setting was paradise for the kids. It also made my commute quite bearable, with a scenic drive over the hills, through the woods, and across the Delaware River before joining the bustling traffic around the commercial hub of Bridgewater, New Jersey.

Without the long commute to New York City, my work-life balance was restored. I had more time to play with the kids, who were five and two by then, and we could afford a second car—making Penelope mobile for the first time since moving out of New York City. It seemed as if we were settling into a long period of stability.

In the fall of 1992, Chelsea was supposed to start kindergarten. However, a routine placement test revealed that her verbal abilities were trailing those of her peers by almost two years. This was a shock and a revelation for me—and from that point on I stopped using "smarts" as the defining criterion in my relationships with other people. I told my colleagues at work, "I think my daughter is a little dummy, but I love her anyway."

It turned out that my "little dummy" was actually hearing impaired and was otherwise sharp as a whip. She had developed the ability to read lips and was fooling everyone around her. Hearing aids and a special education program soon allowed my little princess to catch up with the rest of her class.

+ + +

During the summer of 1994, Penelope and I loaded up the kids for our first family vacation, a visit to Penelope's half-brother and his family in Toronto, by way of Niagara Falls.

As I drove across the Rainbow Bridge into Canada, I was briefly reminded of my previous life as a spy. Only four years earlier, this bridge was to have been my conduit to safety. But that memory was so far removed from my current reality that it seemed to have come from another universe.

But as we were taking in the awe-inspiring views at Niagara Falls, the shadows of the past were descending on our home in Mount Bethel. The name "Jack Barsky" had arrived at the FBI office in Allentown, and special agent Joe Reilly was appointed as lead agent in what was determined to be the most important counterintelligence case by the FBI at that time. While we were away on vacation, a team of FBI agents quietly broke into our house and conducted a thorough search.

The following year, when Penelope made a trip to visit her aging uncle in London, the FBI alerted MI5—the British version of the FBI—and they followed Penelope during the entire week of her stay. Neither she nor I had a clue.

Through a merger and subsequent acquisition at MetLife, my department became part of United Healthcare. I took advantage of the change to advance into the management ranks. My second assignment took me to Minneapolis, and I traveled back and forth on a weekly basis. What I didn't know was that the FBI routinely searched my car while it was parked in the long-term lot at the airport. My transition from undercover spy to normal, everyday American was so complete that I suspected nothing.

✛ ✛ ✛

Over the next few years, what appeared to be a stable and happy family was slowly crumbling on the inside. My relationship with Penelope was not on solid footing. No matter how well I took care of her material needs, she sensed that there was an important ingredient missing: genuine love.

She once told me, "You are a great provider and a great father, but a lousy husband."

I didn't know what she meant by that. She drove the better car, and I brought flowers home on a regular basis. Was it that I didn't want to go with her to the clubs she liked to visit? Or was it my refusal to join her for a Julio Iglesias concert? This lack of understanding reflected the inadequate level of my awareness at the time, but somehow even this thick-skinned German noticed that something was going in the wrong direction.

In an attempt to bring more unity to our family, I agreed to attend Sunday mass with Penelope. For about three years, the four of us attended a Catholic church in nearby Stroudsburg. To an agnostic like me, the Catholic mass was emotionally neutral and intellectually meaningless. It was neither attractive nor off-putting. I enjoyed the organ music and some of the short sermons, but all the rituals that had meaning for the Catholic congregation didn't mean much to me or the children. The kids sat through the hour-long mass in anticipation of the fast-food reward they expected to receive afterwards, and I was always glad when the service was over.

When going to church failed to heal our marriage, I made a proposal. One morning I sat down with Penelope in the kitchen and started the conversation.

"I know that to you there is something missing in our relationship. Can you tell me what I can do to fix it?"

"You can't fix something you broke a long time ago."

"I understand," I said contritely. "But I'm willing to make a fresh start. How about if we renew our vows on our tenth anniversary? This time we can do it in a church with a priest and a real reception afterward. What do you say?"

"You think that all you have to do is put a big Band-Aid on old wounds and everything will be well. You treated me like a nuisance when we first met, and I got used to it. Now you want to fix it by waving a magic wand? I think it's too late for that."

"But can we just agree that the past was bad, but we still have a long future ahead of us? Why not try to make it better?"

"I don't think it's going to work," she said. "We just need to find a way to coexist."

For some time, I had wondered whether I should ever tell Penelope the truth about the years when we were first together and of all my years before that. Frustrated that she wasn't willing to try to work on our relationship—even if, admittedly, it had been bad for a long time—I at least wanted her to understand me. I decided to use my secret weapon.

"I need to tell you something."

Penelope waited, but signs of impatience were evident on her face.

"This should give you an idea of how much I love you, Chelsea, and

Jessie. When I first met you, I worked for the Russians. I was actually a spy. My real name is Albrecht Dittrich, but I have lived in America as Jack Barsky for a long time. Not long after Chelsea was born, the Russians wanted me to return to Moscow, but I couldn't leave you and Chelsea, so I severed my ties with the KGB. Do you know what I've risked for you? I could have been captured or even killed. Does that mean anything to you?"

Penelope's response was totally unexpected. At first, I thought she didn't believe me. I could see her mind working as she processed what I had just revealed. After a lengthy pause, she said, "So what you're telling me is that you're in this country illegally? That means I am not really legal either. What if they find out and throw us both out of the country and take Jessie and Chelsea away from me?"

With that, she ran out the back door crying. My secret weapon had completely backfired.

As it turned out, that backfire caused more damage than I could have possibly guessed. The FBI had bugged our house during their break-in, and they were listening to the entire conversation. They now knew that they had their man, and they even had a taped confession.

PART V

THE CATCHING OF A SPY

35

BY THE MIDDLE OF MAY 1997, warm weather had taken over in the Northeast. It was a Friday, and I wanted to leave work as early as possible, eager for a head start on a great spring weekend in the country. I was especially looking forward to a game of two-on-one basketball with my children, who at the ages of ten and seven had already become serious competition for their aging dad.

At four o'clock, I decided to make a run for it. Cautiously sneaking through the maze of cubicles, taking a circuitous route to avoid the boss' office, I slipped out the door and sprinted to the parking lot.

Four months earlier, I had resigned from United Healthcare and accepted a director's position with Prudential. The fifty-mile drive to our house in Mount Bethel was a welcome change from longer commutes in the past.

Today, as expected, the westbound traffic on I-80 was stop-and-go. After forty-five minutes of battling an army of fellow commuters from the seat of my white Mazda 323, I was finally in the clear. It would be smooth sailing until I hit the Portland-Columbia Toll Bridge just five minutes from my house. As I emerged from the tollgates, a Pennsylvania state trooper waved me over for what appeared to be a routine traffic stop.

"Sir, would you please step out of the car?" he asked when I rolled down my window. I thought this was a little strange, but I still was not alarmed.

Then I noticed another man—in civilian clothes—approaching the car. He was a middle-aged, stocky fellow with a receding hairline. He held up a badge and said in a calm voice, "Special Agent Reilly, FBI. We would like to talk with you."

I'm certain that I looked stunned by these words, which seemed to come from a parallel universe I had left light-years ago. My past had finally caught up with me.

✦ ✦ ✦

What I didn't know yet was that the FBI had started working on the Barsky case in late 1993. When they zeroed in on my location, the case was assigned to the Allentown office, and Special Agent Joe Reilly was put in charge. With his extensive experience in counterintelligence, he was up to the task.

After speaking to Elisha Lee Barsky, whose son Jack had passed away in 1955, it was clear to Agent Reilly that they had their fish on the hook—but they had no idea how big that fish might be.

Even though the Soviet Union had collapsed two years earlier, there was always a chance that a sleeper agent or an entire cell was still operative—or at least ready to be reawakened. Because I had helped Penelope gain citizenship, the suspicion was that we were working as a couple, a frequently used mode of operation by Soviet agents.

Furthermore, I had applied for a US passport via the mail in 1989. Although the passport was issued, I never received it. But the notion that I had emergency cash and a valid US passport raised the possibility that I was a flight risk.

Joe Reilly, however, had come to the conclusion that I had fully integrated into American society and that my affection for my children made it very likely that I would cooperate fully with the American authorities. The plan for the first encounter was to detain me but not arrest me, and to demand my full cooperation without any promises in return.

Of course, I didn't know any of this, and I feared the worst. Reilly later told me that the moment I saw his badge, all the blood drained from my face and I turned white as a sheet. However, he also marveled at my quick recovery and the coolness and fatalistic stoicism I displayed throughout the evening.

The FBI's preparations for the day of the encounter were meticulous. The tollgate was an ideal point to stop me away from my home. For what was to follow, the Reilly team had rented an entire wing of the Pocono Inn at Water Gap in the borough of Delaware Water Gap.

Agent Reilly drove the car, and his partner, David Roe, joined me in the backseat. Noticing that Roe had a gun strapped to his ankle reminded me that this was very serious business. As we made our way north on Route 611, I asked the most important question: "Am I under arrest?"

"No."

That simple answer brought me a glimmer of hope.

Next, I displayed a sense of gallows humor by asking, "What took you so long?"

The answer was suppressed laughter—the ice was almost broken.

After a fifteen-minute ride along a winding country road, we reached the hotel. Inside, I noticed guards at both ends of the hallway as I was escorted to a room in the middle.

Inside the room were a number of thick binders lined up on shelves around the walls. These binders were labeled with bits and pieces of information of my early years in the US. One of the labels contained the Ella Borisch convenience address I had used until 1981. Another one had "Dieter" written in big letters on it.

These props were an obvious psychological trick, which I recognized immediately in spite of the pressure I was under. The binders were indeed empty, but there was nothing the FBI needed to do to convince me that the only way out of this precarious situation was 100 percent full cooperation.

I emphatically volunteered this logic to my captors, and I believe they understood. Other than my family and myself, I had nothing left to defend. By 1997, I had lost any illusions I once had about the Communist ideal. With that gone, any vestige of loyalty to my erstwhile employer and its representatives had melted as well.

After we sat down, Joe Reilly began the debriefing with a simple statement: "Jack, this does not have to be the worst day of your life."

The glimmer of hope became a small flickering flame.

Before the debriefing session began, I was allowed to call Penelope and tell her I was going to be late because of some problems at work. Having studied me in great detail, Reilly knew I was suffering from hypertension. It was quite comforting to hear him ask whether I needed my blood pressure medication.

The first session covered all the basics, such as real name, date and place of birth, education, and recruitment.

After two hours, Agent Reilly told me I'd be released for the night to return to my home. He said I should spend the weekend trying to relax. That was easy for him to say. I wouldn't begin to relax for another few weeks. Just prior to releasing me, Reilly introduced me to the head of the surveillance unit, who said to me with the face and tone of a headmaster addressing an undisciplined student, "Don't even think about running. We will be watching your house, and we have every road and intersection in the area covered. You cannot get away."

That warning wasn't necessary. Flight wasn't an option for me—where would I go? Instead, I spent Sunday, May 18, 1997, my real forty-eighth birthday, wondering where I would celebrate my fiftieth.

✛   ✛   ✛

On the following Tuesday, Agent Reilly and his partner took me to the Allentown FBI facility. As I rode in the back of the car, Reilly turned around with an arm over the seat.

"We need to give you a lie detector test—this test is critical for your future. I think we can believe you, but we need to have a positive test on record to proceed."

I had no idea what to expect. In the movies, those tests are often depicted as a third-degree interrogation with a hostile interviewer and a bright light shining in the subject's face. As I soon found out for myself, a real lie detector test is the most low-key interrogation imaginable. There were no bright lights, all questions were disclosed in advance, and the only answers allowed were a whispered "yes" or "no." The instruments are so sensitive that they can pick up the slightest physiological changes triggered by a lie.

Agent Reilly got us past the guard at the Allentown office, and we walked up to a room that was furnished with a sofa, a table, and four chairs. He introduced me to the examiner, who opened a wooden case and extracted a number of measuring devices that he proceeded to attach to me—a clip on my fingertips, a blood-pressure cuff on my arm, and a curled wire around my chest.

To begin the test, the examiner read all the questions to me. Then there was a practice run, during which he asked all the questions and I answered them. After that, he activated the measuring devices—which collected skin conductivity, blood pressure, heart rate, and other physiological data—and sat down on a chair behind me to start asking the questions.

"Are we in Allentown, Pennsylvania?"

"Yes."

"Is your name Jack Barsky?"

"Yes."

"Is your birth name Albrecht Dittrich?"

"Yes."

"Do you currently work at MetLife?"

"No."

The entire procedure took no more than fifteen minutes, after which the examiner retreated to another room while Agent Reilly and I passed the time with small talk in the examination room. When the examiner emerged a half hour later, he said, "You passed all the questions except for this one," pointing at one of the questions on a sheet of paper. I studied the question—*Have you not severed all ties with the KGB?*—and suddenly it struck me: "This question has an implied double negative. Is that important?"

"Indeed it is," answered the examiner. "I will rewrite the question, and you will have to come back another day to answer it. We need a complete test result."

Agent Reilly dropped me off at a parking lot in the town of Bangor, where my car was parked, and I drove myself home. The polygraph test had made me very nervous—particularly failing that one crucial question. When I arrived home, it was still early in the day, and I was too antsy to just sit around, so I pulled out the string trimmer and went to work on a very steep slope at the edge of my property.

As I was standing with one foot well below the other, attacking the pesky weeds, I suffered a near panic attack. My heart raced, and I found it hard to breathe.

What's going to happen to me?

What if I fail the test again? Will I go to jail after all?

What about Jessie and Chelsea?

Those thoughts continued to play back in my mind. No matter how hard I tried to come up with answers by analyzing what the FBI agents had said and done, there were no answers. All I could do now was hope.

I didn't sleep well that night, and for several nights afterward, but my mood improved radically a week later after I passed the final lie detector question. I knew now that the FBI believed I was telling the truth.

36

OVER THE NEXT SIX WEEKS, Joe Reilly and his partner conducted a number of detailed debriefing sessions with me.

"We're going to start from the beginning—your beginning—and you need to be honest and up front about everything."

"I have nothing more to hide," I said, and that's exactly how I felt. I had lived undercover for so many years with nobody knowing the real me—and often I didn't even know the real me—so now, for the first time, I was able to tell everything without holding back.

We met once or twice a week at the same hotel and went over my entire biography and KGB career with a fine-tooth comb. When we were done, I had the feeling that agents Reilly and Roe knew more about my life than I did.

"You don't know why they recruited you?" Agent Roe pressed me.

"No. It could have been through the Party or maybe my friend Günter or because I won the scholarship. They never told me. Just one day I got that knock on my dorm-room door. I thought the fellow was Stasi, but he could have been a KGB collaborator. He never even mentioned his name."

We took a field trip to New York City, and I showed the agents a number of spots I had used for dead-drop operations. I showed them a rock formation with the word *Styx* on one of the boulders in Cunningham Park, Queens; a hollow tree in Inwood Hill Park on the northern tip of Manhattan; and another hollow tree in Van Cortlandt Park in the Bronx.

Finally, we went to search for my stash of emergency documents—the

Canadian passport and driver's license I had hidden away fifteen years earlier. We drove to an area near the Gun Hill Road subway station in the Bronx and made our way north on a small dirt path that runs through the middle of a one-hundred-yard wide greenbelt between the Bronx River Parkway on the west and Bronx Boulevard on the east. There were overgrown weeds and shrubs on both sides of the path.

At one point, I turned to Joe Reilly and said, "This is going to be tough. I have no idea whether I'll be able to find the spot again."

Five minutes later, I stopped dead in my tracks.

"You got something?" Reilly asked.

I pointed to the remnants of a park bench on the left side of the path. The wood was all gone, but the two concrete legs were still in the ground.

"Just maybe . . ." I said, as I approached the left-hand leg. Reaching down, I pulled hard on the post to expose the bottom, and there it was. The package I had buried underneath that leg fifteen years earlier was still there.

"Pay dirt!" I exclaimed triumphantly, knowing that this discovery proved both my truthfulness and my excellent memory.

✦ ✦ ✦

We returned from New York City and resumed the debriefing process the following week. Every night I went home and acted as if everything was fine, but inside my stress level continued to rise. The FBI was still keeping me in the dark about their plans for the future.

Other than the sessions with Agent Reilly and his partner, my work and home life routine never changed. Remarkably, neither Penelope nor any of my coworkers observed any signs of stress.

Though Reilly wouldn't even hint about my future, he and I seemed to have forged at least a tenuous connection, both intellectually and emotionally. But that didn't mean I wouldn't be put in jail or deported to Germany, with unknown consequences to Penelope and my children, whose innocent lives would be completely disrupted.

During one of our meetings, I asked with some trepidation, "Penelope says she wants to visit her brother in Toronto. Can she go, and can she take the kids?"

A week later, Agent Reilly told me that the Bureau had decided to allow our entire family to cross the border. They did not want to disrupt the normal activities of my family, and it was still too early to let Penelope in on the ongoing investigation.

This seemed to be a very positive sign that they trusted me. Who would allow a former spy to leave the country if they didn't trust him?

It was a hot Thursday in the middle of July. Once again, as I had been doing for the past two months, I drove past the left-hand turn onto the Columbia-Portland Toll Bridge and continued straight ahead to the village of Water Gap for yet another debriefing session.

How much longer can this go on? I asked myself. *We have been through my life forwards and backwards. What else can I possibly tell them?*

I knocked on the door of the hotel room, and when Joe Reilly opened the door he had a big grin on his face.

"Come on in," he said. "Today is your lucky day."

"What do you mean?"

"The United States government has made a decision about your future. In appreciation of your honesty and full cooperation, you will be allowed to stay in the country and so will your family."

This was by far the best news I had received in my entire life. I could barely suppress a loud scream of joy and relief. There was a future for all of us, and it would be a good one!

"The FBI will work on cleaning up your record and providing you with honest and legitimate documentation," Reilly said. "This may take a while because your case is very unusual. Typically, folks like you are given a new identity and put in the witness protection program. However, you are so enmeshed in American society that this option would only disrupt you and your family. So, instead, we will try to clean you in place."

Delirious with joy, I said, "Can I tell Penelope now?"

"I think we should do that," he said.

✦ ✦ ✦

The following Friday, I told Penelope that she needed to be at home on Saturday morning because "some local government officials want to ask us a few questions about land use in the neighborhood." I hoped this lie would be the last one I would ever have to tell.

The "local officials," Joe and Dave, showed up the next morning at 10:00. We took seats at the kitchen table, and Joe opened the conversation.

"Mrs. Barsky, we understand that you're aware that Jack here used to be a KGB agent. We know that too. We're from the FBI."

Penelope's face turned ash gray, but before she could say anything, Joe continued.

"That's not a bad thing. Jack has cooperated with us fully, and the US government has decided not to press charges. Your entire family will be allowed to stay in this country."

Penelope did not grasp everything Joe had said, and with a noticeable tremble in her voice, she said, "I knew there would not be a good ending to this. I knew it!" Turning to me angrily, she continued, "How could you do something like this to me and the children? Answer me!"

At that point, Agent Roe interrupted in a calm voice. "Mrs. Barsky, please take a deep breath. Everything will be fine. You have a beautiful house on Allegheny Road, and you will keep it. Your husband will keep his job, and one day you all will be free to go wherever you want. It will just take a bit of time to go through all the formalities to get Jack documented properly."

When that sank in, Penelope breathed a sigh of relief, but deep inside I knew she was not at peace. Numerous times since my confession to her, she had expressed her anger about my secret. She was married to a spy and a liar, someone she could never really trust.

This visit to my house concluded the main portion of the debriefing. However, Joe and I continued to meet weekly at a diner in the village of Water Gap. He usually came with a few clarifying questions, and I would answer as best I could. Then we would spend another hour or so enjoying a light meal and talking about life, history, politics, and the human condition. We found out we had a lot in common, and after we had met a number of times, I gathered my courage and started asking him a few questions of my own.

"So, how did you guys find me? As you know, I stopped working for the KGB in 1988. So why now?"

"Well," Joe began as he took a sip of coffee, "in 1991, a fellow by the name of Vasili Mitrokhin contacted British intelligence. Mitrokhin had been a KGB archivist, and over the years he had smuggled out thousands of handwritten notes copied from documents stored in the vaults of the KGB. Actually, he contacted the CIA first, but the junior officer who spoke with him did not take him seriously and showed him the door. I can bet you that guy's career is stuck in neutral!"

I followed the story with great interest, leaning forward as the noise of the diner faded into the background. "And there was a reference to me in those notes?"

"Indeed. There was a reference to a Jack Barsky, code name Dieter, who was living somewhere on the East Coast as an illegal. In fact, Mitrokhin mentioned that there were nine volumes on 'Dieter' in the archives, but he was only able to look inside folders that documented Dieter's career through 1984."

"Aha," I said. "That explains why all the information on the outside of those phony binders in the hotel room was so old. So, how did you finally locate me?"

"When I got the case in the fall of 1993, the director of the FBI told me personally that this was the biggest counterintelligence case we had going. An illegal with nine volumes of records at the KGB had to be taken very seriously. After all, we had just gone through the Aldrich Ames debacle."

We paused for a moment as our waitress came and cleared away our plates and topped off Joe's coffee.

"Finding you was not hard at all. Now if your name had been John Miller, that would have caused some problems, but there aren't that many Jack Barskys in the US. When we found out you had obtained a Social Security card in your mid-thirties, had worked as a bike messenger, graduated from college with highest honors, and then went on to have a great career in IT, we knew we had our man. That's just not normal, to say the least."

I couldn't help but chuckle at that.

"By the way, you escaped detection much earlier. A few months prior to your applying for your Social Security card, the FBI canceled a program that required the Social Security Administration to notify us of anyone over thirty who applied for a Social Security card. But because the program hadn't yielded any results, it was scrapped."

"How much time did you spend investigating me? After all, illegals often go through long periods of inactivity. I could have been a sleeper."

"That's what we were afraid of, and for that reason we investigated slowly and very carefully. We didn't want to alert you to the fact that we were looking at you. So, at first I watched your house from the hills across the street. I also went through your garbage on a regular basis—not a pleasant task in the heat of summer. And when the house next to you was put up for sale, the FBI bought it. We had a male and a female agent move in, and they pretended to be a couple."

I wanted to laugh out loud. I pictured Joe going through my trash and watching me with binoculars while I mowed the lawn or read the morning paper.

"Of course, all that effort yielded absolutely nothing." I said with a bit of a grin on my face.

"Yup," Joe sighed. "We could have finished the investigation much sooner, but then we stumbled onto something that made us pause. We found out you were friendly with a fellow who was born in Cuba and had immigrated to the US."

"Who? Gerard at work? He's the smartest guy I ever worked with—what about him?"

"Well, it turned out he owned an apartment in the Bronx that he had rented to a low-level Soviet diplomat. The alarm bells went off. Was this an international spy ring? The alarm bells rang even louder when Penelope took a trip to London. MI5 followed her the whole time."

I shook my head in wonder at all that had gone on without my knowledge. The spy was being spied on and never knew a thing!

"Anyway, with all that going on, we finally got permission from the Justice Department to bug your house. It didn't take long for us to overhear an argument between you and Penelope during which you confessed to her your past affiliation with the KGB. We had our evidence and decided to move in."

Now the pieces of the puzzle were all in place for me. It's not often that the subject of a criminal investigation gets to hear the whole story straight from the investigator.

+ + +

My legalization was only a matter of time, and I knew I had to be patient. Because my case was so unusual, the process was rife with difficulties, and it took several failed attempts before everything went through. While Penelope and the kids retained their original IDs and documents, the process to legalize me was much more complicated. In order to have a record of entry into the US, the FBI drove me across the St. Lawrence River into Canada and turned right back. When I reentered the US, I received a Form I-94, which became the foundation for the green card I received in 2009.

Joe received a letter of commendation from the head of the FBI for his good judgment and judicious handling of my case, and he retired soon after the debriefing sessions officially ended. Subsequently, my connection to the FBI was maintained by three other agents, all professionals of the highest caliber. I was especially grateful to the gentleman who went out of his way to wade through the bureaucratic morass and the many layers of government to eventually finalize my case and allow me to become a US citizen. He's still an active agent, so I won't even mention his first name, but he's a hero to me.

As time passed, Joe and I got to know and like each other even more. We discovered that we had a few fundamental character traits in common. We were both hardworking and quite disciplined in support of our respective causes. However, when the situation seemed to call for flexibility, we were not averse to making ad hoc decisions that were not in the official playbook. I still remember an abrupt U-turn Joe made in Washington, DC, using the entire grass strip on the right-hand side of the road. We also had in common a bare-bones honesty, which in turn made us into very believable liars when the situation required.

One evening in Washington, DC, he and I were taking advantage of the Marriott happy hour prior to a scheduled visit to FBI headquarters the next morning. We got into a conversation with a lively and rather inquisitive young lady, who looked at Joe and asked, "So what do you do for a living?"

Joe didn't miss a beat. With a deadpan delivery, he said, "We're undersea explorers. We go to the bottom of the ocean and recover rare minerals."

It took a huge effort for me not to burst out laughing. There was a certain boldness and recklessness in that bald-faced lie that I could easily relate to. So it was no surprise to me that we decided to stay in touch after Joe retired. Later on, when I took up the game of golf, Joe invited me to join his group for a weekly Saturday morning outing.

I have become an avid, though average, golfer. All in all, I've played more than one hundred rounds of golf with my erstwhile enemy and captor.

PART VI

THE REDEMPTION OF A SPY

37

AFTER GROWING UP in the privations of postwar East Germany, signing up with the KGB, and successfully infiltrating the United States of America, I had cut all ties with the Russians and continued to work my way up the ladder in American society. Just when I thought I was in the clear, I'd been caught by the FBI. Now I was living an upper-middle-class existence in the US, with a very good career in a field I loved, and I was raising two amazing children. This ex-Communist KGB spy was indeed living the American dream.

But there were some things I couldn't walk away from.

Though I believed I had overcome my greatest obstacles, I couldn't escape my greatest enemy—myself. I needed more than an escape; I needed transformation.

Most of my life was filled with material richness and contentment, but there were cracks in the foundation. Soon those cracks would expand, my foundation would crumble, and I would find myself like Humpty Dumpty, in shattered pieces on the ground.

I knew that my marriage was already a broken mess, but we continued on for the sake of the children. I found fulfillment in my job and my support for Chelsea and Jessie.

For six years, I dedicated much of my spare time in support of Chelsea's basketball career, which had begun to take root when she was still young enough to be sucking her thumb.

One day, as she and I were sitting on the couch watching Michael Jordan do one of his Superman impressions on the court, Chelsea sat up straight and asked me, "What is this?"

"Basketball," I said.

"I want to do that."

I was elated, because it finally gave me an excuse to erect a hoop at the end of the driveway and do a little dribbling and shooting myself. Little did I know that eight years later, I would watch my baby drain a three-pointer as a freshman in her first Division I basketball game.

Once Chelsea got a taste of the game, she stuck with it with the same kind of ferocity I had displayed when studying English. Her beginnings were humble—in her very first game, she was hit on the head by a perfectly thrown pass, which reminded me of my own first attempts at the game—but she quickly became the star of her team.

After one season of recreational ball, I signed her up to attend the Donyell Marshall summer camp in the city of Reading, about seventy miles from our home. This was one tough camp, and the staff ran it with near military discipline. When I picked up Chelsea eight days later, she looked scratched, bruised, and totally exhausted.

"Enough basketball for a while?" I asked when we reached the car. The stone-cold look she gave me in response was worthy of Medusa, and from that moment on I knew she was as dedicated to the sport as I had ever been. I spent the next several years supporting her as much as I could—through a disappointing high school experience and two nationally competitive travel teams. From the time she was twelve on, Chelsea never celebrated a birthday at home. There was always a tournament somewhere, and we spent countless hours in the car, driving to gyms near and far.

All this time together deepened our father-daughter relationship and created a special bond. Even as a teenager, she actually seemed to like me. One day, I visited practice at her high school gym. When she saw me standing at the door, she ran to me and yelled, "Hey, everybody, this is my dad!"

We also developed a language that only the two of us could understand. When Chelsea was six years old, she saw me typing without looking at the keyboard. When she asked how I could do that, I responded, "I have little eyes on my fingertips."

Many years later, she returned from basketball practice one day and told me, "Dad, my fingers have eyes now."

She and I were the only two who would know what that meant—though, in the game of basketball, my fingers never had eyes like hers did.

Basketball also made a huge difference in Chelsea's growth as a person. Hard work, discipline, team play, competitiveness, and grace in victory and defeat were only some of the life lessons she learned from the game.

All the dedication and sacrifice eventually paid off. During Chelsea's junior year of high school, we visited fifteen colleges that were recruiting her, including several Division I programs. For me, the highlight was the awesome reception we received at the United States Military Academy at West Point, a quality institution through and through.

✤ ✤ ✤

In late June 2005, three weeks after Chelsea's eighteenth birthday, I drove her to Loretto, Pennsylvania, for an official visit to St. Francis University. I had long since decided that I would tell her about my past when she turned eighteen, and this four-hour drive was the ideal opportunity.

I started hesitantly, fully aware of the bombshell I was about to drop.

"Chelsea, I need to tell you something important. Would you mind taking your earbuds out?"

She looked at me somewhat annoyed and said, "What?"

"Well," I continued. "I used to be a spy."

So there it was, out in the open!

"Huh?" Now she was paying attention.

I spent the next hour in an uninterrupted monologue, telling her the whole story—where I came from, how I got here, what I had done, and how we were all safe now. When I came to the part where I took a huge risk by blowing off the KGB so I would be able to care for her, she broke down and cried.

The disclosure of my past moved our relationship to an even higher level, and after eighteen years I was finally able to share with my daughter the depth of the unconditional love I had for her.

+ + +

One year later, Penelope and I drove Chelsea back to St. Francis to begin her college career. We took two cars so we could leave one with Chelsea, which meant the two ladies rode together and I followed solo. Halfway into the drive, I got a call from a headhunter who was recruiting me for a new job.

"Jack, they're offering you the job, and they've thrown in a nice signing bonus to sweeten the deal."

"Tell them I accept—no need to play games," I responded eagerly.

As soon as I hung up, I called Penelope and shared the good news with her. Her reaction was mildly cheerful, and it took the edge off my excitement. At the age of fifty-six, I had reached the financial pinnacle of my life. In two weeks, I would start a job as the chief information officer for a Fortune 500 company in Princeton, New Jersey, making forty times as much as I had earned as a bike messenger. Not only that, but Chelsea was on a full scholarship, so I had no college expenses. I should have been ecstatic, but I wasn't. The money was great, but it couldn't make up for the continuing deterioration of my marriage.

The drive home with Penelope was awful. She and I barely talked. After we briefly shared our impressions of the campus and the head coach, and discussed where we could pick up some Chinese food on the way home, the conversation fizzled and finally stopped altogether. We had nothing much to say to each other anymore.

In 1999, we had moved into a brand-new home—a McMansion with a walk-in closet bigger than my first apartment in Berlin. This gorgeous house, in Pittstown, New Jersey, had a grand entrance foyer with a huge crystal chandelier, and the backyard featured a granite patio with an in-ground pool and a waterfall.

For the first few years, Penelope had occupied herself by turning the empty shell of a house into her own home. But once all the excitement of feathering the nest was over, she fell back into the doldrums. We were now living more like roommates than a married couple. With Chelsea gone and Jessie only two years away from his eighteenth birthday, the glue that held our marriage together had lost its hold.

I now felt very much alone in this huge house, and the bottle became a trusted companion each evening before I withdrew for the night to my separate bedroom.

✦ ✦ ✦

A few weeks after we dropped Chelsea off at college, I packed my bags for a trip to Pebble Beach, California, for an exclusive, three-day conference that included top-notch speakers, great golf, entertainment, and food in what many consider a paradise on earth. Spouses were invited, but Penelope refused to go.

"You just go and be with your people," she said.

After a six-hour flight into San Francisco, I rented a car and drove south on the Pacific Coast Highway, arriving at Pebble Beach just after sunset. The concierge at the lodge parked my car and showed me to my room on the second floor. I walked straight to the window and opened the curtains to reveal a picture postcard view of the eighteenth hole, with a white sand bunker in front, the churning ocean in the background, and the silhouette of a magnificent cypress tree off to the left.

Looking at all this beauty, I was suddenly struck with sadness. How I wished to be able to share this moment with somebody. I went to bed feeling that loneliness would be an unwelcome partner during my stay at this marvelous place.

The next morning, after a magnificent breakfast buffet, I attended an interactive session with Stuart Varney, an economic journalist I'd seen on television many times. Digging deep into some past memories, I asked some questions about the future of the nation state and the role of the Trilateral Commission. At the intermission, Varney looked at me quizzically and said, "I would not expect these kinds of question from an IT executive."

There's a lot more to me than meets the eye, I thought.

We teed off after lunch. My group started on the famous seventh hole, which features a one-hundred-yard shot into a peninsular green surrounded by crashing waves. As luck would have it, I was up first.

Nervously, I took a tentative swing—oh no, a bad hit! However, as if guided by magic, the ball ran onto the green, rolled forward, and came to rest about three inches from the hole.

Of course, that's exactly what I intended to do, I thought as the other golfers applauded my shot. In the end, my team won second prize, and I took away a marvelous crystal vase as a souvenir.

The next two days were filled with conference sessions in the morning and golf in the afternoon. I played both Spyglass Hill and Spanish Bay, and it was indeed paradise on earth. On the final evening, the farewell party included a performance by Rain, with their incredible Beatles tribute. Both their sound and appearance were so authentic that it felt as if I were at a real Beatles concert, something I would have given all my possessions for when I was in high school. But the desire to share all of this with someone only grew, and the ache nearly outweighed the enjoyment.

The next morning, it was time to say good-bye to paradise. There was a fine mist in the air as I got into the rental car to drive back to San Francisco. As I drove through the town of Watsonville, I suddenly started crying and couldn't stop. I felt both stunned by my emotion and overwhelmed by my grief for something I couldn't quite identify. Where was this sadness coming from? Was it just a letdown from having to leave this great place after such a wonderful experience? Or was it something else? It seemed the trip had not refilled my tank, but had only made me more aware of its emptiness.

✦ ✦ ✦

A few days after my return, Penelope and I had an emotionally charged argument, and it became clear that even our unspoken roommate arrangement could not survive. A week later, I filed for divorce and subsequently moved into a two-bedroom apartment near my job. My only companion was Barney, an African grey parrot, who greeted me every time I came into view with, "You moron!"

In a matter of weeks, I had gone from being on top of the world to the depths of despair, hitting rock bottom. Without a specific reason, I cried myself to sleep every night. After plodding through so many times of loneliness in my life, I didn't understand why I couldn't rise above it this time.

As life continued in an empty new rhythm, a good friend who had unusual insight into my psyche suggested I start dating again.

My response was curt and simple: "I'm done with that stuff."

"No, Jack, seriously," she said. "I might know you better than you know yourself. First and foremost, you are a lover."

"That may well be true," I said with a sigh, "but love is a two-way street, and I always seem to wind up on one-directional roads. Let's not talk about this anymore."

I pushed the idea away and didn't give it any more thought as, little by little, I managed to crawl out from the pit I was in. At work I was able to function, but there was little joy in my life. The only things that deadened the pain of loneliness were my nightly drinking and the game of golf.

What I couldn't guess was that the biggest change of my life was just around the corner.

38

ONE EVENING, just a few days after Jessie's eighteenth birthday, he and I met Chelsea at the Clinton House, our favorite restaurant. I had already told Chelsea that I was going to reveal my murky past to Jessie.

"I can't wait to see his face," she said, remembering her own reaction when I had told her.

As soon as the waitress had taken our orders, I cleared my throat and started my confession.

"Jessie, I've got something to tell you. I might as well come out with it straightaway—I used to be an undercover agent for the Russians."

Jessie stared at me. Chelsea leaned forward with a slight grin on her face.

"You're joking, right? There's no way," Jessie said, looking at Chelsea to gauge the truth of my story. I told him about Berlin, Moscow, and coming to the United States, and he asked questions as he followed the tale. It took a while for it to fully sink in.

"Dad, you've got to write a book—and if you don't write it, I will," he said. There was a sense of pride in his voice that I'd never heard before. I remembered overhearing him tell a friend one time, after a 'bring your child to work day" event, "My dad doesn't really do any work. He just sits in his office and talks to people all day." Suddenly, the boring office worker had been elevated to some kind of action hero in my son's mind.

Before we went our separate ways that night, I reminded Jessie that I would always be there for him if he needed anything. The divorce had turned into a mess of lawyers and disagreements and further stress. I could only guess how life at home was for Jessie.

✦ ✦ ✦

Two weeks later, Jessie decided to come live with me at the apartment. He and a friend conspired to load up his belongings and leave the house at a time when Penelope wasn't home. This wasn't necessarily the best way to handle the situation, but it reflected the emotional climate at the time.

Soon after Jessie moved in, he enrolled at Mercer County Community College to lay the foundation for a potential four-year degree. With my son now living with me, I wasn't alone anymore. The time we had together also gave us the opportunity to bond with each other as adults.

I still had no interest in dating, and I played as much golf as I could—on Saturdays with Joe Reilly and his gang, and on Sundays with colleagues from work. My nighttime sleep aid helped me evade the dire emotional reality of my life.

Work, at least, was going well. Besides golf, it was the only bright star in my otherwise dark sky. In early fall, I decided I needed to hire an assistant: The human resources department screened some candidates and handed me the résumés of two finalists. After initial phone interviews, I invited both candidates to come in so I could meet them. My only concern with one of the applicants, a young woman named Shawna, was that she had volunteered during the phone interview that she was a Christian.

I hope she's not a Holy Roller, I thought to myself. But then I reminded myself that I had worked with some good employees who had been open about their Christian faith. They almost always turned out to be honest, hardworking people, the kind you never had to worry about.

Shawna was sitting at the table with her back to the door when I entered the small conference room for the interview. When she turned around and we made eye contact, I was instantly in love. I know that sounds extreme, but it was as if I'd been slapped by the invisible hand of God. Nobody—and I mean *nobody*—had ever made that kind of impression on me.

Impeccably dressed in a charcoal-gray business suit, with her head held straight and her shoulders square, she exuded elegance in every way. But what struck me the most, from the moment I first laid eyes on her, was the glow that seemed to emanate from her face. Her smile was neither seductive nor superficial; it was calm, even serene, reflecting a great amount of self-confidence. She was also twenty-four years my junior.

It wasn't the first time I had fallen in love, but each time before had always been a process. Even with Gerlinde, whose beauty had so captivated me on the dance floor, it wasn't love at first sight. And over the years, I had seen many beautiful women, but their outward beauty never managed to touch my soul the way Shawna did the very moment I saw her.

I managed to retain my poise and conduct the job interview; it was no surprise that Shawna aced it. Her impressive résumé included a stint with the United Nations as a bilingual secretary. She carried herself with class and dignity, and I later found out that she had attended a British-style finishing school in her native country of Jamaica. She answered all my questions, showed a well-developed ability to think on her feet, and even asked some good questions of her own. In the end, it was an easy decision to offer her the job.

So I now had a new assistant, but I had to keep my attraction for her under wraps. I had no business falling in love with a much younger woman, especially one who reported to me. Besides, I was still in the middle of divorce proceedings with Penelope.

I kept my feelings for Shawna hidden, but I also found ways to be helpful to her whenever possible. I soon learned that she was the head of a three-person household that included her mother, who had come to the US late in life, and a son who had just started high school.

✦ ✦ ✦

Our company encouraged bosses to take new employees out to lunch, so after her second week, I took Shawna to her favorite Mexican restaurant. This was a sacrifice for me because I really don't like Mexican food. At one point, the conversation veered into the realm of faith when I asked her what gave her the inner peace that I and the others in the office had noticed and been drawn to.

"As I told you during the interview," she said, "I get my strength from Jesus."

I remembered that she had said that, but I still found it odd. How could she draw strength from someone she had never met, let alone someone who died two thousand years ago?

I explained my philosophy to her in a straightforward fashion.

"I used to be a radical atheist with extreme hostility toward the church and Christianity. However, I've since met too many good Christians to retain my hostility toward your faith. So now my motto is 'live and let live.' As long as you don't proselytize me, I won't criticize you."

She smiled, as if unfazed by my words.

Encouraged by her silence, I continued to explain my belief system.

"Atheism seems to be just as foolish as Christianity. One maintains that there is a God, and the other says there isn't. But neither side can prove their hypotheses, which are ultimately statements of faith. I believe in reason, but my ability to reason is not developed enough to understand the universe. I'll stand with Socrates, who said, 'I know that I know nothing.' So, there may well be a God, but—"

Without finishing the sentence, I shrugged my shoulders and boldly (today I'm more inclined to say cowardly) declared myself an agnostic.

Back in the car on our way to the office I wanted to be sure that the line was clearly drawn.

"You may believe whatever you like, but please don't think for one minute that you'll make a convert out of me."

In response, Shawna, who had already seen the care and kindness I extended to the team I supervised, made a bold statement: "You are already a Christian; you just don't know it."

I had no comeback for that one.

✦ ✦ ✦

Throughout my career as a manager, I always tried to help others develop to their fullest potential, even if it meant losing them as they went on to explore other opportunities within—or even outside of—our company. So when Shawna told me that she had enrolled at Philadelphia Bible

College in pursuit of a bachelor's in biblical studies, I became curious about her writing skills, thinking that one day I could help her advance to higher positions in the company.

When I asked her to share a sample of her writing, she handed me a recently completed essay on the biblical book of Ruth. I read the essay and found her writing to be fundamentally sound, but I didn't know whether it did justice to the original source.

"I guess I have to read the original to see if your paper makes sense."

Ever the alert evangelist, Shawna produced a Bible from her bag and handed it to me. I took it home, and as I sat down to read it, I realized this was the first time since my early attempt to read Genesis from Opa Alwin's Bible that I had opened a Bible.

As a man, I didn't find the book of Ruth to be the most inspiring text I'd ever read, but it was enough to get me interested in finding out more. When I mentioned it to Shawna, she came back with a set of CD recordings of the entire Bible, proving once again that she was prepared for any eventuality.

I can listen as I drive to work, I mused as I set the CDs next to my briefcase. *That's not a bad idea . . .*

I decided there was no reason to be closed-minded about the Bible. After all, it was the most-read book in the history of mankind. Besides, I'd had about enough of the shtick put out by the radio talk show crowd that I usually listened to during my hour-long commute. This was an opportunity to fill a gap in my knowledge of the world, and it would come at no additional cost in time or money.

As I began to listen to the Old Testament, there were many sections I didn't understand and many questions I would have asked if I'd had a teacher by my side. So I asked Shawna if she could help me grasp some of the material better. In an instant, the boss–employee relationship was turned on its head. Shawna became my teacher, and I was the beginner student. She gave me Bible passages to read at night, and we began to meet every weekday morning, a half hour before the official start of the workday, to discuss the various subjects she had picked. We commandeered a small conference room at the office, and the entries in both our calendars read: *Logistics Planning*.

During these discussions, which I considered purely academic,

Shawna always managed to sneak in a few remarks about a church service she had attended the previous weekend. What she described sounded significantly different from the Catholic mass I had experienced.

Shawna spoke in such glowing terms about her church that I became curious, and when she invited me to accompany her one day, I accepted.

We decided to meet on a Saturday at Zarephath Christian Church for their afternoon service. I arrived in the parking lot right on time, but Shawna was running a little bit late. I waited patiently in my car—there was no way I would enter the church by myself without knowing what to expect.

Shawna arrived in time for us to catch the tail end of the worship set, and we took seats in one of the back rows. I was surprised at how professional and pleasing the music was—a delight for my discerning ears.

When the pastor stepped up to the podium, he exuded the same glow that I had gotten used to seeing on Shawna's face. Even today, my vocabulary is not rich enough to do justice to that look—it is angelic and otherworldly, yet completely present and engaged with real life. It projects a serenity that seems to say, "I have found inner peace and nobody and nothing can disturb it."

As he began the message, I found myself captivated in a way I could not have anticipated. The reverence in the pastor's calm and quiet delivery was a welcome contrast to some of the fire-and-brimstone, in-your-face sermons I had caught glimpses of on TV. He spoke about God's love for His people. I had never heard God described in such a way. His statements about God's love transcended logic. They were absolute. You either accepted it or you didn't; there was no middle ground. I had long felt a yearning for unconditional love, the type of love I had been surprised by when Chelsea was born; the type of love I still felt for her and for Jessie. Was it possible that someone could love *me* in the same way?

At the end of the service, I did something unexpected and out of character. Feeling a strong need to speak to the pastor, I rose to my feet and I walked toward the altar.

Of course, at six foot three, I was hard to overlook, and the pastor immediately stepped forward to greet me.

"You have a phenomenal delivery," I said, as if I were critiquing a TED Talk.

The pastor thanked me and then asked me some questions about myself. We talked for about five minutes, and when he had gathered enough background on me, he called over an assistant pastor and asked if it would be okay if they prayed for me.

I shrugged and said, "Why not?"

As they prayed, they placed their hands on my back and shoulders. Surprisingly, my discomfort with that was minimal. It seemed that, in little more than an hour, I had overcome most of my emotional resistance to the church.

Before I left, the pastor went to the back of the sanctuary and returned with two books, *The Case for Christ* by Lee Strobel, and a Bible bound in red. I read the Strobel book the next day and read through the Bible during the following year. I wasn't entirely convinced by *The Case for Christ*, but it planted a seed. For the first time in my life, I was open to the possibility that Jesus Christ was not only a special human being but also God's Son, who had been crucified and had risen from the dead. You might say the door to faith was ajar.

When I shared my thoughts with Shawna, she pointed me to a weekly half-hour radio program called *Let My People Think*, featuring a speaker named Ravi Zacharias. I decided to investigate it the next time I had a chance during my drive to work. Ravi Zacharias turned out to be a highly intelligent, deeply philosophical thinker, who laid out his faith in a way that fully engaged my mind. And the message he conveyed simply blew me away.

What I found especially appealing was his logical argument that there could be no morality without a power external to humanity. By now, I had learned enough about human nature—with myself as Exhibit A: always wanting to be good, and yet failing so often—that I agreed fully with his reasoning. As I listened to Ravi in the privacy of my car, I found myself responding out loud: "Yes, exactly!"

These radio broadcasts also disabused me of a notion I had held since my youth—that religion, especially Christianity, was only for the intellectually weak and those who responded with their heart rather than their head.

Ravi Zacharias watered the seeds planted by Lee Strobel, but ultimately it was C. S. Lewis who nudged me over the line to faith in God.

In short order, I read both *Mere Christianity* and *The Problem of Pain*. The argument that impressed me the most came from *Mere Christianity*:

> I am trying here to prevent anyone saying the really foolish thing that people often say about Him: "I'm ready to accept Jesus as a great moral teacher, but I don't accept his claim to be God." That is the one thing we must not say. A man who was merely a man and said the sort of things Jesus said would not be a great moral teacher. He would either be a lunatic—on a level with the man who says he is a poached egg—or else he would be the Devil of Hell. You must make your choice. Either this man was, and is, the Son of God: or else a madman or something worse. You can shut Him up for a fool, you can spit at Him and kill Him as a demon; or you can fall at His feet and call Him Lord and God. But let us not come with any patronising nonsense about His being a great human teacher. He has not left that open to us. He did not intend to.[4]

I was now an intellectual Christian—historical facts and Socratic dialogue had gotten me there. My soul had yet to follow, but I had opened myself up to Christian thought and culture. I attended church regularly, reviewed Shawna's Bible college essays, and helped out with some of her research. All of these activities drew me inexorably toward an emotional, spiritual, and intellectual destination.

Of course, one cannot become a Christian through only experience and logic. The cornerstone of Christianity is faith—which includes, but transcends, experience and logic. As it says in Hebrews 11:1, "Faith shows the reality of what we hope for; it is the evidence of things we cannot see." Accordingly, faith cannot be attained by study alone, and it cannot be forced.

I was soon to learn, however, that when faith finally blossoms, it can happen quite suddenly. For me, it happened on the golf course, of all places.

One weekend morning, as I waited for my playing partner to hit his shot, I was staring up at a massive white cloud formation that soared against the bright blue sky. Just then, I felt a sensation similar to what

I had felt before my first kiss, only much stronger. All the nerves in my body came alive and were tingling as a profound and otherworldly awareness began to grow in me.

He is!

Was this a manifestation of the Holy Spirit? I couldn't say. All I knew was that it was real, and it came without warning at a time when all I was thinking about was how to advance a little white ball on a stretch of green grass.

✦ ✦ ✦

Not long after that, God had another surprise for me. The church I attended was not in the habit of making altar calls. However, one day at the end of the service, as the pastor was lingering near the pulpit, a powerful but unexplainable force caused me to march down the left-hand aisle toward the front.

This was not a casual stroll through the auditorium. My approach was resolute and purposeful, and the pastor quickly noticed me. When I reached the front of the room, he said, "You look like a man on a mission. What can I do for you?"

"I'm here to give my life to Jesus Christ."

I have no memory of what followed, but Shawna later told me that the pastor reactivated his microphone and addressed the audience that was slowly filing out. As soon as he began to speak, people stopped in their tracks and began to listen. The pastor then spent about five minutes sharing my background as an atheist who had grown up behind the Iron Curtain (which I had shared with him and a few others at an earlier time). He finished by thanking God for another saved soul, and the people responded with loud and extended applause.

I remember none of it.

39

AFTER MAKING MY DECLARATION OF FAITH that Sunday morning, I began to reflect on the extraordinary transformation that had happened to me. The long journey I had been on from rigid atheism to born-again Christian seemed an altogether unlikely path. Or was it?

How could a person receive the message of the Bible and observe the truth revealed in nature without coming to the conclusion that God is real? I was thoroughly grounded in a scientific approach to everything in life, and it was logical thinking that started my conversion. Yet science has never reached the absolute and is not likely to ever do so. Over the centuries, scientists have tried to explain the world. And as many times as they believed they had found the answer, they've had to correct themselves.

Albert Einstein, arguably the most brilliant scientist in history, never fully embraced the validity of quantum mechanics—proving there's always more to learn even for the greatest minds.

The big bang theory consists of a number of highly complex mathematical equations that only a select few can understand. I'm convinced that those formulas, too, will one day be enhanced, corrected, or even replaced.

Though humanity's search for knowledge is noble and good, our claims to absolute knowledge are nothing but arrogance.

Born again. What did that mean to me? Outwardly, I was still the same person. But inwardly I began to notice changes. The most radical change was my growing acceptance that I would never be fully in control of my life—no matter how hard I worked at it. Once I began to reflect on this, I understood why Ravi Zacharias calls God "The Grand Weaver." There were decisions made by others that acted as switches for the tracks of my life—such as Rosi's decision to break up with me, the KGB's decisions regarding my deployment, and the FBI's decision not to prosecute me. These were all massively life-changing events over which I had absolutely no control.

Looking back, there were many moments when I was in grave danger of being arrested—or perhaps even killed—but somehow God's protective hand shielded me during my entire high-risk life. I should have been caught when my first application for a birth certificate failed. I could have become a victim on the South Side of Chicago. I was fortunate that the FBI canceled their over-thirty notification program with the Social Security Administration just a few months before I applied. I dodged another bullet when I was able to retrieve my application and documents from the clerk at the passport office. I should have been investigated after paying cash for a last-minute ticket on the Concorde. And on and on it goes.

Finally, there were impossible coincidences that changed my course or direction—such as the tailor-made sermon the pastor preached on my first morning at church; Gerlinde showing up at my apartment in Berlin just after I returned from Moscow; the failed final dead-drop operation, Joe Reilly being appointed lead agent on my case; and Shawna appearing in my life when I was in desperate need of an evangelist, even though I didn't know it. These are but a few examples of the overwhelming evidence in my life of a highly complex tapestry woven by an all-powerful God.

The acceptance of my own weakness in contrast with God's all-surpassing power finally gave me a measure of inner peace. Though I have always been—and likely will continue to be—a very active and involved individual, I finally began to understand the meaning of the word *relax*. It means to let go. It means to do what I have to do, but without the urge to control everything and without biting my nails for fear that my plans may go awry. It means not burying my troubles inside or dumping them onto others, but instead taking them to Jesus—who is living and active and sharp.[5]

Though I was definitely a work in progress—and still am today—

I found myself becoming a friendlier and more patient person. In the supermarket, I stopped racing the person with the overflowing shopping cart to get ahead of her in line. I would bend down and pick up garbage in the parking lot, and I said *please* and *thank you* far more often than ever before.

Finally, I did away with my "sleep medication," the half bottle of wine I used to consume every night. For the first time in almost thirty years, I realized that I could fall asleep without a sedative. I also kept up my church attendance, continued to study the Bible, and audited a course on C. S. Lewis at a local Christian college. *The Screwtape Letters* was one of the most delightful pieces of literature I had ever read. Its powerful message that the business and noise of our daily lives can make us lose sight of what is truly important resonated strongly with me.

+ + +

In early 2008, while I was chatting with Pastor Rob after church, he asked, "Are you ready to go public with your faith?"

"I'm not sure what you mean?" I responded with a half question.

"Baptism in water. We have a baptism scheduled in March."

I had to think about that for a while. It was likely that some of the people I knew, who had the same prejudice against the Christian faith that I had carried for decades, would appreciate me less if I openly proclaimed my faith. But did that really matter? I decided that it didn't. If I wasn't ready to stand by my faith openly and publicly, it would mean I was a phony or a coward. Those were not options I was willing to consider.

On March 16, 2008, I arrived at the church early, went to a back room, and put on shorts, a T-shirt, and rubber sandals. When it was my turn, I stepped onto the platform and into the water-filled tub, where I relinquished control in more ways than one.

Pastor Rob and an assistant held me steady, and after a brief prayer, they leaned me backward and fully immersed me in the water. I emerged dripping and grinning. There it was for all who cared to see: *Former Soviet spy Jack Barsky was a Christian!*

Pastor Rob heard more about my background when I helped his niece with a history paper and told her some details about my experience as a spy. Inspired by the arc of my story, he approached me a month before Easter 2009 and asked, "Would you be willing to give your testimony at the Easter service?"

"Yes," I replied, without thinking about the circumstances or possible consequences.

The pastor showed himself to be a man of great faith when he asked me to speak at all three Easter services without seeing a draft of my testimony. There was no rehearsal; he just handed me the microphone.

There was one service on Saturday and two on Sunday. At the second Sunday service, Jessie and Chelsea, as well as Shawna and her family, were present. This is the first time my two children saw me openly and publicly testify to my faith.

I shared with the congregation my journey from atheism to agnosticism to Christianity, and I illustrated how God had been at work in my life all along, even though I didn't know Him. In conclusion, I recited a poem, titled "Loneliness," that I had written when I was in the depths of despair in 2005, shortly after my return from the conference in Pebble Beach.

Loneliness is a stampeding multitude that tramples down the seeker of solace lying on the desert floor with one arm extended towards the heavens in a desperate plea for mercy
Loneliness is a prison cell with walls made of the fabric of fear
Loneliness cries out in anguish to the world only to be tortured by the magnified echo of the futile cry
Loneliness is a mirage of all that is good, a mirage close enough to be sensed but far enough to remain tortuously unattainable
Loneliness is the vision of a shoulder to lean on, always to be withdrawn at the last moment, resulting in a frightful eternal freefall towards utter darkness
Loneliness is a silent scream for a healing hand
Loneliness is the certitude that there is no healing hand
Loneliness is a demon who knows only himself

In my original version of the poem, I had ended with a plaintive cry of desperation in all caps: *I AM LONELY!* But when I recited the poem on Easter, I finished on a more hopeful note:

Loneliness is Jesus at the Cross betrayed by Man.
Rejoice brother, Christ rose again—and He extends His Love to You.
The Love of Christ overcomes the Specter of Loneliness—
He who is with Christ cannot be lonely.

Rob's belief in me proved to be justified, but what I found even more remarkable was that I had shared my testimony with about a thousand people during those three services, many of whom lived and worked near my home and workplace, and yet miraculously, none of my testimony trickled out into the public realm. No local journalists picked up my story, and it seemed that no one from work had attended any of the three services. If the news about my background had reached my company, I would have been subject to immediate dismissal.

At the time, in spite of the fact that I had the full support of the United States government, my legal status had not yet been resolved. I could only conclude that God both protected me and determined that my time to go fully public had not yet come.

✦ ✦ ✦

As my faith in God continued to grow, so did my relationship with Shawna. Her words, "You are already a Christian, you just don't know it," turned out to be prophetic. One day, God answered my prayer and turned this growing friendship into a deepening love. Shawna had asked me to stop by her apartment on my way home to help her fix some things around the house. I have always been rather handy with a hammer and a screwdriver, so I looked forward to displaying my manly skills to this woman I so admired and loved.

I was standing on a chair, fixing a loose curtain rod over a window, when suddenly I heard these words spoken in a low-key, seemingly disembodied voice: "I love this man. I can't help it. I love this man."

I did not respond, but the ice was broken. When I left her apartment, I asked for a hug, and she gave me one. I felt like running all the way back to my house. My entire life was turning around in a way I could never have expected.

Over the next eighteen months, our relationship continued to grow, and on September 12, 2009, Shawna and I were married in the same sanctuary where I had accepted Christ and was baptized. Jessie and Chelsea attended, along with Shawna's mother and her son, Carmellau. We were now a new family made up from rather disparate parts, yet we were the most functional family I had ever been a part of.

Two years later, at the age of sixty-two, I became a father again when Shawna delivered a beautiful little girl, whom we named Trinity. I asked Joe Reilly, who had long since retired from the FBI, to be Trinity's godfather. He and I still enjoyed periodic phone conversations, with topics ranging from history to world affairs, and from sports to politics. Throughout history, many people have been killed in wars by someone who could have been their best friend under different circumstances. And to me, there's no better proof that friendship has the capacity to triumph over enmity than my relationship with Joe.

The first years of marriage brought numerous struggles, not the least of which was being laid off from my job at the same time that Shawna found out she was pregnant. There are very few employment opportunities for executives in their sixties, and when I wasn't able to find a new job right away, my faith wavered and I turned once again to my old companion: alcohol. But God was faithful and answered my prayers. After eighteen months of forced idleness, I landed a good full-time job that would allow me to take care of my entire family. After one year of a weekly two-hundred-mile commute, we were able to sell our home in New Jersey and move to a lovely house on the Hudson River, just north of Albany, New York.

But God wasn't finished with me yet. In fact, He still had some major life changes in store. Just when I thought the past was securely behind me, God brought it back again.

40

I NEVER WOULD HAVE SOUGHT OUT a final assignment to wrap up the loose ends of my life. I was hoping that the process of becoming a legal US citizen would finally come to a close, but there was no urgency to that. Thoughts of returning to visit the country of my birth were no more than a fuzzy notion. Germany had become a foreign country to me, or so I had convinced myself.

But God decided to use Chelsea to crack open a door to the other side of the Atlantic. I had told her that she had a half-brother in Germany named Matthias. Sometime in 2009, and unbeknownst to me, she began a systematic Internet search to find him. For months and months, that search yielded nothing. But one day in the spring of 2010, I received a phone call from Chelsea.

"Hello?"

"I found him."

"What? Found who?"

"Matthias, of course, and he's coming to visit me in a month. He doesn't want to see you, though." Her voice tailed off with disappointment, but that was just fine with me. I wasn't ready to burst the American bubble I had been living in for years and face the past—or the little boy I'd left behind in Germany.

But once Matthias was in the US, he changed his mind and told Chelsea, "I want to meet my father."

On a Friday evening, Chelsea called and said, "Dad, Matthias and I are having dinner at the Clinton House, and we would like you to join us."

Considering that the Clinton House was only three miles from my home at the time, a refusal to join them for dinner would have branded me a coward. Chelsea had forced my hand.

When I entered the restaurant, the two half-siblings were waiting for me near the entrance. Matthias just stared at me for a long time without saying a word. This was the oddest reception I had ever received from another human being. After we took our seats at the table and ordered our meals, we began to talk, and the initial awkwardness soon gave way to a free-flowing conversation—mostly in English, for Chelsea's benefit, but also because Matthias's English was much better than my rusty German. When our meal was finished, we decided to continue the conversation at my home.

There was only so much time we could spend on pleasantries and small talk before I had to address the most delicate issue between us— my *choice*. The unvarnished truth was that I had chosen one sibling over the other, and now they were both in my presence—one waiting for an explanation and the other a much interested audience.

I picked the only approach that I thought would resonate with Matthias, explaining to him the raw logic behind my thinking, namely that Chelsea needed my support much more than he did. He agreed. He told me that the KGB had taken good care of him and his mother while I was still in their employ. They hand-delivered my salary to Gerlinde until early 1990, more than a year after I cut ties with them. Matthias remembered at least two all-expense paid vacations with Gerlinde to Moscow and Yalta, a city on the Black Sea. Finally, and this was very important to me, when Matthias told me that the KGB had delivered my $60,000 bankroll to his mother, I was ecstatic. I saw it as yet another link in the chain of events that could only be held together by God's protective hand.

When Matthias and I said good-bye, I felt a tenuous thread of hope that we might be able to build a relationship—something we'd never had. But with my application for US citizenship still stuck in a bureaucratic quagmire, some of that hope would have to be deferred. Still, I had my son back, thanks to Chelsea's enterprising persistence.

✦   ✦   ✦

It seemed that my paperwork had fallen down a rabbit hole somewhere in the offices of the United States Citizenship and Immigration

Services. Phone inquiries about the status of my application yielded no results, and even the FBI couldn't get a straight answer. Like a page out of Franz Kafka's *The Castle*—a tale of horror describing the frustrations of an individual in his dealings with a large faceless bureaucracy—this seemed to be a case of finding the right person who knew the right person who knew the right person. Had it not been for the unflagging efforts of my FBI liaison, to whom I am forever grateful, my papers might still be stuck in a bureaucratic graveyard, slowly taking on the yellowed look of ancient historical documents.

But on the morning of August 20, 2014, against all hope, I got The Phone Call at work.

"This is Officer Cahill from Homeland Security, the Albany office. Would you be able to come in tomorrow morning?"

The creature of habit in me responded, "Let me check my calendar." Then it hit me: I had been waiting thirteen years for this moment!

"What am I saying? Of course I can come over. What time do you want me to be there?"

The next morning, I met Officer Cahill, who took my oath. Ten minutes later, I walked out a proud—and official—American citizen.

On my drive back to the office, I reflected on the circuitous journey I had taken to get here—from the little village of Rietschen in East Germany to Moscow, via Jena and Berlin, to my final home in the USA. What I had not expected was my emotional reaction. It felt really good to call a country my home again.

✦   ✦   ✦

After I became a US citizen, I applied for the elusive document I had been so eager to acquire three decades earlier. On the day the passport arrived in the mail, I opened the envelope and pulled out the navy-blue booklet. After having had my picture pasted onto so many forgeries over the years, it was odd to see it once and for all at home on a genuine American document.

Well, Alex and Sergej and everyone else, I finally have a real US passport.

Now that I had the prized document in my hands, the idea of return-ing to Germany for a visit came bursting from the back of my mind and began to gather steam. Finally, I told Shawna, "I have to go, and I have to go as soon as possible!"

By that time, I had established e-mail connections with a number of old friends from high school and university, and soon a plan took shape for a journey into the past that included meeting seventeen people in nine locations over a span of two weeks. Those plans did not include my family of origin. My mother would have been ninety-four by then, and it was unlikely she was still alive. I hadn't talked to my father since I was seventeen, and I had lost contact with my brother back when I was still living in Berlin.

There was another wrinkle to this trip—the German media. The year before, Shawna and I had received an unlikely visitor—her half brother, Richard. He had grown up in Germany, and Shawna had never met him. When Richard found out I was German, he inquired about my background.

"So how did you get here?" he asked as we took a walk around the pond on our property. I'd expected this question at some point.

"Well, I had some help from the government," I answered a bit slyly.

"Which government?" Richard probed. "The Germans or the Americans?"

"Neither one, to tell you the truth. It was actually the Russians."

"Huh?"

"Well . . . I'm a retired Soviet spy."

"What?" Richard stopped in his tracks.

This was the stock reaction I received from people in response to my initial disclosure. But then Richard continued, "Let's go back to the house. I want to write this down."

After he finished taking two pages of notes, he said enthusiastically, "I promise, this is going to be huge."

Sure, Rich, I thought to myself, suppressing the urge to roll my eyes. How in the world would an employee of the German railroad be able to make my story public?

Well, I underestimated Richard. He had a friend who was close to Susanne Koelbl, a journalist for *Der Spiegel*—a top German publication and the very magazine I had studied diligently to learn about Western culture during my training in Berlin and Moscow. Frau Koelbl and I talked by phone a few times, but we agreed that nothing would be done until my legal status in the US was clarified. Shortly before my scheduled departure, I located my brother online and gave his information to *Der Spiegel.* A reporter spoke to Hans-Günther, who confirmed that our mother had passed away. The reporter also obtained some old family photos, which he passed along to me. Hans-Günther was interviewed by Der Spiegel TV and appeared briefly in a documentary they produced. When I tried to contact my brother directly, he sent me a brief e-mail updating me on his current situation in life, but he concluded by saying, "After thorough consideration, I have determined that I do not want to have a relationship with you."

✦   ✦   ✦

On the morning of October 17, 2014, I closed my suitcase, kissed Shawna and Trinity good-bye, and set out on yet another adventure.

The flight to Germany was a painful reminder that today's airline seats are not designed for anyone over six feet tall. But as I limped toward the line for passport control at Berlin Tegel Airport, the cobwebs in my head were blown away. This was my first border crossing in twenty-eight years, and this time I would be presenting a genuine passport, not a forgery. But what if the Germans knew that I was actually Albrecht Dittrich? What if I had been declared an enemy of the state and would be arrested on the spot?

I approached the passport control agent with the same nervous feeling I'd felt decades earlier, but he passed me right on through. I may have surprised him with my accent-free German, but in any case my entry into the country was routine.

The plan was to leave my bags at the hotel and connect with Richard to spend the day just wandering around the city. Yet, as my tired, aching legs dragged me slowly down the main concourse, I noticed a handful of people looking directly at me.

Is there something wrong with me? Am I so disheveled that I would attract the attention of strangers?

Next, I spotted Richard leaning against a wall some sixty feet ahead of me.

Why is he not making an effort to greet me?

The answer became clear when a microphone was suddenly thrust in my face and I noticed a handheld professional camera pointed at me. Three days before my trip, I had e-mailed Susanne Koelbl to let her know I would be in Berlin and that we could meet for a cup of coffee if she was interested. Being the good journalist that she is—who clearly has a flair for the dramatic—she did not want to miss the historic moment of my return to German soil.

She asked her first question in German, but my attempt to answer coherently in my mother tongue was so garbled that my first words upon returning to my homeland were later charitably laid to rest on the cutting-room floor.

Thankfully, Frau Koelbl switched to English and my answers were recorded for broadcast on German television. My responses betrayed the physical and emotional fatigue and the trepidation I felt regarding this entirely new adventure. A lot of questions were swirling around in my head, and some of the possible answers were frightening. Would I be rejected by friends and family? Would they, in typical German fashion, tell me to my face that my choices had been morally wrong, even disgusting and despicable? How could I leave my mother, wife, and son, and disappear without a trace? Would I be able to answer those questions honestly and credibly? I now realized that this visit could potentially turn into another high-stress moment in my life.

Thankfully, once the interview was completed, the conversation turned to the logistics of the day and pushed the dark thoughts aside. We left my bags at the hotel and ate breakfast at one of the many cafés found on almost every block in Berlin. The German coffee was strong and tasty, and the pastries took me back fifty years. The bakers had not lost their touch.

✢ ✢ ✢

For the next two days, Richard, Frau Koelbl, and I roamed the streets of Berlin. Except for the area between the Brandenburg Gate and Alexanderplatz, East Berlin was hardly recognizable. Older buildings had either been replaced or prettied up, and there was construction going on everywhere. I could not even recognize the apartment building in Lichtenberg where I had lived forty years earlier. Germany was still making massive investments in their attempts to restore Berlin to its former glory as the nation's capital.

The Berlin Wall is typically one of the first places where visitors want to go. For me, it was the first time I had taken a close look at the monster that for thirty-eight years had divided the country. At the time the wall was erected, I lived in a remote part of East Germany. We had no family in the West, and I didn't know anybody who did. All through my growing-up years, and well into my time with the KGB, I accepted the wall as a necessary evil designed to protect the fledgling Communist state from the Nazi-infested ruling class of West Germany. My life was going so well in East Germany that I never had even a fleeting thought of going over to the West. Thus, it never occurred to me during those years that the primary purpose of the wall was not to keep the Westerners *out*, but to keep the East Germans *in*.

It was all the more eye-opening for me to visit the Berlin Wall Museum and finally become aware of the evil this death strip represented. Hundreds of East Germans had been murdered for something Americans take for granted—the God-given freedom to choose where to go and where to live.

There was yet another shadow that followed me on my travels—the ghost of the Stasi, the East German secret police. It began with a visit to the Stasi Museum.

Years earlier, I had read *Man without a Face*, the autobiography of Markus Wolf, the head of the Stasi's main directorate for reconnaissance. Many in the international intelligence community regard Wolf as the greatest spymaster of the twentieth century. One of his operatives, Günter Guillaume, caused the downfall of West German Chancellor Willy Brandt in 1974. I found nothing new in that book about the methods and tactics employed by undercover agents, but I was completely unprepared for what I found at the museum. I was appalled by the lawless activities the Stasi had employed to monitor and control the citizens of East Germany.

At the height of its power, the Stasi had about 80,000 full-time employees and 170,000 signed volunteers—one agent for every forty adult citizens of the country. A majority of those agents spent their time watching and reporting on friends, neighbors, and even family. According to my German friends, the movie *The Lives of Others* is an accurate depiction of the insidious activities of the Stasi.

The massive amount of data collected by the Stasi was too much to be destroyed on the day the wall came down, and what survived has still not been fully processed to this day. I walked out of that museum with feelings of guilt, shame, disgust, and anger. The Stasi and the KGB had been partners in crime, and I had been a loyal employee and willing participant in their scheme.

The foundation of my Marxist-Leninist ideology had long since crumbled, but my visit to East Berlin and the Stasi Museum was another step in cleaning up the toxic rubble. I saw God's hand in guiding this trip to help me become whole and to reconcile my American present honestly and cleanly with my German past.

41

MY NEWLY ACQUIRED PERSPECTIVE of the Stasi horrors became a silent companion on my trip to Jena, the town where I spent my university years.

My college buddy Günter met me in Berlin and we made the trip together. Forty-five years gives Father Time plenty of opportunity to make his mark on people, and Günter was no exception. During our college years, he had been slight of frame with long arms, a thick head of black hair, and a mustache. Now his frame had almost doubled in size, and most of his hair was gone. But his bright, slightly mischievous eyes were a dead giveaway—this was still my good friend Günter.

The next two and a half hours in the car together were delightfully entertaining. Günter is one of the best storytellers I've ever met, so he mostly talked and I mostly roared with laughter. And because he still had the accent of his hometown, Jena, his tales took me back emotionally to the time of our youth.

Most of Günter's stories had to do with his professional past. In the 1970s, the East German government had overestimated the demand for highly trained chemists. As a result, Günter had difficulty finding a job after college, as did many of his fellow doctoral students. Finally, he found employment as a scientist with the Stasi forgery department—which, with the exception of money, forged everything worth forging. Given that engineering is in the German DNA, it's not surprising that Günter and his colleagues became world class at their devious craft. Because of his outstanding work, Günter wound up heading the entire department.

After the wall came down, the West Germans recognized the

excellence of Günter's operations, and while the Stasi itself was smashed to pieces, his department was fully integrated into a unified all-German intelligence service. To his consternation, Günter was forced into early retirement, and as an ex-Stasi member he saw his government pension cut in half. But thanks to his wife's pension from her career as a teacher, the two still manage to live comfortably in a suburb of Berlin.

✢ ✢ ✢

When we arrived in Jena, it was already dark. Günter and I checked into our hotel and proceeded to the restaurant where we would meet my son Günther; his mother, Edeltraud; and his stepfather, Bruno. Two years earlier, Günter had connected me to Edeltraud via e-mail, and my son had come to visit for two weeks at my house in New Jersey. Much like my experience with Matthias, that initial reunion started out feeling awkward and uncomfortable but ended with a genuine hope for a new beginning. Now I was here to meet him again and to reconnect with his mother some forty years after we had last seen each other.

It was an unusually warm October evening, and Günther, Edeltraud, and Bruno were sitting at an outside table waiting for us. As we approached the table, Günther suddenly became animated. He stood up, pointed at Günter, and asked his mother, "Who is that?"

When she responded, he became furious.

"Either he goes or I go!"

There was no reasoning with the young man. Apparently, Edeltraud had told him that Günter was ex-Stasi, and there was no way that my son would break bread with a hated former agent. Forced to choose between my friend and my son, there was really no choice to be made. I sat down with my son and his parents, and Günter had to leave the scene. We made plans to reconnect the next day to visit some other friends, and he walked off defeated and somewhat befuddled. But such was the hatred that most East Germans felt toward the Stasi even twenty-five years after the wall came down.

Even though we are now ideologically worlds apart, Günther and I were able to rekindle our friendship and are likely to continue to be friends as long we're on this earth.

+ + +

History has been kind to the dreamy little city of Jena, one of the few East German towns that truly thrived after reunification. Unlike Berlin, which has undergone a radical face-lift, Jena still presents itself to the world much as it did fifty years ago. Most of the buildings I remembered from when I lived there are still standing, but they've been spruced up and are a lot more attractive. I had no problem finding all the old haunts from my college days: the five-hundred-year-old headquarters of the university where Professor Siegmund Borek recruited me for the Communist Party, the Rosenkeller student club where I spent countless Saturday nights, the dormitory where I was first approached by the KGB, the auditorium where I listened to many chemistry lectures, the building with the lab where I set myself on fire, and the yard where I conducted the mustard gas experiment.

Even the restaurant Die Sonne, where I met my first KGB handler, was still in business, albeit freshly painted on the outside and completely redone inside.

That evening, I had dinner with four of my former basketball teammates. This was a raucous event that took me back to the days when we would celebrate a win or mourn a loss with full steins of excellent beer.

I spent some time with the journalists from *Der Spiegel* and time with some other friends. I was also afforded the opportunity to finally apologize to Edeltraud for the immature and cowardly way I had treated her during her pregnancy and after Günther was born. Amazingly, she forgave me.

I spent my final evening in Jena exclusively with my son Günther, and the next morning I said good-bye to Jena with a heavy heart.

+ + +

After Jena, I made forays into Rietschen, Bad Muskau, and Spremberg, with a quick stop at Reichenbach that yielded an unexpected treasure— a certified copy of my birth certificate. Though I had no documentation to prove that I was indeed Albrecht Dittrich, I knew too much about the people who had lived in Reichenbach during my childhood to have been a fake.

Unfortunately, Opa Alwin's high school was no longer in use. The magnificent building was boarded up, testimony to the decay that befell this part of Germany after the reunification. Similarly, the school building in Rietschen, the village where we lived during my first ten years, was also empty and boarded up.

The house in Bad Muskau, where I spent the second decade of my life, was still there, freshly renovated and painted, but quite recognizable. The front door with the mail slot that Rosi's good-bye letter came through was still in its original state. But gone were the outhouse and the Russian writing on the north wall. A chat with an eighty-year-old resident who remembered my mother yielded some interesting information about the fate of other neighbors, but there was really not much to do or see, so I continued my trip northward.

During my last few days in Berlin, I reconnected with Matthias and his lovely wife, Désirée, and I continued to marvel at how Chelsea had single-handedly managed to bridge the gaps between our family members. However, the one relationship that seemed beyond repair was with Gerlinde. I wanted to try, but how could I even begin to explain, much less justify, my betrayal of her? Matthias and his wife asked me not to contact Gerlinde, to avoid reopening barely healed wounds of the past, and I knew I had to respect their request.

✦ ✦ ✦

Before I left Berlin, there was one more surprise in store for me, one more opportunity to tie up a loose end.

I was sitting in Matthias's apartment, going through some printed material that my classmate Jürgen had given me, when I noticed a list of addresses and phone numbers. I saw that Rosi was on the list and that she had a Berlin address.

"Should I give her a call?" I wondered out loud.

Matthias looked at me quizzically, but when I explained to him the role that Rosi had played in my life, he put on his most wicked grin and said, "Of course you must call her. This should be interesting!"

Without giving it any more thought, I dialed the number.

"Hallo?"

"Guess who this is. . . . Take a deep breath," I said. "This is Albrecht."

Fifteen seconds of silence were followed by a shriek. "Oh my! Are you serious? I have to sit down!"

Apparently, like many others, Rosi had believed the rumors that I had perished in a rocket accident in Kazakhstan. When I called her, it was as if I had come back from the dead. We agreed to meet over coffee the following afternoon.

When I arrived at the agreed-upon place, Rosi was already there, sitting on a worn park bench in front of Zion Church. There was no mistaking her identity; it was still Rosi. The beautiful features I had fallen in love with fifty-five years earlier still shone through, though like all of our faces, hers had weathered with time.

For me, the past fifty years had completely healed any wounds that were caused by the abrupt breakup of our relationship. I was driven more by my innate curiosity to know how her life had been.

Rosi, on the other hand, was quite emotional. Without any prompting, she volunteered, "You know I made a really bad mistake when I let you go. We were simply too young to appreciate what we had."

As a tear slowly made its way down her cheek, I said, "That's okay, no hard feelings. You know, they say that things happen for a reason." Rosi's confession felt like an apology that was neither requested nor needed, but it still felt good.

On my last day in Berlin, Matthias and I did something we should have done thirty years earlier: We went to a soccer game together. Befitting the situation, he was the one who took me, not the other way around.

✛ ✛ ✛

On my way to the airport, I had one more Rip Van Winkle moment. Much like the mistakes I had made in Montreal and New York due to cultural ignorance, I now provided some inadvertent comic relief in the country I once called home.

Before returning the rental car, I had to fill the tank with gas. But when I pulled into the self-service gas station, I couldn't find the slot for the credit card on the pump. So I went inside and asked the young woman behind the counter quite sincerely, "Can you tell me how this works?"

Given that I was asking in perfect native German, she looked at me as if expecting a hidden camera to pop out at any moment. Then, figuring she would just play along with the joke, she explained slowly, "First you remove the gas cap. Then you take the nozzle, stick it in the tank, and press the lever."

When her explanation reminded me of the twist-top bottle cap episode in Montreal from way back when, I burst out laughing and explained my dilemma to her. I don't know if she believed me, but I did learn that in Germany one always pays inside after pumping gas.

In spite of all the memories, and the good food and excellent beer that resulted in a seven-pound weight gain, Germany was not my home anymore. Albrecht had his taste of the past, and he was satisfied, but he was also quite happy to merge with Jack as a whole person who lives in the United States. Miraculously, this Humpty Dumpty was being put back together again.

On my return to the US, I landed at Newark Airport, which is one of the worst places in the country to fly in to. The dingy facility and horrendous service makes you feel as if you've just landed in a Third World country. But nevertheless it was home.

No matter what challenges we face in our nation, as long as the beacon of freedom still shines, that's where my home will be. America has always stood for the freedom to pursue our dreams and our faith; the freedom to come and go; the freedom to think and to express our thoughts without fear; and, most important of all, the freedom to fail.

I pray that this mind-set will continue to prevail in the one great bastion of freedom on earth—the United States of America.

✛　✛　✛

Two days after my return from this eventful trip, I got a call on my cell phone while I was at the office.

"Hello, Jack? My name is Draggan Mihailovich, producer at *60 Minutes*."

Fortunately, I was somewhat prepared for the call. Frau Koelbl had gotten in touch with Steve Kroft, whom she had met two years earlier at a seminar in the US. She told me that *60 Minutes* might be interested in my story.

Mr. Mihailovich was very professional but also very insistent, "My assistant and I would like to come to your place and tell you a little bit about what we want to do here. How about this coming Saturday?"

I agreed and immediately called Shawna.

"Guess what—*60 Minutes* just called."

"What? *60 Minutes*? You're delusional!" she responded.

"This is real. I don't know what they have in mind, but they're coming to our place for a visit."

The fact that Mr. Mihailovich knew about me and my story was the final link in the series of improbabilities that would ultimately allow me to share my story with the world.

When the bell rang on Saturday, I opened the door, and as Mr. Mihailovich walked in, he waved a copy of *Unbroken* in the air as an introduction. He told me that he had discovered and interviewed Louis Zamperini, the hero of that book, and he had a hunch that he was onto another story worth pursuing. After a three-hour interview, Draggan seemed excited about featuring my story on his program.

To work with some of the world's best journalists in the news and entertainment industry was an adventure in itself. But the most important aspect of this production was that it gave me an opportunity to take my two adult American children to Germany and show them where I grew up. In April 2015, I again invaded Germany—this time in the company of a CBS crew and Jessie and Chelsea.

In contrast to my previous visit, the weather in Germany was absolutely rotten, with cold rain and wind every day. There was even a crippling hurricane, an extremely rare occurrence in Germany. But the weather did nothing to dampen our fun and excitement. We traveled in style, but the company we were in was more fascinating than the Mercedes limousines.

It was great to show my kids all the places of my youth. To the amusement of our driver, the three of us constantly talked over one another and bickered about everything that could be bickered about—thus revealing a genetic predisposition toward argumentativeness. But unlike in the past, this time we didn't take things too seriously. We laughed a lot, and when things got a little tense between two of us, the third one would jump in as a mediator.

The final exclamation point of our trip was a grand family reunion with Matthias and Günther. When Jessie had to fly home earlier than Chelsea and I, Günther came up from Jena to bid him good-bye. When we took Jessie to the airport, we were able to take the one and only picture that features all four of my adult children and me. Now that this family has been reunited, we will persist in our relationships regardless of the ocean that separates us physically.

✦ ✦ ✦

The *60 Minutes* story aired on May 10, 2015. Not surprisingly, the board of directors at my company became uncomfortable with the revelations of my past. As a result, I was laid off, effective May 18, 2015—one more significant life event that fell on my actual birthday. Losing my job wasn't part of my plan, but I have become accustomed to "interference" from God, and I've stopped fighting fights that I'm certain to lose. I've learned that when God overrides my plans, it is typically in my best interest. And I am learning how to trust Him with everything in my life. My departure from a job I truly loved has turned out okay. It gave me time to write this book and spend much more time with my little girl, Trinity.

Today, I strongly believe that God opens the doors He wants us to go through, and He shuts those He wants us to avoid. The challenge is to find the doors that are clearly marked with an Enter sign and avoid the pain caused by butting our heads against the ones that are shut tight. The signs are there—and they always have been—but now I'm paying attention. I sense that God is not quite finished with me yet on this earth, and I'm looking forward to what He has in store.

✦ ✦ ✦

On June 1, 2016, Chelsea's twenty-ninth birthday, I was sitting on my front porch watching Trinity and her mother walk around the pond on our property. Trinity was stabbing her net into the water hoping to catch a fish. *How many times have I told her that she has no chance of catching a fish this way?* But she just does not give up.

My thoughts were wandering into the past, to the day when Chelsea was born, when suddenly a scream disrupted my reverie.

"Daddy, Daddy, I caught a fish!"

"Are you sure? It could be a piece of wood," I yelled across the pond.

"No, Dad. It is a fish, come see," she hollered back.

I slowly rose from my chair and walked closer to take a look at her catch.

Miracle of miracles, Trinity was proudly holding a ten-inch bass with both hands. I was flabbergasted.

"How did you do this?" I asked in disbelief.

"Magic, Daddy. I have magic."

Magic, I think as I watch Trinity's beaming smile. *Yes, little one, you have magic.* Only God could create something so beautiful, and I love you so much.

Thank you, God.

EPILOGUE

HAVING BEEN BORN FOUR YEARS and ten days after Germany's unconditional surrender in World War II, my life's trajectory has its roots firmly planted in that war and its results. As such, I have always had a great interest in the history of Germany in the twentieth century. How was it possible that one of the most civilized countries on the planet could succumb to the wiles of such clownish ghouls as Adolf Hitler, Hermann Göring, and Joseph Goebbels? Why on earth did the German people go along for the ride that would end in mass murder and the biggest war in history? Why would they turn a blind eye to the storm troopers who pulled Jewish neighbors out of their homes in the middle of the night? Why?

Of course, I wasn't alive when all that happened, so I felt justified in not sharing the burden of the guilt and moral dilemma that plagued the German people. More so, the country I grew up in—East Germany—was led by men with bona fide credentials as fighters against the Nazi evil. The state and its leaders used the word *antifascist* as the single most important descriptor of their mission. This epithet was extremely successful in rallying an entire country behind its leadership. As a young person, I was absolutely convinced that I was aligned with the most righteous movement in the history of mankind. But was I really?

As I prepared to write this book, I did much research—for the first time—on the history of the Soviet Union as well as the KGB and its predecessors. I had read about those subjects in my younger years, but in those days all the available material had been carefully scrubbed and

whitewashed to depict the glorious struggle of Communist revolutionaries in pursuit of a socialist paradise. In that context, it was quite
plausible that the security apparatus had to occasionally resort to harsh
measures to fight the enemies of the revolution.

When the denunciation of Stalin finally happened, it was focused
primarily on condemning the cult of personality, and it certainly did
not extend to an indictment of his inner circle—some of whom went
on to inherit power after the dictator died. During my years in the
Soviet Union, there was nothing I could have found that would have
contradicted the notion that I was in a good place and serving a
noble cause.

My "silent defection" in 1988 was purely a personal and emotional
decision, devoid of ideological underpinnings. And for the next twenty-
five years, I deliberately withdrew from the stage of world events as I
pursued my American dream. When the Berlin Wall came crashing
down, I watched from an emotional and physical distance. All I wanted
was my shell of privacy, where I could live out my life in peace with my
new family in the United States.

My discovery by the media changed all that, and my hiding
between the folds of the curtain of history came to an end. I had to
come to terms with my background and my place in the events of the
Cold War. The results of my research were disappointing at best, and
often heartbreaking. Given my personal experience, Vasili Mitrokhin's
revelation that the first directorate of the KGB was fundamentally
ineffective during the second half of the Cold War was not a surprise. However, a deeper dive into the history of the Soviet Union
became an eye-opener of unanticipated proportions. In particular,
the book *Stalin and His Hangmen* by Donald Rayfield, a 600-page
treatise describing the murderous ways of Stalin's regime, shook me
to the bone.

During the Red Terror, which was conducted shortly after the
Russian Revolution by the Cheka, the forerunner of the KGB, people
were killed because they were considered enemies of the revolution.
Later, people were killed for all imaginable and unimaginable reasons:
They belonged to an ethnic minority; they were suspected to be foreign
spies; they spoke a foreign language; they had visited a foreign country;

they wrote prose or poetry that was suspect; they owned too much property; or they were family members, or even just friends, of those who were killed.

In the end, the monster ate itself from the inside out. Five out of nine heads of the Soviet security organization—all of whom had murdered hundreds of thousands of people—were themselves executed, together with many of their close associates. And the killing continued . . .

Having read the word *shot* for the umpteenth time, I broke down in tears as I finally realized that I had made a pact with the devil. The KGB I had joined was the successor to the band of murderers responsible for the deaths of at least 10 million citizens of the Soviet Union—though the actual number killed by Stalin and his henchmen is still in dispute. The people I worked with were all highly educated, clean-cut professionals, and I'm sure their hands were clean—because the dirty work (there *was* still dirty work being done, albeit on a much reduced scale) was left to others.

In those days, I didn't know, and perhaps did not want to know, what was happening around me. But ignorance does not absolve me from guilt. I have always tried to be a good person and please others, starting with my parents. When I signed up for the KGB, I justified my often immoral actions with the excuse that I was serving a greater good. But as the mantle of ideological righteousness began to fall away in tatters during my early years in the United States, I was finally able to do the right thing. I could have walked away from Chelsea as I had done with Günther and Matthias. But I had no excuse that could stand up to the power of unconditional love.

So how is it that somebody who wants to be good—and do good— could wind up dedicating a large part of his life to a fundamentally evil cause? The answer is simple: We are not, and cannot be, good as autonomous selves. Try as we might, without guidance from God we have no moral focal point and no consistent frame of reference to determine what is good and what is not. If I'd had a relationship with God in my younger years, I might have been more circumspect. I might have asked some basic questions, the answers to which may have made me uncomfortable, but likely would have influenced my decision. But I didn't ask those questions because I was so convinced of the power of my own goodness that it became a source of pride, essentially an idol. And therein, I believe, lies the answer to the question of why the Germans went along with Hitler. (And I must confess that I probably would have done the same thing.) Without God, man cannot achieve goodness; without God, man is lost.

Fellow Christians have asked me how I have become a different person after committing my life to Jesus. The answer to this question may be a bit unusual, but it is my answer. By the time I reached my fifties, I had in me all the right behavioral and attitudinal ingredients to pursue the Christian walk. All that was needed was for me to get to know and understand Jesus. As Shawna remarked after observing me in action for a few weeks as my administrative assistant, "You are already a Christian; you just don't know it."

When I began to learn about Christianity, I found it fit me like a glove. To draw an analogy: When your hand is ice cold, it has no feeling. It neither desires a glove nor even knows about the existence of the glove. When the hand begins to thaw, it starts to feel pain. That is when the soothing glove is most welcome.

Christ has taken away much of my pain, and I can live out my life on earth knowing that my sins, committed knowingly or unknowingly, have been forgiven by the enormity of His sacrifice. That is where I have landed. I am finally *home*.

Because I am allowed to leave behind a documented legacy of my unusual life, I'm praying that this legacy will be described by a single word: *LOVE*. I am so grateful to Jesus Christ for the most loving action any person could take on behalf of another. I thank my wife for helping me grasp that truth. And I want to encourage my children to live lives filled with love for God and their neighbors. There is no other way.

AFTERWORD
BY SPECIAL AGENT JOE REILLY, FBI (RETIRED)

I FIRST "MET" JACK BARSKY IN THE SUMMER OF 1993. We were about five hundred yards apart across a verdant meadow of wildflowers, weeds, and grasses in a little valley awash with hawks, doves, jays, woodpeckers, and other winged creatures. He was on the other end of my field glasses, working in his backyard.

I was pretending to be a bird-watcher, but I was actually a special agent with the FBI, and Jack Barsky was a deep-cover secret agent sent to the US by the Soviet Union. By then, he had been operating on American soil for more than ten years, and we were anxious to find out what he was up to. Was he running a spy ring, stealing secrets of scientific, political, or military value? We had to find out.

I positioned myself alongside a little-used dirt road on a hill overlooking Jack's home. From this vantage point, I had a good view of his modest two-story country house, which sat on two acres of green lawn. After setting up a cheap folding table and covering it with books on ornithology, I set my chair in just the right spot, took out my field glasses from their case, and watched "the birds." Few cars ever passed, and no one ever inquired about what I was doing.

I followed this routine, intermittently, on weekends and holidays during the warm months of summer and fall. Though I saw an abundance of birds much more often than I saw Jack and his family, I learned a great deal about the Barskys. I knew when Jack would be home, and I wanted to get a better read on this mysterious and sinister person.

Our surveillance team had followed him to and from work and to other places, but I wanted to know more about the man himself. What kind of person was he? I knew that someday we were going to arrest him and try to recruit him to work for us. I wanted to be in the best position to overcome any resistance on his part.

I was surprised by what I learned from just watching him. He worked hard in his yard, planting trees and shrubs. He did most of his own landscaping with some help from his wife and his young daughter. On hot days, they swam in their aboveground pool. He also had a two- or three-year-old boy, who also played in the grass and splashed in the pool.

Barsky seemed quite attached to his children. He often stopped working to play with them. In the evening, he taught his daughter how to play basketball in their driveway. He seemed to be patient and understanding. Often, after a long day of activity, he would emerge from his house wearing jogging clothes and run five miles through the countryside. At first, we followed him, very discreetly, to be sure he wasn't meeting anyone or engaging in nefarious activities. He wasn't. In those early months of our investigation, I came to believe that Barsky loved his children, but his relationship with his wife was perfunctory, if not downright cold. In time, these observations proved to be true.

Our investigation during the many months that followed revealed that Barsky was an energetic, focused, and intelligent man who would do well in almost any undertaking, except perhaps diplomacy. He was advancing quickly at his job and was well liked and respected. An ideal spy! But what was he actually doing for the Russians, or what had he been doing for them? We were well aware that the KGB's internal operations were in disarray after the collapse of the Soviet Union, but how did this affect Barsky? Was he still receiving instructions, or had he been put in sleeper mode?

Months turned into years of investigation and surveillance. At one point, we even purchased the house next door to the Barsky's to better observe him. We saw nothing to indicate that he was still active. I became convinced that if we arrested him he would cooperate. He seemed to be thoroughly Americanized. He continued to make progress at his job, and he had close friends. He seemed comfortable in his home and loved his children. I did not believe he would give up all of this and go to prison out of devotion to a bankrupt ideology and a failed state. But FBI headquarters did not agree, and the investigation dragged on.

The Justice Department (DOJ) became another source of delay. Their lawyers refused to support our efforts to place listening devices in Barsky's home. We wanted to know for sure whether his wife was involved with his spying operations. She had entered the US from South America, and her past life was clouded. The DOJ refused to support us because we could not show that our spy was actually spying. They readily accepted that he was a Soviet agent who was in the US illegally, and that he was using the identity of a deceased American child to further his mission. But because we couldn't provide evidence that he was currently spying, they wanted to protect his "constitutional rights."

If this sounds bizarre to you, I'm glad. It certainly did to me and my team. In fact, I got the distinct impression during a contentious meeting one time in Washington, DC, that some of the lawyers at the DOJ considered the FBI to be a greater threat to the US than Jack Barsky or the KGB. Finally, after the FBI director intervened on our behalf, common sense prevailed. The Justice Department supported our petition to the court based on FISA—the Foreign Intelligence Surveillance Act. We were immediately authorized to conduct electronic surveillance.

On a weekend when we knew that Jack and his family were away, we entered the house and placed microphones in the kitchen and family room. This was expertly done and the bugs were never found. Within weeks, a conversation in the kitchen between Barsky and his wife, Penelope, broke the case open. She was not happy to be married to a man who was not what he pretended to be. He was asking her to understand his position. At first, he couldn't tell her who he really was or where he was from. He was in constant danger of being arrested as a spy or "silenced" by the KGB for deserting them. This told us a great deal, and we finally received authorization to pick him up.

My personal relationship with Jack Barsky began with his arrest. Well, technically we didn't arrest him. We simply detained him until we were certain that he would cooperate with us—which he did, completely. During the weeks and months of his debriefing by a team of intelligence experts, Barsky and I became friends. He is, indeed, a fascinating man, who as a young man embarked on what he believed would be a great adventure—an adventure that rendered all other human concerns secondary. As his devotion to Marx and Lenin faded and the world of human love could no longer be suppressed, Jack Barsky the spy became Jack Barsky the human being, and his world became more complicated and painful, full of regrets, hurtful memories, and doubts about the future. A lesser person would have fallen apart under the weight of it. Failed marriages, abandoned children, lost causes, financial uncertainty—all the detritus of a spy's life—failed to crush an inner spark of optimism that continues to drive Jack toward the next new chapter in his life.

Jack Barsky's old life, growing up in postwar Germany surrounded by physical and spiritual destruction, was filled with the gospel of Marx and Lenin. According to this new religion, a brave new world would be built on the ashes of the old. The previous generation of young Germans had worshiped at the altar of National Socialism. Jack's generation prayed to the gods of international Communism. There were no other choices, and like most of his friends, Jack was no heretic. As he and I talked about many things over the years, we discovered that life, like the waves of the ocean, has a way of wearing down the sharp edges of early beliefs until only the bright coral remains—at least, for those who have eyes to see it. Jack Barsky is a man who will never stop looking.

This book takes you through many adventures and reveals much about the world of the Cold War. But the most interesting parts are about the man himself. Flawed though he is, and scarred by many of life's cuts, he soldiers on without complaint, trying to be responsible, trying to do the right thing. It is a great irony, but nonetheless true, that our country could use more people like Jack Barsky.

NOTES

1. "Dialectical materialism," Encyclopædia Britannica, www.britannica.com/topic/dialectical-materialism.
2. Ben Macintyre, *A Spy Among Friends: Kim Philby and the Great Betrayal* (New York: Crown, 2014), 42.
3. "The world's most beautiful metro just got better," *The Telegraph*, 13 Apr 2016; www.telegraph.co.uk/travel/rail-journeys/Moscow-Metro-80-years-of-the-worlds-most-beautiful-underground.
4. C. S. Lewis, *Mere Christianity* (New York: Macmillan, 1952), 55–56.
5. See John 1:1-4 and Hebrews 4:12.

ACKNOWLEDGMENTS

Though there were many Germans who contributed to the formation of Albrecht Dittrich, these acknowledgments are dedicated by Jack Barsky to my American friends and collaborators.

My first set of thank-yous goes to two friends of long standing, both immigrants who made me feel welcome in our country early on. Joseph Contino, a Sicilian by birth, was the very first individual who extended his hand to welcome me to his world. Gerard Bu, who fled to the US from Cuba, taught me how to dream and reignited my ambition to be the best I could be.

Had it not been for Joe Reilly's humanity and his keen insight into my personality, I might have been separated from my family and deported to a land that was no longer my own. When Joe retired, he handed the baton to another FBI special agent, who did not rest until all hurdles had been cleared and I could finally call myself a proud citizen of the United States of America.

Chelsea's stubborn determination is the reason that I now have an extended family that reaches across the Atlantic. And then there is Richard, my brother-in-law. He believed in my story from the moment he heard it, and he got the ball rolling. Without Richard this book would probably not have been written.

Susanne Koelbl from *Der Spiegel* spent hours digging into me without mercy, forcing me to honestly come to terms with all aspects of my past. Draggan Mihailovich of *60 Minutes* continued the grilling. He told my story with integrity, compassion, and excellence.

This book would not have been possible were it not for my agent Eric Myers of Dystel, Goderich, and Bourret. He not only discovered me, but he also taught me the fundamentals of writing a memoir. His tireless work on the book proposal and his willingness to act as a sounding board throughout the entire creative process is much appreciated.

I was lucky to be able to work with two excellent writers: Cindy Coloma, my collaborator, and Dave Lindstedt, my editor. Both worked hard to meet almost impossible deadlines, particularly in light of the fact that I threw an enormous amount of raw material at them. Cindy breathed life into my story, and Dave used his outstanding talents to create a cohesive tale.

I would like to express my gratitude to the staff at Tyndale Momentum—beginning with executive publisher Jan Long Harris and continuing with associate publisher Sarah Atkinson, senior marketing director Nancy Clausen, acquisitions editor Jillian Schlossberg, "chief hand holder" Sharon Leavitt, and the many others who worked behind the scenes. This team represents true excellence, something so rare that it must be cherished. Because of the warmth and caring this team has shown me at all times, I now consider Tyndale Momentum part of my extended family.

But in the end, it is my lovely wife, Shawna, who deserves the most recognition. She was a beacon of light during my implausible spiritual journey, and she puts up with this occasionally grumpy German, who has trouble dealing with tremendous stress at an age when most of his contemporaries are sailing happily into retirement. Thank you, my darling!

And may God bless you all!

ABOUT THE AUTHOR

JACK BARSKY was born, raised, and educated in the former German Democratic Republic (East Germany). He started a brief career as a college professor, teaching chemistry and math at Friedrich Schiller University in Jena. His life took a sharp turn when he was recruited by the KGB for an undercover mission. After four and a half years of training in Berlin and Moscow, he was launched on an undercover assignment into the United States.

Jack created an American identity for himself and went on to become an ordinary member of American society. After a two-year stint as a bike messenger in Manhattan, Jack entered Baruch College, graduating three years later with a degree in business administration. He started his professional career as a computer programmer but soon advanced into the ranks of management and executive management.

Jack unilaterally severed his relations with the KGB in 1988 and was captured by the FBI in 1997. After a lengthy debriefing process, Jack and his family were allowed to stay in the United States. Jack became a Christian in 2007 and was baptized in March 2008. He became an American citizen in 2014. In the spring of 2015, *60 Minutes* ran a story on Jack's unusual life. Subsequently, he decided to retire from corporate life and concentrate on his book and public appearances.

Jack has two adult sons in Germany and an adult son and daughter in the United States. He lives with his wife, Shawna, and their five-year-old daughter, Trinity, in Covington, Georgia.